THE BIOARCHAEOLOGY OF MUMMIES

The modern manifestation of mummy studies began to take shape in the 1970s and has experienced significant growth during the last several decades, largely due to biomedical interest in soft tissue pathology. Although this points to a vibrant field, there are indications that we need to take stock of where it is today and how it may develop in the future, and this volume responds to those demands. In many ways, mummy studies and skeletal bioarchaeology are "sister-disciplines," sharing data sources, methodologies, and practitioners. Given these close connections, this book considers whether paradigmatic shifts that influenced the development of the latter also impacted the former.

Whilst there are many available books discussing mummy research, most recent field-wide reviews adopt a biomedical perspective to explore a particular mummy or collection of mummies. *The Bioarchaeology of Mummies* is a unique attempt at a synthetic, state-of-the-field critical analysis which considers the field from an explicitly anthropological perspective.

This book is written for both skeletal bioarcheologists that may not be familiar with the scope of mummy research, and mummy researchers from biomedical fields that may not be as acquainted with current research trends within bioarchaeology.

Kenneth C. Nystrom is an Associate Professor in the Department of Anthropology at the State University of New York at New Paltz, USA. His research interests center on examining the interaction between biology and culture and how we can reconstruct behavior in the past by studying human remains.

THE BIOARCHAEOLOGY OF MUMMIES

Kenneth C. Nystrom

Routledge
Taylor & Francis Group

NEW YORK AND LONDON

First published 2019
by Routledge
52 Vanderbilt Avenue, New York, NY 10017

and by Routledge
2 Park Square, Milton Park, Abingdon, Oxon, OX14 4RN

Routledge is an imprint of the Taylor & Francis Group, an informa business

Library of Congress Cataloging-in-Publication Data
Names: Nystrom, Ken, author.
Title: The bioarchaeology of mummies / Kenneth C. Nystrom.
Description: Abingdon, Oxon ; New York, NY : Routledge, 2018. |
   Includes bibliographical references and index.
Identifiers: LCCN 2018025835 | ISBN 9781611328387 (hardback : alk.
   paper) | ISBN 9781611328394 (pbk. : alk. paper) | ISBN 9780429842467
   (web pdf) | ISBN 9780429842443 (mobi/kindle) | ISBN 9780429453359
   (ebk.) | ISBN 9780429842450 (ePUB)
Subjects: LCSH: Mummies. | Forensic archaeology.
Classification: LCC GN293 .N97 2018 | DDC 599.9—dc23
LC record available at https://lccn.loc.gov/2018025835

ISBN: 978-1-61132-838-7 (hbk)
ISBN: 978-1-61132-839-4 (pbk)
ISBN: 978-0-42945-335-9 (ebk)

Typeset in Bembo
by Apex CoVantage, LLC

This book is dedicated to my family for their patience and support and to Dr. Arthur Aufderheide for his friendship and guidance.

CONTENTS

FIGURES

TABLES

INTRODUCTION

The modern manifestation of the mummy studies field began to coalesce in the 1970s. Largely stemming from a biomedical interest in soft tissue pathology, mummy-based research has experienced significant growth. Though this points to a vibrant field, a number of issues reflect a rapidly expanding discipline that lacks a formal structure and unifying research paradigm. Researchers are beginning to reevaluate fundamental methods of data acquisition, analysis, and interpretation. There are calls for establishing fieldwide research protocols and ethical guidelines. Though these are significant issues, Arthur Aufderheide, one of the primary architects of modern mummy studies, captures what I believe to be the biggest challenge facing the field:

> Due to their spectacular nature, mummies have often been decontextualized, because interest in the preserved body has overridden the importance of archaeological contexts. Integrative, hypothesis-driven, multidisciplinary approaches . . . are essential to a more holistic understanding of these remains.
> *(2013: 134)*

In the same publication, Aufderheide said that for mummy studies to survive, it must join with a related discipline. To be honest, this statement always gave me pause because I considered mummy studies to fall within the umbrella of biological anthropology. I believe his comments underscore the fundamental 'fork-in-the-road' that the field faces. Clarifying research protocols, reporting standards, and establishing a code of ethics are necessary and vital but will not serve to produce more holistic research agendas. In my opinion, the adoption of a biocultural paradigm, one that more explicitly incorporates consideration of archaeological and anthropological contexts, would draw the field closer to anthropology and will ultimately ensure continued vitality of the discipline.

Because this is a critical period for the field, it is important to consider its development, where it stands today, and how it may proceed in the future. Mummy studies was emerging at the same time as bioarchaeology in the United States, and given the close connections between them today, I consider whether the paradigmatic shifts experienced by bioarchaeology also impacted mummy research. That is, to what extent has mummy studies managed to successfully merge biomedical and anthropological paradigms that were structuring skeletal biology and paleopathology in the closing decades of the twentieth century? The historical development of modern mummy studies is such that many researchers are coming from biomedical sciences and therefore do not have the same connection to, or background in, anthropological and archaeological method and theory. The strongly interdisciplinary makeup of mummy studies, although a strength, has also resulted in fragmentation. The main argument I make in this book is that whereas as a field mummy studies has experienced considerable growth over the last forty-five years, it has done so while remaining in large part isolated from the historical trajectory of bioarchaeology and current research trends therein.

This book is really intended for two audiences. On the one hand, it is written for skeletal bioarcheologists who may not be as familiar with the scope of mummy research. Though I would bet that most skeletal bioarcheologists own *The Cambridge Encyclopedia of Human Paleopathology* by Arthur Aufderheide and Conrado Rodríguez-Martin, Aufderheide's other tome, *The Scientific Study of Mummies*, may not as frequently grace their bookshelves. Despite some larger collections, mummies are rare, and, therefore, opportunities to work with mummies will tend to be infrequent for most bioarcheologists. Although the educational background of most bioarcheologists likely includes some training in soft tissue anatomy and physiology (most of us have likely taken gross anatomy), it is not the main focus of our graduate training. As I will point out, mummy-related articles are published in a broad range of journals, the majority of which are not standard outlets for bioarchaeological research. Indeed, only a small fraction of mummy-related articles have been published in what can be considered the main journals for bioarchaeological research. Given this, some of the chapters—for example, Chapters 1 and 4 where I discuss the basic mechanisms of mummification and current methodological trends—target this audience. These chapters are meant to serve as an introduction to mummy studies and as an enticement to become further engaged.

This book was also written for mummy researchers from biomedical fields who may not be as familiar with current research trends within bioarchaeology. The history and dominant research paradigm of mummy studies is such that it has attracted the involvement of a diverse range of biomedical professionals. Indeed, many of the key players in the development of modern of mummy studies were medical doctors, pathologists, and medical imaging experts. Although their skills and knowledge grant them a unique ability to extract information from mummified soft tissue, their training most likely does not include courses on anthropological or archaeological method and theory. Therefore, some of the chapters, notably Chapters 2 and

5, target this audience. Again, these chapters are meant to serve as an introduction to the field and as an enticement to become further engaged.

Narrative Outline of Book

Although it may seem straightforward, there is some ambiguity in what actually constitutes a mummy. At the most basic level, mummification results from either environmental or human/cultural intervention in the process of decomposition. No minimum amount of soft tissue preservation is necessary to make a set of remains a 'mummy,' though the corpse generally "resembles its living morphology" (Aufderheide 2003: 41). In the first chapter I discuss how the term 'mummy' is defined and operationalized, the criteria used to classify mummies, and the mechanisms that can lead to mummification. In the last part of this chapter I will discuss several case studies where research has focused on reconstructing the environmental and anthropogenic factors and processes impacting soft tissue preservation.

In Chapter 2, I discuss the historical development of bioarchaeology and mummy studies. Several recent publications have taken a retrospective look at bioarchaeology while also providing critical analyses of where the discipline is and where it might be going. Since the term "bioarchaeology" first appeared in the literature in the 1970s, it has focused on the contextualized analysis of human remains—predominantly skeletal remains. The breadth of research that calls itself bioarchaeology has expanded significantly, with distinct foci and 'schools' emerging (Rakita 2014). Because my educational background and research fall within the Buikstra 'school' of bioarchaeology, my perspective is one in which data derived from skeletal remains are articulated with social theory and archaeological data within a problem-orientated biocultural research design.

Several recent publications have focused on the history of mummy studies, the closely allied field of paleopathology, and key figures in the development of these fields. The scientific study of mummies has long been dominated by medical professionals such as physicians, anatomists, and pathologists, who, due to their knowledge of soft tissue anatomy and physiology, had the necessary skills to examine fleshed remains. This chapter ends with a brief look at a selection of on-going mummy projects: interdisciplinary research programs that focus on the investigation of specific groups of mummies or the investigation of a specific topic.

In Chapter 3, I discuss publication patterns in mummy studies. I first discuss the visibility and representation of mummy-related research in edited volumes. The remaining portion is devoted to the analysis of mummy-related articles published in peer-reviewed academic journals between 1970 and 2015. These data will be examined in the following manner: distribution of research based on journal type, a synthesis of publication trends and patterns within specific journals, and finally what type of research questions are most commonly being addressed. By identifying publication patterns and by considering them in reference to current publication trends in bioarchaeology, I hope to identify areas where the connections between the disciplines can be accentuated and amplified.

The next chapter considers the degree to which mummy studies have engaged with social theory. As used here, social theories are "bodies of general knowledge about sociocultural phenomena expressed in postulates, premises, assumptions, principles, and models" that "ostensibly answer *how* and *why* questions about human behavior and societies" (Schiffer 2000: 1, emphasis in original). Within bioarchaeology, the integration of social theory is reflected in a number of recent volumes (e.g., Argarwal and Glencross 2011a; Baadsgaard et al. 2011; Geller 2017) and journal articles (e.g., Duncan and Schwarz 2014; Knudson and Stojanowski 2008; Marsteller et al. 2011). This research is notable in its emphasis on reconstructing aspects of identity and interactions between the body, social identity, and culture. Arguably, the integration of social theory is one area in which mummy studies and skeletal bioarchaeology are most distinct. Therefore, I will highlight areas where mummy research has more explicitly integrated theory as well as areas where the incorporation of theory can provide significant new avenues of investigation.

In Chapter 5 I focus on three methodological advances that have stimulated research: biogeochemistry, paleoimaging, and paleogenetics. Beyond the relatively standard biogeochemical and molecular methods familiar to skeletal bioarcheologists, mummy studies commonly incorporate a fairly staggering array of highly specialized investigative tools such optical interferometry (Vargiolu et al. 2013), atomic force microscopy (Maixner et al. 2013), gas chromatography–mass spectrometry (GC-MS) (Echeverría and Niemeyer 2013). Although these methodological advances have no doubt spurred mummy research, it is important to consider how they have been implemented and if they have stimulated the development of novel research questions that expand the discipline.

In the final chapter I bring this all together to discuss the current state and future of mummy studies. The field is at a critical juncture as it faces a number of fundamental challenges including methodological standardization, the generation of ethical guidelines, the question of curation standards, and efforts to provide training opportunities. As the field moves to address these issues, however, it cannot lose sight of the concern expressed by Arthur Aufderheide quoted earlier: the field needs to integrate a more holistic, problem-orientated approach. Through this and by explicitly adopting a biocultural perspective, mummy studies can not only elaborate on its current focus on health and disease, it can also broaden its scope.

1

MUMMIES

Definition and Mechanisms

When contemplating mummies, many folks may automatically conjure up images of a linen-wrapped, well-preserved, and life-like body: there is, however, quite a bit of variability in what may be considered 'mummified.' Mummified remains exhibit some degree of soft tissue preservation, though the boundary between 'mummy' and 'skeleton' is somewhat ill-defined and fuzzy.[1] Lynnerup (2007: 441) writes that a body is a mummy when the "soft tissue preservation is so pronounced that body parts, or the whole body, have somewhat intact skin and some preserved internal structures such as muscle fasciae, ligaments and maybe even tissue of internal organs and muscle." Aufderheide (2003: 41) defines a mummy as "a physically preserved corpse or tissue that resembles its living morphology but resists further decay for a prolonged postmortem interval." These definitions permit some flexibility regarding what may be classified as a 'mummy.' While no one would question the 'mummy' status of remains such as Ötzi the Tyrolean Iceman (see Figure 4.9) or the Ice Maiden from Peru (see Figure 1.2), it becomes less clear when discussing bodies that are not as well preserved. For instance, the remains described by Gaudio and colleagues (2014) and Alt et al. (2003) appear to be mostly skeletonized (Figure 1.3), with only remnants of skin and connective tissue preserved. To take this even further, while some of the prepared Chinchorro bodies have been completely stripped of flesh, they are generally considered and discussed as 'mummies.' Thus, while Lynnerup's definition emphasizes soft tissue preservation, Aufderheide's definition focuses on the final appearance of the remains and perhaps permits a bit more latitude regarding what may be considered 'mummified remains.' Because there are no minimum standards for being a 'mummy,' the decision to describe remains as mummified is effectively left up to the investigator. As will be discussed later, however, there have been recent attempts to create more systematic methods for assessing and describing the degree and amount of soft tissue preservation.

Regardless of the extent of soft tissue preservation, mummies are categorized in two ways: the physical and/or chemical processes by which soft tissue is preserved, and the degree to which these processes result from either human action or environmental factors. Categories defined by the mechanisms of mummification are based on (1) taphonomy and (2) the manner and degree to which the natural sequence and timing of tissue decomposition has been altered. Research on the taphonomy of soft tissue preservation draws heavily from the natural and biomedical sciences (e.g., Mayer et al. 1997). Research in the latter category hinges upon the reconstruction of behavior based on the presence or absence of evidence for intentional human intervention. Here the primary distinctions made are between anthropogenic and spontaneous mummification and draws more explicitly from anthropology and archaeology speaking to the broader social and environmental context in which mummification occurred.

Mechanisms of Mummification

Mummification results from the interruption of decomposition. Decomposition encompasses three different processes: autolysis, putrefaction, and decay (Carter et al. 2007; Tibbet and Carter 2008). Autolysis ('self-digestion') can begin almost immediately after death (Vass et al. 1992) and is due to the release of hydrolytic enzymes that begin to digest the body's tissues. This leads to putrefaction—the breakdown of lipids, carbohydrates, and proteins and the accumulation of organic acids and gases (Tibbet and Carter 2008). Autolysis and putrefaction characterize the 'fresh' and 'bloated' phases of decomposition, respectively; rupturing of the skin marks the onset of active decay (which in turn can be subdivided into different stages, Tibbet and Carter 2008). During this phase, most of the mass of the corpse is lost through purging of cadaveric fluid. In forensic contexts, establishing the postmortem interval is dependent upon reconstructing the sequence and timing of these stages and the potential influence of environmental and anthropogenic variables.

A host of environmental factors can influence the progression of decomposition and subsequently increase the likelihood of mummification. These include the presence/absence of an aqueous medium, acidity, temperature, substrate specificity, and the presence of inhibitors such as heavy metal ions. Aufderheide (2003: 43) has identified seven primary, though not necessarily mutually exclusive, mechanisms of mummification: desiccation, thermal effects, chemical effects, anaerobiasis, excarnation, miscellaneous, and indeterminate.[2] I will provide a short summary of each of these mechanisms and refer the reader to Aufderheide (2003) for a fuller treatment.

Desiccation

The most important environmental condition that influences whether soft tissue is preserved is the speed at which water is removed from the body. Desiccation is the most common mummification mechanism and involves the removal of water from the body via evaporation, osmosis, or the application of heat (Aufderheide 2003) and may be encouraged through both human/cultural intervention and environmental factors.

Human intervention in the decomposition process, including evisceration, excerebration, chemical treatments (e.g., immersion in natron), and exposure to heat, fire, or smoke, increases the likelihood of mummification by reducing the amount of water in the body or accelerating water loss. A more unusual example of intentional desiccation is the 'self-mummification' documented in some Buddhist priests (Hori 1962; Ritzinger and Bingenheimer 2006). It has been suggested that a gradual reduction in food and water intake resulted in dehydration and loss of body fat, which, upon death, would have encouraged mummification. In most instances, these antemortem steps were accompanied by additional postmortem measures to ensure preservation (Cuong 1982–84; Gildow and Bingenheimer 2002; Sakurai et al. 1998).

Spontaneously desiccated mummies have been described from a wide range of arid environments, from hot deserts to cold mountain-top sites. Examples of spontaneously desiccated mummies include some of the remains from the Romano-Byzantine period cemetery site of Kellis-1 in Egypt (Aufderheide et al. 2004a), the remains from the Hets Mountain cave site in Mongolia (Figure 1.1; Turner et al. 2012), the Late Horizon Volcano Llullaillaco mummies from Argentina (Figure 1.2; Ceruti 2015), and remains from Muktinath Valley in the Himalayas, Western Nepal (Figure 1.3; Alt et al. 2003).

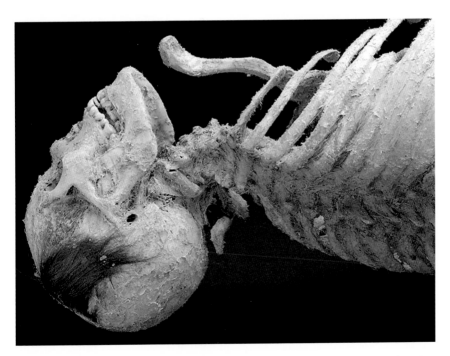

FIGURE 1.1 Spontaneously desiccated mummified remains recovered from the Hets Mountain Cave site in Mongolia (Turner et al. 2012).

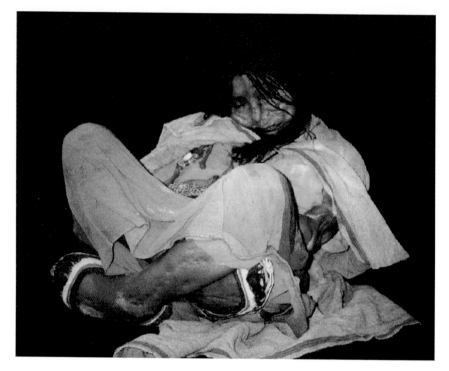

FIGURE 1.2 The Llullaillaco Maiden. Photo by Maria Constanza Ceruti 2015.

Thermal Effects

Enzymatic and bacterial activity are highly dependent upon temperature, with lower temperatures reducing, and ultimately halting, bacterial activity. Freezing environmental conditions can result in frozen 'wet' mummies, such as Ötzi the Tyrolean Iceman and members of the Franklin Expedition, where tissues remain hydrated (Janko et al. 2012). Alternatively, cold temperatures can also result in freeze–drying through sublimation of water, such as is observed in the Inuit mummies from Greenland (Hart Hansen and Nordqvist 1996). Exposure to heat can inhibit bacterial activity, but this may be secondary relative to the acceleration of water loss (Aufderheide 2003). Exposure to the sun or heat from a fire has been suggested to be involved in the production of the Guanche mummies (Rodríguez-Martin 1996).

Chemical Effects

Several different chemical processes can result in soft tissue preservation including the presence of heavy metals, chelation, smoking, and adipocere formation. In many

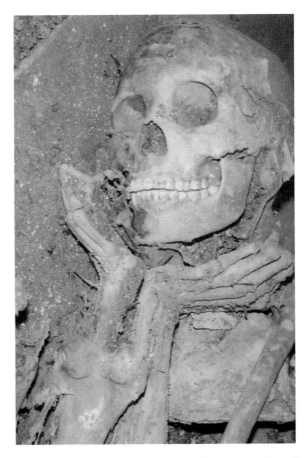

FIGURE 1.3 An example of a spontaneous mummy from the Muktinath Valley in the
Himalayas, Western Nepal (Alt et al. 2003).

cases, these chemical effects are likely secondary relative to other mummification
mechanisms such as desiccation.

Heavy Metals

The presence of heavy metal ions such as arsenic, mercury, and copper reduces an
enzyme's ability to bind to a substrate that inhibits decomposition (Aufderheide
2003). The presence of mercury has been suggested to be responsible for tissue
preservation observed in a 320-year-old mummy from Japan (Yamada et al. 1990)
and may have been used during the Han Dynasty in China as a preservative (Werning 2010). Preservation of the "Copper Man" from Chile (Bird 1979) and a corpse
from British Columbia (Schulting 1995) may be due to the presence of copper,

but desiccation is likely the primary mummification mechanism in both instances (Aufderheide 2003). Recently, the presence of copper plates has been implicated in the preservation of soft tissue observed in a young child from the Zeleny Yar necropolis in Russia.[3] Although results have not been published, news articles on these remains indicate that the body was wrapped in fur and then covered with copper or bronze plates. The investigators suggest that soft tissue preservation was accidental and due to burial in permafrost and the presence of copper plates. Based on the photos and descriptions provided, however, the copper plates do not appear to be in direct contact with the soft tissue and thus their contribution to the mummification process would seem to be limited.

Chelation

The preservation of soft tissue observed in bog bodies (Figures 1.4 and 1.5) results from the action of sphagnan, a pectin-like carbohydrate polymer produced by sphagnum moss. The sphagnan binds calcium ions, which not only results in the characteristic decalcification of the bones in bog bodies but also makes calcium unavailable for bacterial metabolism. Sphagnan also reacts with free amino groups and reducing sugars in what is called a Maillard reaction. This reaction results in the cross-linking of collagen fibers and in a preservation process akin to tanning (Aufderheide 2003).

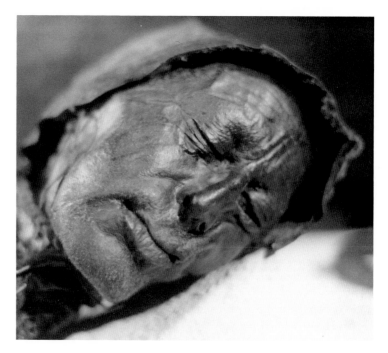

FIGURE 1.4   The face of Tollund Man, a bog body from Denmark, discovered in 1950. Photo by Sven Rosborn.

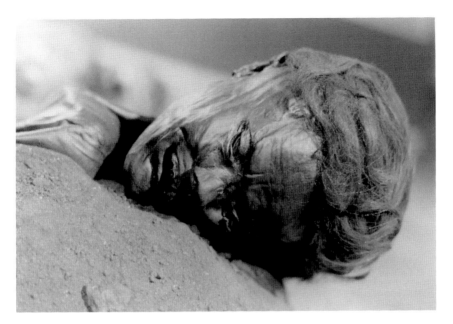

FIGURE 1.5 The bog body known as Grauballe Man. Photo by Sven Rosborn.

Smoking

Mummification among the modern Anga of Koke Village in Papua New Guinea involves keeping the body in a hut with a smoky fire for approximately thirty days (Beckett et al. 2011a, b). The increase in temperature encourages desiccation, but the formaldehyde in smoke creates cross-linkages between collagen fibers that can also promote soft tissue preservation. Other mummification traditions in which smoking may have played a role are the mud-coated Chinchorro mummies (Arriaza 1995a) and the protohistoric Maori (Orchiston 1971).

Adipocere

Adipocere, more commonly known as grave wax, results from the conversion of body fat by microbial activity (species of the *Clostridium* genus) into saturated free fatty acids with even-numbered carbon atoms: predominantly myristic acid, palmitic acid, stearic acid, and 10-hydroxystearic acid (Bereuter et al. 1997; Mayer et al. 1997). The environmental conditions conducive for adipocere formation can be quite variable, though typically it is associated with wet or damp environments. Forensic research has demonstrated that key factors in adipocere formation include mildly alkaline reducing anaerobic conditions, warm temperatures, and some source of moisture (Fiedler and Graw 2003; Forbes et al. 2005a, b). Adipocere has been demonstrated to develop in cold, acidic environments as well, though its formation may be slower (Forbes et al. 2005a).

Aufderheide (2003: 53) considers adipocere as a form of mummification because it can be quite stable and can "resist subsequent chemical change and thus tends to preserve the tissue's gross morphology," though there is some disagreement (see Ubelaker and Zarenko 2011 for a brief summary). Adipocere has been observed in bodies in which preservation of soft tissue is quite good (e.g., Bereuter et al. 1997; Dickson et al. 2004; Murphy et al. 2003) as well as in instances in which remains are mostly skeletonized.

Fiedler et al. (2009: 1328) describe a substance recovered with the skeleton of a child from the Late Roman period in the city of Mainz, Germany (Figure 1.6). Most of the body was covered in a thick layer of adipocere, with only the skull and distal extremities being skeletonized. The remains were contained in a stone sarcophagus, buried in moist clay soil adjacent to the Rhine. The authors suggest that periodic flooding may have filled the sarcophagus with water, creating an anaerobic environment that led to the formation of the adipocere. Chemical analysis demonstrated that the substance in question had only traces of the fatty acid methyl esters typically found in adipocere, but the ratios in which they were found is similar to that of modern adipocere (Fiedler et al. 2009: 1332).

Surprisingly, given the high lipid content of the brain and the remarkable number of brains that have been recovered from archaeological contexts (Kim et al. 2008; Papageorgopoulou et al. 2010; Prats-Muñoz et al. 2012; see O'Connor et al. 2011 for a complete list), only two instances have occurred wherein preservation has been explained as resulting from adipocere formation. Tkocz et al. (1979) note that frequent flooding and an alkaline anaerobic clay soil at the medieval churchyard in Svendborg, Denmark, likely facilitated adipocere formation and the brain preservation. Papageorgopoulou et al. (2010) describe the brain recovered from the

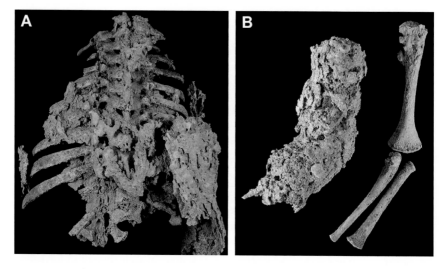

FIGURE 1.6 The crusty 'puff pastry-like' adipocere described by Fiedler et al. (2009).

FIGURE 1.7 Lateral (A) and medial (B) view of the brain recovered from Quimper-Bretagne, France (Papageorgopoulou et al. 2010).

skull of an eighteen-month-old infant from a thirteenth-century site in Quimper-Bretagne, France (Figure 1.7). This individual was wrapped in a "leather envelope and deposited into a wooden coffin" in an acidic clay soil. Clay soils produce a "less stable" and "not as advanced" adipocere product (Forbes et al. 2005a: 42) and may be why adipocere formation was limited to the brain in these instances.

Excarnation

One mechanism that initially appears a bit odd to include in a discussion of mummification is excarnation, or the removal of soft tissue. If we accept that a mummy is defined by the preservation of soft tissue, then technically the removal of soft tissue really does not result in a 'mummy' at all. In these instances, calling a set of remains a 'mummy' does not so much rest on the presence of soft tissue but rather on the reconstruction of mortuary behavior and the intention behind the behavior. Given this, excarnation is the only mummification mechanism discussed by Aufderheide (2003) that is strictly due to human activity, whereas the other mechanisms discussed earlier could derive from either environmental, human agency, or some combination thereof. It is the reconstruction of remains into something that approximates the living individual that warrants its inclusion as a mummification mechanism.

Two examples of excarnation include the overmodelled skulls from Vanuatu and the Chinchorro, which will be discussed in more depth later. Aufderheide (2003) discusses the mummification practices of the inhabitants of Vanuatu where the body is allowed to progress through all stages of decomposition. Individual features were modeled in clay and a vegetal fiber paste and affixed to a wood and paste effigy (Aufderheide 2003: 63). He also reports on similar overmodelled skulls from Papua New Guinea, Colombia, Ukraine, Jericho, and several Middle Eastern countries (Aufderheide 2009).

Intentionality

Mummies are also categorized based on the degree of human intervention in the process of soft tissue decomposition. These categories include:

Anthropogenic or artificial mummification—This process involves human or cultural actions that intentionally interfere with the decomposition processes and increase the likelihood of long-term soft tissue preservation.
(Aufderheide et al. 2004a; Lynnerup 2007).

Spontaneous or natural mummification—This occurs when soft tissue is preserved due to environmental conditions and occurs without any human intervention.

Spontaneous-enhanced mummification—Soft tissue preservation that is due to favorable environmental conditions that may have been 'helped' or 'encouraged' by humans.

This classification scheme is based on researchers' ability to identify evidence for deliberate interference in the normal progression of decomposition. My colleagues and I have argued elsewhere (Nystrom et al. 2010) that this is inherently biased toward anthropogenic processes such as evisceration or excerebration because these are more visible in the archaeological record. Alternatively, corpses in which there is no evidence of direct intervention are commonly considered to be the result of spontaneous mummification. For example, the remains of the young children recovered from the summit of the Volcán Llullaillaco in Argentina are considered "natural mummies" (Wilson et al. 2013: 1). Although these individuals were not eviscerated or excerebrated, intentionality should be evaluated within a broader mortuary context. Although it is impossible to say for sure, the Inca were probably aware that mountain-top burial would result in preservation of the soft tissues, and although no archaeologically visible steps (e.g., evisceration) were taken to ensure preservation, this does not negate the possibility that preservation of the body was the intention. Beyond potentially influencing the interpretation of the social context of mummification, concluding that a mummy is either spontaneous or anthropogenic may significantly influence research design and tissue sampling, a topic I will return to later in this book.

Anthropogenic Mummification

Anthropogenic mummification occurs when people take deliberate steps to preserve soft tissue. Many examples of anthropogenic mummification exist from a wide variety of contexts and time periods, from the Chinchorro tradition in Chile (5000 BC, Arriaza et al. 2005) to the Italian Renaissance and the preservation of Neapolitan nobles in the fifteenth and sixteenth centuries AD (Fornaciari G. et al. 1999, 2003, 2009). The following examples were chosen to illustrate the temporal and spatial breadth of anthropogenic mummification. Although there is variability in how preservation was accomplished, fundamentally they share several features in common.

Egyptian Anthropogenic Mummification

No doubt due to a combination of a long history of archaeological investigation and popular fascination, Egyptian mummification is likely the most commonly recognized anthropogenic mummification tradition in the world. A considerable amount of information is available on Egyptian mummification, from both textual sources including Egyptian papyri (e.g., Papyrus Vindob 3873, Vos 1993), classical texts (Herodotus [ca. 484 BC to ca. 425 BC], Diodorus [1st century BC)]), and bioarchaeological investigations (e.g. Aufderheide 2009; Elias et al. 2014). Descriptions of the features and developmental phases of Egyptian mummification are common (e.g., Aufderheide 2003; Ikram and Dodson 1998), the basic parameters of which included

- The beginning of anthropogenic mummification is associated with pharaonic Egypt, beginning in the Old Kingdom.
- The brain was removed through the nose (i.e., transnasal excerebration).
- The abdominal organs were removed through a cut made in the abdomen (i.e., transabdominal evisceration).
- There were different types of mummification based on socioeconomic variables.
- The heart was always preserved and, if damaged, replaced by a heart scarab.
- Varying amounts of a plant-based (coniferous) resin were applied.
- The naturally occurring salt known as natron was used as a desiccant.

A number of recent articles have expanded on our understanding of time depth and variability in Egyptian anthropogenic mummification practices. Predynastic Egyptian mummies are considered to be spontaneous mummies with soft tissue preservation resulting from desiccation (Aufderheide 2003; Ikram and Dodson 1998), whereas features associated with anthropogenic mummification (e.g., resin-soaked wrappings, evisceration) beginning to appear during the Old Kingdom (2686–2181 BC) (Ikram and Dodson 1998). Jones and colleagues (2014), however, have recently documented the use of resin as a preservative during the Late Neolithic and Predynastic periods in the Badari region of Upper Egypt (c. 4500 BC—3350 BC). The authors analyzed samples of textiles taken from cemeteries at the site of Mostagedda using conventional gas chromatography (GC-MS), sequential thermal desorption–gas chromatography–mass spectrometry (TD-GC-MS), and pyrolysis–gas chromatography–mass spectrometry (Py-GC-MS). They determined that the textiles were impregnated with a substance consisting of a plant oil or animal fat base with smaller amounts of conifer resin, aromatic plant extract, wax, and plant gum, making it quite similar to the resin used in the mummification process in later Egyptian periods. These results would push back this feature of Egyptian anthropogenic mummification 1500 years (Jones et al. 2014).

Texts by Greek historians Herodotus and Diodorus Siculus have had a significant structuring influence on our understanding of Egyptian mummification in both popular and academic spheres, creating stereotypes that have not been systematically tested until recently. For instance, based on these historical sources, it is assumed that excerebration was limited to the elite and was performed through the nasal cavity with an iron hook. Similarly, evisceration through an incision in the abdomen was reserved for the elite, whereas for commoners this was accomplished by the transperineal introduction of chemicals (Wade and Nelson 2013b). These historical accounts create a sense of standardization and uniformity, yet Wade and colleagues have demonstrated that there was considerable variability in excerebration and evisceration in terms of technique as well as social, geographic, and temporal factors.

South American Andes

The South American Andes have yielded an astonishing number of mummified remains, including some of the oldest anthropogenic and spontaneously mummified remains in the world (Arriaza 1995b; Ovalle et al. 1993). Along the Pacific Coast, the Andean mountain chain creates a rain shadow that results in extreme aridity, facilitating extraordinary preservation of otherwise perishable material such as textiles and flesh. Mummified remains have also been described from a variety of other contexts including the altiplano (e.g. Knudson et al. 2005), mountain-top peaks (e.g., Ceruti 2015), and the *ceja del selva* (the "eyebrow of the jungle"; Guillén 1998). There are three groups in which anthropogenic mummification has been documented: Chinchorro, Chiribaya, and the Chachapoya. The last group I will discuss in this section are the Inca, though to date no Inca mummies have been discovered and described.

Chinchorro Mummification

The Chinchorro were a group of pre-ceramic, fisher-gatherer societies that inhabited the Pacific coast of southern Peru and northern Chile between ca. 7020 and 1110 BC (Arriaza 1995b). Archaeological (see Santoro et al. 2005 for a recent synthesis) and bioarchaeological research on the Chinchorro is extensive and has looked at diet (e.g., Aufderheide et al. 1993; Reinhard et al. 2011), trauma (Standen et al. 2000, 2010), and health (e.g., Reinhard and Urban 2003; Rivera et al. 2008; Standen et al. 1984, 1997). Four different anthropogenic mummification styles have been identified and described: Black, Red, Bandage, and Mud.

The Black Chinchorro mummies are the oldest examples of anthropogenic mummification, though there is some temporal overlap between the categories (Arriaza et al. 2005). The process of creating Black mummies involved the removal of nearly all of the soft tissue from the skeleton. The head and appendages were detached from the trunk and some of the skin, including the scalp, was separated from the body, though retained and ultimately replaced. The viscera, soft tissue, and the brain were also removed. Hot coals or ash may have been used to dry the thoracic cavity, which was then filled with a mixture of animal hair, grasses, and ashes. The body was reassembled, using sticks that ran the length of the axial and appendicular skeleton secured to the bones with reed cord. The entire structure was then covered with a white-ash paste. Any retained skin was put back into place, or replaced by sea lion or other animal skin, and the entire body was painted with black manganese paint.

The body was not as completely disassembled in the production of Red Chinchorro mummies. Although the body was decapitated, the arms and legs were not separated from the trunk. Incisions were made in the abdomen, groin, shoulders, and legs to remove viscera and muscles. The skin of the arms and legs appears to "have been rolled down like a sock" (Arriaza 1995b: 46) and then rolled back up following the removal of the muscles and the introduction of stuffing material. Similar to the Black mummies, the cavities may have been dried out using hot ashes or coals and then stuffed. The body was reinforced with sticks inserted under the skin. The head received more attention than in Black mummies; a white ash paste 'helmet' was applied to the skull, which was then covered by skin and painted with black manganese or red ocher. A human-hair wig was attached to the back of the skull with manganese paint. Both adult and subadult Red mummies have been identified. In some instances, efforts were made to model individual features including breasts, eyes, nose, and mouth (Arriaza 1995a; Standen 1997).

Bandage mummies are a variation of the Red mummies, a style that has been observed in only three infants and at least one adult (Arriaza 1995a, b). The body was treated in the same manner as described earlier, though there is no evidence of incisions in the subadults; the main difference is that the pieces of either human or animal skin were reattached in strips that are approximately 2 cm wide.

The first step in preparing a Mud-coated Chinchorro mummy involved either smoking the corpse or drying it with coals. There is some evidence of evisceration,

TABLE 1.1 Distribution of Chinchorro mummies by type and location

Site	Anthropogenic			Spontaneous	Total
	Black	Red	Mud		
Morro I	8	27	25	36	96
Playa Miller 8	1	9	0	0	10
Morro 1-6	0	0	0	69	69
Morro 1-5	0	17	0	1	18
Morro Uhle	0	9	2	1	12
Arica	2	0	0	0	2
Chinchorro 1	2	0	0	0	2
Maestranza 1	7	0	0	4	11
Quiani	0	1	0	0	1
Maderas Enco 1	3	0	0	0	3
TOTAL	23	63	27	111	224

Source: Adapted from Arriaza et al. 2005.

but the body does not appear to have been reinforced in any way (Arriaza 1995a). Mud, mixed with some sort of protein binder such as blood, sand, or vegetal fiber, covered the body, effectively affixing it to the ground. Adults and subadults of both sexes were afforded this treatment.

The complexity and variety of these mummification types, coupled with the presence of spontaneously mummified bodies, led to the development and testing of two hypotheses regarding their association with Chinchorro social organization. Vivian Standen (1997) suggested that Chinchorro mortuary behavior was selective and that not everyone was mummified. This presents several possibilities, including that different mummification styles may correspond to within-group membership and may indicate the existence of a social hierarchy. Alternatively, Bernardo Arriaza (1995a) argued that Chinchorro mummification was egalitarian and explains the coexistence of different mummification styles as signifying reuse of space through time. To test these hypotheses, Arriaza and colleagues (2005) generated radio-carbon dates from fifteen Chinchorro mummies from four different cemeteries (Morro Uhle, Morro I, Playa Miller 8, and Maestranza). The results indicated a temporal pattern: Black style mummies are the oldest, followed by Red, and then Mud-coated mummification. Spontaneously mummified bodies were found to be contemporaneous with Black and Red styles. These results demonstrated that not everyone was artificially mummified (Table 1.1). In fact, the authors note that at Morro I, 63% of the recovered individuals were artificially mummified in some manner. It is noteworthy that all infants recovered archaeologically were accorded complex mummification treatments (see also Standen et al. 2014), which suggests that mummification may reflect "ideological-circumstantial treatment of the dead" (Arriaza et al. 2005: 670). Although it appears that artificial mummification was not afforded to everyone, it does not seem to be based on vertical social hierarchies.

The Chiribaya

Chiribaya is the name given to the culture that inhabited a series of sites, predominantly situated in the coastal Ilo Valley, in the Osmore drainage in southern Peru during the Late Intermediate Period (ca. AD 1000–1350). Interpreted as a *señorio* (a polity composed of loosely integrated communities), the Chiribaya consisted of biologically and culturally distinct coastal *pescadores* (fisher-folk) and inland *labradores* (agriculturalists) (Lozada Cerna et al. 2009; Lozada Cerna and Buikstra 2005). Although this intersite economic specialization appears consistent for valley sites, archaeological excavations along the coast north of the Ilo Valley have documented intrasite economic diversification (Zaro 2007; Zaro and Alvarez 2005; Zaro et al. 2010).

The information available on Chiribaya anthropogenic mummification is limited. Arthur Aufderheide examined 134 mummies from Chiribaya cemeteries and does not report on any evidence of anthropogenic mummification (Aufderheide 2003). Sonia Guillén (2004), however, reports that there is a small sample of anthropogenically prepared mummies from the sites of Chiribaya Baja, Loreto Viejo, and Algodonal. Guillén provides only general details but indicates that the bodies were eviscerated through an abdominal incision. The cavity was then filled with raw wool and food (e.g., corn, manioc, coca leaves), and the incision was closed with wool yarn. She also indicates that the skin may have been treated in some manner to deter insect activity.

The Chachapoya

In 1997, over 200 mummy bundles were recovered from the Chachapoya site known as LC1 at the Laguna de los Cóndores (Figure 1.8, Guillén 2004). Incorporated into the Inca Empire during the Late Horizon (ca. AD 1470–1532), the Chachapoya inhabited a region in northern Peru bounded by the crest of the Central Cordillera of the Andes to the west and the Río Huallaga to the east. The mummies recovered from LC1 have been described as anthropogenic because there is evidence that the internal organs below the diaphragm were removed via the rectum and that the skin may have been treated with some form of natural antiseptic (Guillén 2004; Wild et al. 2007).

Based on a radiocarbon dates from the LC1 site, Guillén and colleagues (Guillén 2004; Wild et al. 2007) have suggested that anthropogenic mummification was introduced by the Inca when they conquered the region. In her 2004 article, Guillén calls them "Chachapoya-Inca" mummies and characterizes Chachapoya mortuary behavior as centered on the secondary interment of dry bones. Chachapoya mummies, however, from other sites predate the Late Horizon and the Inca conquest. Mummies from the Laguna Huayabamba, radiocarbon-dated to between 1017 and 1219 AD, are very similar to the LC1 mummies in terms of textiles, body position, and overall structure (Nystrom et al. 2010). One potentially significant difference is whether or not the Huayabamba mummies were eviscerated. Though I was unable

FIGURE 1.8 Anthropogenic mummy from the Laguna de los Cóndores (Wild et al. 2007).

to conduct an internal examination of the Huayabamba mummies, I did observe a prolapsed rectum in one of the mummies. This is most likely due to the buildup of decomposition gases, suggesting that at least this individual had not been eviscerated (Figure 1.9).

Because Laguna Huayabamba is a pre-Inca site, some form of mummification was present in the Chachapoya region prior to the Inca. Although the Inca may very well have introduced changes in Chachapoya mortuary behavior, based on the presence of mummies at the Laguna Huayabamba, they did not replace a mortuary focus on dry bones with mummification. Rather, my colleagues and I have suggested that the presence of both disarticulated bones and mummified remains points to an extended mortuary practice, one in which mummified remains, while visited and cared for, gradually degraded and become disarticulated dry bones (Nystrom et al. 2010).

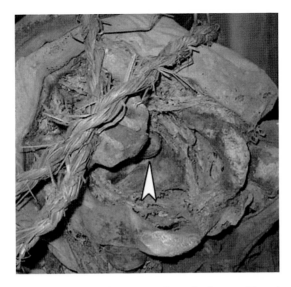

FIGURE 1.9 The perianal region of a mummy from the Laguna Huayabamba (Nystrom et al. 2010). The white arrow points to a prolapsed rectum, which could have resulted from the postmortem buildup of intra-abdominal gases, suggesting that this individual was not eviscerated like those from the Laguna de los Cóndores.

The Royal Inca

Royal Inca mummies are generally assumed to be anthropogenic based primarily on the description of early Spanish chroniclers, though a royal Inca mummy has yet to be recovered or studied by bioarchaeologists (Aufderheide 2003; Bauer and Rodríguez 2007). Despite this, it is worth spending some time considering them for several reasons. The sociopolitical and economic influence the Inca emperors retained in death make them an excellent example of 'dead body politics' (Buikstra and Nystrom 2015; Verdery 1999). Although there are no royal Inca mummies to study, numerous examples of other Late Horizon mummies provide some insight into Inca mortuary behavior and imperial policies, including mountain-top sacrifices (Ceruti 2015), the Chachapoya (Guillén 2012), and Puruchuco-Huaquerones (Williams and Murphy 2013). In some cases, Inca conquest and imperial policies may have had a significant impact on regional mortuary traditions.

In Spanish Colonial Peru (1599), Juan Polo de Ondegardo was placed in charge of stamping out what was considered to be idolatry among the native populations. This consisted in large part of locating and destroying mummies (Bauer and Rodríguez 2007). Polo de Ondegardo located all of the royal Inca mummies as well as the bodies of several Inca queens (*qoyas*) and other ritual artifacts. Although most were destroyed, Polo de Ongegardo secretly kept five royal mummies. In 1560, twenty-eight years after the initial Spanish entrada, Garcilaso de le Vega had the opportunity to view these Inca mummies and wrote this description:

> The bodies were perfectly preserved without the loss of a hair of the head or brow or an eyelash. They were dressed as they had been in life, with *llautus* [royal headbands] on their heads but no other ornaments or royal insignia. They were buried in a sitting position, in a posture often assumed by Indian men and women: their hands were crossed across their breast, the left over the right, and their eyes lowered, as if looking at the ground. . . . I remember having touched one of the fingers of Huaina Capac, which seemed like that of a wooden statue, it was so hard and stiff. The bodies weighed so little that any Indian could carry them in his arms or [on] his back from house to house. . . .
> *(Garcilaso de la Vega. 1966: 306 308 [1609: pt. 1. bk. 5, ch. 29],*
> *translated by Bauer and Rodríguez 2007: 4)*

Other accounts tend to support the assumption that the Inca mummies were anthropogenic:

> The body [of Pachacuti Inca Yupanqui] was so well preserved, and treated with a certain resin, that it seemed alive.
> *(Acosta 1986: 364 [1590: bk. 6, ch. 21], translated by*
> *Bauer and Rodríguez 2007: 6)*

> He was embalmed and well preserved, as were all those that I saw
> *(Polo de Ondegardo 1990 [1571], translated by*
> *Bauer and Rodríguez 2007: 6)*

> His [Huayna Capac's] mother was much esteemed. She was called Mama Ocllo. Polo sent her body and that of Huayna Capac's, well-embalmed and cured, to Lima.
> *(Acosta 1986: 424 [1590: bk. 5, ch. 22], translated by*
> *Bauer and Rodríguez 2007: 6)*

Historical documents suggested that these royal mummies may have been buried on the grounds of the Hospital of San Andrés in Lima. Despite archaeological excavations in 1868, 1877, 1937, and more recently in 2001 and 2005, they have not been located (Bauer and Rodríguez 2007). Consequently, while the earlier quotes may provide tantalizing hints as to the nature of royal Inca mummies, the mummification process and the steps taken to ensure preservation remain unknown.

Historic Anthropogenic Mummies

The term "embalming" is often used interchangeably with anthropogenic mummification. For instance, the above translations of sixteenth-century Spanish

Chroniclers describe Inca remains as embalmed. In their study of "embalmed bodies, dating to the Renaissance and coming from Italy" Valentina Giuffra and colleagues (2011: 1949) focus "on the mummification techniques used to treat these bodies." Guillén (2004: 150) states that "almost all the Chiribaya mummies were preserved naturally" and that investigators did not "report any embalmed bodies." Embalming should be considered a specific form of anthropogenic mummification, and it would be best to avoid conflation of the terms. Key features of the former involve the chemical treatment of the soft tissue and immersion and/ or injection of chemicals, whereas not all anthropogenic mummification involve chemical treatment.

Some of the earliest embalming methods (mid to late AD 1500s) involved evisceration and immersion in aqua vita (an aqueous solution of ethanol). Beginning in the seventeenth century and the emergence scientific study of anatomy, embalming involved the arterial injection of a chemical cocktail (Aufderheide 2003; Brenner 2014). Embalming exclusively as part of funerary behavior began in the mid-1800s in the United States during the Civil War (Brenner 2014).

A number of prominent historical figures have been embalmed including Vladimir Lenin and Eva Peron, but these have not received any systematic scientific investigation (Aufderheide 2003). There is, however, a rich body of literature on the embalmed remains of historical figures (e.g., Fornaciari G. 1999; Piombino-Mascali et al. 2010) from the Italian Renaissance.

Gino Fornaciari and colleagues (e.g., Fornaciari G. 1999; Fornaciari G. et al. 2009) examined twenty-seven bodies recovered from the Basilica of San Domenico. Fourteen of the individuals were leading figures of the Italian Renaissance such as Maria of Aragon (1502–1568), Ferrante I of Aragon, King of Naples (1431–1494), and Isabella of Aragon (1470–1524). These individuals were eviscerated via an incision that extended across the full anterior thoraco-abdominal wall. Secondary cuts were observed running transversely at the level of the umbilicus, and in six individuals the calotte was cut off, allowing the removal of the brain (Figure 1.10).

During renovation of the hospital of Santa Maria della Scala in Siena, Italy, the mummified remains of two individuals were recovered; Salimbene Capacci (1433–1497), the rector of the hospital in the late fifteenth century, and his wife, Margherita Sozzini (?–1511). Valentina Giuffra and colleagues (2011) examined the mummies to reconstruct the embalming procedures, ultimately comparing the process to contemporaneous documentary evidence and the remains discussed above from the Basilica of San Domenico (Figure 1.11a, b, c).

The body of Capacci was eviscerated via an incision made on the left side of the thoracic and abdominal walls whereas Sozzini was eviscerated through an incision that ran from the upper thorax through the sternum and down to the pubis. Contrary to some of the other examples discussed here, the brains were not removed. In both instances, the body cavities were stuffed with vegetal material which including sage, rosemary, foxtail, and flax, though there is a distinct difference between the individuals, which Giuffra et al. (2011) suggested may be related to the social rank of Capacci relative to his wife as well as potentially the season in which they died.

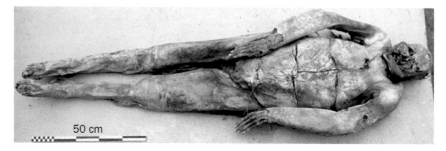

FIGURE 1.10 The mummified remains of Maria of Aragon (Fornaciari G. et al. 2003).

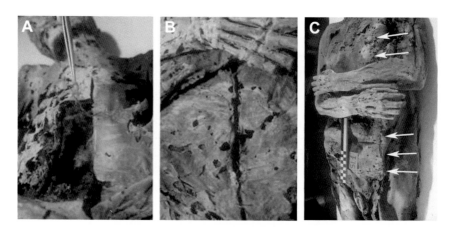

FIGURE 1.11 (A) and (B) are anterior views of the body of Margherita Sozzini demonstrating the vegetal material used to stuff the body cavity and the incision through the thorax and abdominal wall for evisceration. The white arrows in (C) indicate the left lateral incision made on the body of Salimbene Capacci (Giuffra et al. 2011).

Spontaneous/Natural Mummification

The defining feature of spontaneous mummification is that there is no evidence of any intentional steps taken to intervene in the decay process. Preservation in these instances is due solely to environmental conditions that delay the process of decomposition, and as discussed earlier, is most commonly due to desiccation. Examples of spontaneous mummies include Ötzi (see Figure 4.9), Kwäday Dän Ts'ìnchí (Dickson et al. 2004), the Greenland mummies (Figure 1.12), the mountain-top sacrifices (see Figure 1.2) and Chiribaya mummies from the South American Andes, early Egyptian mummies (Aufderheide et al. 1999; Aufderheide et al. 2004a), and the remains of the sailors from the Franklin Expedition.

Despite the direct connection between spontaneous mummification and environmental conditions, research on soft tissue taphonomy has been limited

FIGURE 1.12 Spontaneously frozen mummy of Inuit child from Qilakitsoq burial in Greenland (Edwards et al. 2002).

(Aufderheide 2011). As will be discussed in Chapter 3, however, this type of research appears to be increasing in frequency including both comparative (e.g., Prats-Muñoz et al. 2013) and experimental taphonomic studies (e.g., Gill-Frerking 2010).

A significant amount of research has been devoted to reconstructing the environmental conditions that led to the mummification of the corpse that has come to be known as Ötzi. Briefly, the perimortem scenario that has been reconstructed for Ötzi's last few days suggests that for some unknown reason, he fled to the mountains, was pursued, was shot in the back with an arrow, and died due to hemorrhagic shock (Pernter et al. 2007). Several hypotheses follow regarding the environmental factors that may have resulted in the remarkable degree of soft tissue preservation observed in Ötzi:

- The body was rapidly desiccated by an autumn föhn, a warm wind (Rollo et al. 2000) and then covered by snow.
- The body froze rapidly then was covered by snow resulting in desiccation and freeze-drying.
- The body was frozen due to the buildup of ice in the soil.

Analyses seeking clues about what led to Ötzi's preservation have been conducted on his skin (Bereuter et al. 1997; Makristathis et al. 2002; Williams et al. 1995), dermal collagen (Janko et al. 2010), brain tissue (Maixner et al. 2013), gut contents (Dickson et al. 2009; Rollo et al. 2002), red blood cells (Janko et al. 2012), and mtDNA (Handt et al. 1994; Olivieri et al. 2010). Further, investigators have examined the bacteria living on his skin (Rollo et al. 2000), mouth (Maixner et al. 2014), colon, and stomach (Cano et al. 2000) to try to reconstruct the postmortem environmental conditions.

Evidence that speaks to the taphonomic history of the body includes the complete loss of epidermis, hair, and nails (though Capasso 1994 reports some nails were recovered), although with no signs of advanced putrefaction (Bereuter et al. 1997). Adipocere was observed underneath the dermis on the face, the formation of which is generally associated with wet conditions. Several studies have demonstrated that the collagen in the dermal layer of Ötzi's skin was structurally well preserved (Hess et al. 1998; Janko et al. 2010; Williams et al. 1995). Janko and colleagues (2010) examined the micro- and ultrastructure of collagen bundles from the dermal layer using atomic force microscopy (AFM) and Raman spectroscopy measurements. These researchers observed slight changes in the mechanical behavior of the collagen as determined by AFM, increasing from 3.2 ± 1.0 GPa recorded in modern collagen to 4.1 ± 1.1 GPa in the samples obtained from Ötzi. The authors suggest that this small shift in the mechanical properties of the collagen—in effect, the collagen became stiffer—may be due the creation of more cross-linkages following dehydration of the tissue (Janko et al. 2010). Additionally, the results of the Raman spectroscopy analysis indicate very little degradation of the collagen fibrils, a result that is not expected if the fibers had undergone cycles of freezing-thawing or microorganism activity.

Based on these data, it appears that shortly after death the corpse was covered by snow and ice, thus protecting it from scavengers. The body was found in a shallow depression below a rocky ledge, which likely prevented it from being crushed by the glacier. At some point, possibly during the Roman period, the ice thawed and the body became submerged in meltwater for several months, followed by desiccation (Bereuter et al. 1997). It was at this point that most of the postmortem damage listed above may have occurred.

Spontaneous-Enhanced Mummification

There is a fine line between the above category and what Aufderheide called 'spontaneous-enhanced' mummification. What exactly constitutes spontaneous-enhanced mummification is a bit unclear though, because Aufderheide (2003) does not actually provide an explicit definition of the term. I would offer the following as a definition: soft tissue preservation that is due to favorable environmental conditions that may have been 'helped' or 'encouraged' by human intentional or unintentional alteration of the natural or built environment. In this manner, the category bridges the gap between spontaneous and anthropogenic mummification.

In the two examples discussed next, it is the nature of the built mortuary environment, the tombs and structures in which the dead were interred, that facilitated soft tissue preservation. In one instance, features of the tomb were intentionally constructed to encourage preservation, whereas in the other case, soft tissue preservation appears to be unintentional. I think it is in this category where it is beneficial to consider an expanded definition of intentionality. Although these mummies do not exhibit the classic signatures of anthropogenic mummification (e.g., evisceration, excerebration), by considering the body within its broader mortuary context, it may be possible to infer the intentionality traditionally limited to artificial mummification.

Palermo Catacomb Mummies

Between the sixteenth and eighteenth centuries, burial practices among Capuchin friars living in the city of Palermo, Italy, resulted in one of the largest collection of mummified remains. The deceased were brought to a special preparation room known as *colatoio* (plural: *colatoi*, from the Latin *colum* which means drain (Piñar et al. 2014)). Inside were racks of terra-cotta tubes; bodies were placed on top of these tubes, which served to drain away decomposition fluids. The *colatoi* were sealed for approximately one year, after which the body was washed with vinegar, clothed, and either placed in a coffin or put on display (see Figures 2.1 and 4.8). The manner in which the *colatoi* were constructed, along with a dry environment and stable temperature, led to spontaneous desiccation. Long-term preservation of the bodies may have also been due to ventilation within the catacombs' corridors. It is this coupling of a human-made burial structures and environmental factors that makes this an example of spontaneous-enhanced mummification. As noted by Piombino-Mascali et al. (2010: 359–360), the original intent behind the construction of the *colatoi* was not mummification but rather was an attempt to accelerate decomposition to "reach the 'dry and pure' status that Hertz postulates." Thus, the *colatoi* represent an instance in which unintentional consequences of tomb construction (i.e., dry, cool ambient climate) and intentional features of the tomb (i.e., the terra-cotta tubes) converged to facilitate mummification via desiccation. In time, a variety of additional intentional steps were introduced, including dipping in lime, evisceration, and arterial injection of chemicals (Piombino-Mascali et al. 2010).

Joseon Dynasty Mummies

During the last decade a number of articles have been written about mummies from the Joseon Dynasty (1392–1910 AD) of Korea (Figure 1.13) (Chang et al. 2006; Kahila Bar-Gal et al. 2012; Kim et al. 2008; Lee et al. 2007; Seo et al. 2010; Shin et al. 2009; Song and Shin 2014). During the Joseon Dynasty, coffins had a layer of charcoal while the space between the coffin and the pit walls were filled with a lime-soil mixture (Shin et al. 2003a).

FIGURE 1.13 Medieval Korea mummies: (A) Andong (Kim et al. 2014), (B) Hadong 1 (Hershkovitz et al. 2014), and (C) Hadong 2 (Shin et al. 2012).

How mummification happened in these instances is not fully understood (Shin et al. 2008) though it is possible that the presence of lime played a role. Lime (CaO) can have several preservative effects, including a high affinity for water, heat-induced desiccation, and the retarding of enzymatic activity through increased pH (Aufderheide 2003). The presence of lime has been implicated in mummification in several instances, either being directly applied to the body or in the form of lime-stone architecture (Aufderheide and Aufderheide 1991; McKinley 1977; Yamada et al. 1996). It is also possible that the lime-soil mixture created a physical barrier protecting the burial from the introduction of water. Other environmental variables are almost certainly involved as well, because many examples of remains recovered from lime-soil tombs that are not mummified exist (Kim et al. 2008).

Mummification in these instances could be categorized as examples of 'spontaneous-enhanced' in that preservation results from the unintentional creation of favorable environmental conditions by human activity. There was no intent to preserve soft tissue, and in fact, Shin and colleagues note that, "descendents (sic) hoped that the corpse of the ancestor would be completely decayed" because "medieval Koreans believed in misfortunes correlating with the incomplete disintegration of the corpses of their ancestors" (Shin et al. 2003a: 377 and 382).

Chapter Summary

My colleagues and I have previously discussed biases in the categorization of mummies as either anthropogenic or spontaneous (Nystrom et al. 2010). Our primary concern was that this distinction rests upon the observation of relatively gross morphological evidence, such as excarnation and evisceration. Because anthropogenic mummies are considered to be the product of the intentional preservation of soft tissue, they are a distinct and observable manifestation of mortuary behavior. Alternatively, preservation in spontaneous mummies is not intentional and therefore is not considered to reflect human behavior. In this instance the body itself becomes irrelevant, and we may rely exclusively upon the built environment or material culture to reconstruct mortuary behavior. This bias may inadvertently influence the reconstruction of the social context and the significance of the body in a culture.

This distinction between intentional and unintentional mummification may also influence research design and tissue sampling. Researchers may have greater reluctance to conduct invasive analyses or to take tissue samples from a mummy that is considered to be anthropogenic, whereas the same may not apply to those mummies categorized as spontaneous. As will be discussed in more depth in the section on ethics, some authors have discussed how the decision to take tissue samples may be influenced by the distinction between anthropogenic and spontaneous mummification.

Reliance upon this distinction also neglects intentional steps taken to enhance soft tissue preservation that are more ephemeral archaeologically. Research conducted by Michael Parker Pearson and colleagues on bog bodies from Bronze Age Britain serves as an important example as it destabilizes the distinction between these categories.

The Bog Bodies of Cladh Hallan

Despite the fact that there is evidence that bodies were intentionally deposited in bogs, soft tissue preservation in these instances is considered to represent spontaneous mummification as it occurred "without any human intervention: the process appears to be completely natural" (Gill-Frerking 2010: 62). Alternatively, research by Parker Pearson and colleagues suggests the intentional use of the bog to preserve soft tissue.

Parker Pearson and colleagues (2005) excavated a series of three Late Bronze Age to Iron Age roundhouses (ca. 1100–200 BC) at the site of Cladh Hallan, South Uist, Outer Hebrides. They recovered remains of two adults and a child in the north house, one child and two dogs in the central house, and finally one child in the southern-most house (Parker Pearson et al. 2005). Several features of the skeletons and burials suggested to the researchers that the bodies were preserved above ground for a period of time before their final interment (Figure 1.14). First, there was a discrepancy in the radiocarbon dates produced from the skeletons themselves and the optically stimulated luminescence (OSL) dates from the base of house walls, with the former significantly predating house construction. There was also evidence for postmortem manipulation of the bones. Most tellingly, osteological and isotopic analyses indicate that the adult male skeleton from the north house is composed of three separate individuals (Parker Pearson et al. 2007). Similarly, molecular

FIGURE 1.14 The female 'mummy' from Cladh Hallan (Hanna et al. 2012).

analyses of the female skeleton from the same house demonstrate that the mandible, humerus, and femur all come from different individuals (Hanna et al. 2012).

The researchers employed several different methods to reconstruct the taphonomic history of the remains, including mercury intrusion porosimetry (HgIP), short-angle X-ray scattering (SAXS), and Fourier transform infrared spectroscopy (FTIR). Both the FTIR and SAXS analyses indicated that the bone surfaces were only slightly demineralized and were distinctly different from other bones recovered from the same context. The results of the HgIP analyses indicated that the porosity observed in the tibia of the male skeleton recovered from the north house was significantly less than what was observed in a contemporaneous dog skeleton.

Further, microscopic examination of a section of the male's femur indicated a sharp and distinct boundary of microbial activity.

Based on these results the authors conclude that the decay process had been interrupted through exposure to an acidic environment. Parker Pearson and colleagues (2005: 544) suggest that the remains were intentionally immersed in a bog to preserve them, leading the authors to speculate that "artificial mummification was far more widespread in prehistoric societies than hitherto realised." By discussing these remains as examples of artificial mummies, the authors run counter to the general classification of bog bodies as natural mummies. Although clearly these remains do not fit into our definition of 'mummy' because they no longer have soft tissue, the careful reconstruction of the taphonomic history of the remains suggests that they may have had preserved soft tissue at one point. On one hand, these results have some serious implications for the interpretation of other bog bodies. More broadly, this example illustrates the difficulty in identifying intentional human intervention in the decay process.

Notes

1. On December 17, 2014, a news story that carried the catchy title "Cemetery with One MILLION Mummies Unearthed in Egypt" proceeded to garner a lot of attention on social media. The site with this massive cemetery, Fag El Gamous, dates to the Roman and Byzantine period of Egypt and has been excavated by researchers from Brigham Young University for the last twenty-eight years. The possibility that the cemetery contains a million mummies was based on the density of burials already excavated and the estimated extent of the cemetery. Although several aspects of the project, as reported in this news story, are questionable from a bioarchaeological perspective (the researchers suggest that a eighteen-month-old was female based on the presence of a necklace and bracelets; they noted that there may be some internal division of the cemetery, with clusters of individuals with blonde hair and with red hair), it is a statement made by the director of the project, Kerry Muhlestein, professor of Ancient Scripture at BYU, and the reaction of Egyptian Antiquity Department officials that is most pertinent to the focus of this chapter. Despite the fact that the title of the news story is about mummies, Muhlestein states, "I don't think you would term what happens to these burials as true mummification" but that "If we want to use the term loosely, then they were mummified."

   On December 20, however, Youssef Khalifa, head of Egypt's Ministry of Antiquities, halted the excavation and states that "there are no million mummies, a mummy definition to begin with means a complete mummified body . . ." and further describes the remains the BYU team are recovering as "only poor skeletons." (http://luxortimesmaga zine.blogspot.com/2014/12/mummy-curse-strikes-again-msa-stops-byu.html, accessed February 9, 2015; www.dailymail.co.uk/sciencetech/article-2877855/Cemetery-one-MILLION-mummies-unearthed-Egypt-1-500-year-old-desert-necropolis-largest-found.html, accessed January 31, 2015).
2. Aufderheide (2003) also provides short discussions on other, less common, mummification mechanisms including salt, tree coffins, bat guano, ventilation, anaerobiasis, and plaster mummies, as well as instances in which the mechanism is indeterminate.
3. Siberian Times, http://siberiantimes.com/science/casestudy/news/n0314-mummy-of-a-child-warrior-from-lost-medieval-civilisation-unearthed-near-arctic/, accessed August 21, 2015.

2

HISTORY OF BIOARCHAEOLOGY AND MUMMY STUDIES

The fields of mummy studies and bioarchaeology were both crystalizing during the early 1970s. Though they shared (and continue to share) key events and personnel, they ultimately followed different trajectories. Bioarchaeology developed out of the synergy between processual archaeology and skeletal biology with a focus on problem-oriented research grounded in a biocultural perspective in which the body and culture are considered to be intimately connected. From the beginning, mummy studies have been allied more closely with the biomedical fields and have principally focused on questions related to detection and diagnosis of soft tissue paleopathology, paleoepidemiology, and disease evolution.

In this chapter I briefly outline the history of the two fields, noting both commonalities and distinctions. Understanding the historical background is important because it directly influences research trends and challenges faced by the fields. Mummy studies were developing within the same milieu as bioarchaeology and is currently experiencing some of the same challenges that skeletal paleopathology experienced in the 1980s and 1990s. In many ways, paleopathology transitioned through these challenges due to greater integration of the biocultural perspective offered by bioarchaeology (Buzon 2012; Armelagos 2003; Zuckerman et al. 2012). Therefore, my hope is that by detailing the history of the disciplines, discussing both areas of intersection and divergence, I can highlight the potential for more fully integrating the problem-orientated biocultural perspective.

History of Bioarchaeology

Bioarchaeology is the contextualized analysis of human remains and encompasses a range of research perspectives diverse in emphasis and scope (Argarwal and Glencross 2011b; Buikstra et al. 2011; Goldstein 2006; Knüsel 2010; Larsen 2002, 2006; Martin et al. 2013). Bioarchaeology developed independently in the United States and United Kingdom in the early 1970s as several key publications introduced the basic problem-oriented research structure and perspective (Buikstra 2006a).

In the United Kingdom, Grahame Clark (1972) used the term in reference to the interdisciplinary research of archaeologically recovered faunal remains. This was followed closely by Vilhem Møller-Christensen's (1973) description of proper 'osteo-archaeological' excavation techniques for human skeletal material. Whereas Møller-Christensen's paper was principally outlining a methodological approach, his emphasis on the involvement of specialists trained in osteology in the excavation of skeletal material ensured not only greater recovery of skeletal elements but also recovery of vital contextual information. In the UK, bioarchaeology encompasses the analysis of paleobotanical, faunal, and human remains, with 'human osteoarchaeology' often used to differentiate the analysis of human remains (Knüsel 2010). Human osteoarchaeologists and paleopathologists are often employed in archaeology departments and are separated from their social anthropology colleagues. These disciplinary divisions have resulted in human osteoarchaeology/bioarchaeology establishing deeper connections with the natural sciences, whereas theoretical and funerary archaeology fostered a closer relationship with the social sciences (Knüsel 2010).

In North America, bioarchaeology refers specifically to the analysis of human remains recovered from archaeological contexts. Bioarchaeologists are most commonly found in anthropology departments due to a longer history of a four-field approach (archaeology, cultural anthropology, biological/physical anthropology, and linguistic anthropology). In spite of this, the subfields have experienced separation, motivating biological anthropologists to cultivate closer connections with archaeology and social anthropology. This integration between the subfields has deep roots in the United States, and a number of scholars (e.g, Earnest Hooton, Washington Matthews, Cordelia A. Studley, Mildred Trotter, Ruth Sawtell Wallis, Jeffries Wyman) recognized the importance of integrating archaeological and skeletal data in problem-orientated research (Beck 2006; Buikstra 2006a; Powell et al. 2006; Rakita 2006). Key contributions during this formative stage of bioarchaeology in the United States includes Wilton Krogman's (1935) reconstruction of 'life histories' from skeletal material and his emphasis on the need for greater integration between archaeology and physical anthropology. Additionally, the earliest "explicitly labeled strategy-conjoined archaeological-human osteological study" was J. Lawrence Angel's social biology (Buikstra 2006b: 349).

Although preceded by these scholars, the main paradigmatic shifts that led to the formation of bioarchaeology occurred during the mid-twentieth century. Sherwood Washburn's (1951) articulation of the "New Physical Anthropology" emphasized a holistic, problem-oriented, and population-based perspective (Buikstra 2006a). He characterized the 'old physical anthropology' as primarily a technique, where the "common core of the science was the measurement of external form with calipers" (Washburn 1951: 298). In contrast, the New Physical Anthropology "is primarily an area of interest" and is focused on the population (Washburn 1951: 298). Washburn recognized that research questions should be informed by an understanding of context and that the field would require the "active collaboration of many specialists" and a deeper connection "between the branches of anthropology" (1951: 299).

Additionally, Lewis Binford's (1962) "New Archaeology" called for archaeology to become more anthropological and scientific. Dissatisfied with cultural-historical archaeology, Binford advocated that archaeology more fully integrate the goals of anthropology to "*explicate* and *explain* the total range of physical and cultural similarities and differences of the entire spatial-temporal span of man's existence" (Binford 1962: 217, emphasis in original). According to Binford, although archaeology has made significant contributions to explication (i.e., making something clearer), it had made no contribution to explanation.

Coinciding with Grahame Clark's use of the term "bioarchaeology" in the UK, Frank Saul (1972) formulated his forensics-inspired osteobiographical approach. Focusing initially on the generation of a broad suite of data (e.g., diet, pathology) from an individual, the data ultimately led to population-level descriptions and thus reflect the goals and perspectives of bioarchaeology (Buikstra and Scott 2009). Again, though principally methodological in focus similar to the osteo-archaeology of Møller-Christensen, it was explicitly problem-orientated and recognized the importance of archaeological and historical contextualization (Buikstra and Scott 2009).

As it manifested in the United States, the term "bioarchaeology" was first defined by Jane Buikstra (1977) in her contribution to a volume edited by Robert Blakely. In the introduction to the volume, Blakely (1977) explicitly argued for a holistic biocultural approach to the analysis of human remains from archaeological contexts. In her paper, Buikstra advocated for a biocultural, multidisciplinary research design that established an equal partnership between archaeologists and anthropologists. In addition, this bioarchaeology engages much more explicitly with mortuary theory, social theory, and contextual issues (Buikstra et al. 2011; Goldstein 2006). This holistic biocultural paradigm dominates the field today even as it diversifies in scope and emphasis.

Beginning in the 1980s, Clark Larsen's (1981, 1987, 2002, 2006) use of bioarchaeology focused on questions pertaining to quality of life, behavior and lifestyle, biological relatedness, and population history. With an emphasis on adaptive and behavioral changes, it is more bio-orientated and speaks to an audience outside anthropology, facilitated by an increasing incorporation and articulation with the natural sciences. This research program has been very successful, but it has also been criticized as being disconnected from archaeological data and for not being as deeply invested in social theory (Goldstein 2006; Knüsel 2010).

The biocultural bioarchaeology of George Armelagos, Alan Goodman, and Thomas Leatherman adheres to the same basic premises (i.e., population perspective, hypothesis testing) as the bioarchaeologies described above but emphasizes the idea that "cultural systems, such as technology, social organization, and ideology, can inhibit or encourage biological processes such as undernutrition and disease" (Zuckerman and Armelagos 2011: 21). Molly Zuckerman and George Armelagos

(2011: 20) characterize the main distinction between biocultural bioarchaeology and the other manifestations of the field in that the former "explicitly considers social and cultural components of the environment, as well as physical, in regards to human adaptation." Further, advocates of this perspective consider the biocultural perspective as a bridge between biological and sociocultural anthropology leading to holistic analyses of the political economy and political ecology of social inequality (e.g., Harrod et al. 2012; Stone 2012).

The osteobiographical approach is still very much present within bioarchaeology but has expanded in scope and theoretical engagement. In their introductory chapter to the *Bioarchaeology of Individuals*, Ann Stodder and Ann Palkovich (2012: 2) note that the population-centric and increasingly laboratory-focused research of much bioarchaeology has somewhat distanced "the study of skeletal remains from the lives of the people we study." An analytical focus on the individual does not limit the broader significance of the research, however. Indeed, the ability to produce such a detailed reconstruction of a single individual's life and death is predicated upon the detailed reconstruction of context. A focus on reconstruction of an individual's life history is "a complementary component to the populational framework of bioarchaeology" (Stodder and Palkovich 2012: 2).

Beyond a detailed osteological analysis of an individual, osteobiographies "are set apart by their humanistic, even experiential, interpretations of skeletal data" (Boutin 2012: 113). Boutin (2012) takes a narrative approach in her analysis and reconstruction of the individuals and mortuary events from a tomb at the Middle Bronze Age/Late Bronze Age site of Alalakh in Syria. Although loosely based on Saul's original concept, John Robb's (2002: 155) formulation of osteobiography emphasizes the cultural understanding of events rather than on specific individuals and attempts to reconstruct the "cultural idea of what a human life should be."

Although there has been diversification of bioarchaeological approaches to the past, the biocultural model remains the core paradigm. Bioarchaeologists, irrespective of their 'brand' of bioarchaeology, examine the manner in which the body and culture are connected by reconstructing the phenomenological lived experiences of an individual or group, generating data on disease prevalence (Shuler 2011), nutritional inadequacies (Ortner et al. 2001), activity patterns (Havelková et al. 2011), nonspecific indicators of stress (Andrushko et al. 2006), trauma (Murphy et al. 2010), and the biogeochemical signatures of diet (Torres-Rouff et al. 2012) and mobility (Stojanowski and Knudson 2014). Bioarchaeological research is also increasingly incorporating archaeological and social theories that touch on such issues as structural violence (Klaus 2012; Nystrom 2014), sickness ideology (Marsteller et al. 2011), identity (Gowland 2006; Sutter 2005), feminist and gender heteronormativity (Geller 2008, 2009), fragmentation and the self (Duncan and Schwarz 2014; Geller 2012), and embodiment (Baadsgaard 2011).

In their discussion of the development of bioarchaeology, Argarwal and Glencross (2011b) identify three waves of theoretical engagement. The first wave was characterized by a population-based approach that considered skeletal indicators of health and disease as manifestations of adaptive responses to environmental and cultural stressors. Key works include Mark Cohen and George Armelagos' (1984) *Paleopathology and the Origins of Agriculture*. The second wave was twofold. First, research focused on new and emerging methodological tools including isotopic and DNA analyses. Secondly, researchers began the "critical examination of the nature of archaeological skeletal samples themselves," characterized by James Wood and colleagues (1992) discussion of the osteological paradox (Argarwal and Glencross 2011b: 2). The last wave was "anchored in the greater contextualization of archaeological skeletal remains" and the integration of "elements from biological, behavioral, ecological, and social research" (Argarwal and Glencross 2011b: 3). Although the incorporation of mortuary theory within bioarchaeological research would appear to predate this third wave, with the work of Saxe (1970), Binford (1971), and Brown (1971a) influencing the analysis of social correlates within mortuary contexts, the field does seem to be experiencing a recent florescence of research grounded in a wide range of theoretical frameworks.

History of Paleopathology

Because the development of mummy studies parallels the development of paleopathology, and a considerable amount of mummy research is still focused on the subject, it is necessary to identify key moments in the recent history of paleopathology. In the late 1960s, paleopathology was critically evaluated by Saul Jarcho (1966) and Don Brothwell and A.T. Sandison (1967). These authors expressed dissatisfaction with the state of the field and their critiques were "attempts to overcome the mid-century doldrums" (Buikstra and Cook 1980: 434). In his *Human Palaeopathology* volume, Jarcho noted several features of paleopathology that pertained to mummy studies. In particular, he noted that little attention was paid to preserved soft tissues. Further, newly developed techniques in the biomedical sciences were not being applied to the study of ancient tissues, and paleopathology was not regarded as valuable or contributing to medical science.

   Over the intervening fifty years, the state and history of paleopathology has been evaluated by a number of different researchers. In 1980, Buikstra and Cook noted positive developments in many of the areas identified by Jarcho. Although paleopathological reports frequently languished in the appendices of archaeological reports, the authors noted greater interdisciplinary participation. With respect to mummy research, Buikstra and Cook stated that research falls into two categories: the intensive "communal examination of single specimens" and more population-based epidemiological research (1980: 460). Interestingly, in the same year, Dastugue (1980) struck a much more pessimistic note, effectively dismissing the potential contribution of mummy studies to paleopathology. Aufderheide (1981: 867), however, was much more optimistic in his discussion, and although he focuses on anatomical methods, he presages the importance of biochemical and immunological work: "Imagine the legacy of information available about ancient infectious diseases were it possible to identify antigens of or antibodies to bacterial and viral agents in mummy tissue!" Still, the fact that Aufderheide made this statement in 1981, indicates that Jarcho's original criticism about the integration of techniques from the biomedical sciences, which remained apt fifteen years later. Indeed, as will be discussed in Chapter 4, integration of biochemical and genetic methods in the examination of paleopathology did not begin until the mid-1990s.

Ortner and Aufderheide (1991: 1) provided another glimpse into the development of paleopathology and discussed two key areas where the field has "reached a plateau beyond which significant further progress cannot be made without major changes in the type of research we do and the methods we use to do it." In particular, they highlighted the need to shift from a focus on description and classification to the biocultural context of disease itself and the lack of theoretical development (Ortner 1991). It is important, however, to distinguish between Ortner's use of the term 'theory' and how theory is operationalized in this volume. By calling for paleopathological work to be grounded in theory, Ortner (1991: 10) was referring specifically to the interpretation of data relative to evolutionary and biocultural adaptive frameworks:

> Resolution of many of these questions regarding the meaning of our data and observations involves complex issues and knowledge inherent in several disciplines. Nevertheless, it is essential that paleopathology make a significant effort to move beyond the diagnostic phase of research, and ask questions about the biological and evolutionary significance of our findings. At the very least, we need to clarify the role disease has played in the complex process of adaptation between human groups and their environment.

In his review of the Ortner and Aufderheide volume, George Armelagos (1994: 239) argues that the authors "ally paleopathology with medicine rather than with anthropological science with its biocultural perspective." Further, Armelagos (1994: 240) states that "the delayed development in paleopathology is also due to the lack of a problem orientation and a reliance on the newest technology to drive the research."

In 2000, Aufderheide provided a brief summary of progress in soft tissue paleopathology, focusing much of his discussion on new biochemical and genetic methodologies. At the time, these methods were facilitating population-based epidemiological studies of Chagas disease in South America and schistosomiasis in Egypt (Aufderheide 2000: 2573). Other recent reviews of the discipline also focus on advances in the detection and diagnosis of soft tissue pathology (Lynnerup 2007; Zimmerman 2014).

Two recent articles discuss the development and current state of paleopathology. Because the focus of these articles is skeletal paleopathology, they serve as important benchmarks upon which to consider and evaluate the future of soft tissue paleopathology. Both articles begin by providing a synthesis of the development of paleopathology as it moved from a principally descriptive, case-study discipline to "an interpretive, interrogative, and independent one" that increasingly adopted a population-based, hypothesis-driven approach that incorporated consideration of sociocultural and environmental/ecological factors (Zuckerman et al. 2012: 37). Buzon (2012) highlights how this bioarchaeological approach facilitates the examination of the impact of social roles, social status, the living environment, activity patterns, infectious disease, diet, injuries, and trauma on the interpretation of paleopathological data. Zuckerman and colleagues (2012) focus their discussion on how researchers have not fully integrated an evolutionary perspective. That is, the discussion of paleopathological data should be "interpreted in an adaptive context" considering how cultural strategies may buffer, or fail to buffer, in the face of social/cultural and environmental/ecological factors (Zuckerman et al. 2012: 35).

History of Mummy Studies

The history and development of mummy studies is intimately tied to the history and development of paleopathology by scholars and methods derived from the biomedical sciences. Several recent publications provide both general and more in-depth accounts of particular periods and people in the history of mummy studies. Aufderheide (2003) develops a deep and broad view of the main phases and scholars of mummy studies, whereas Lynnerup et al. (2012) provide a view of modern developments as observed through the lens of the World Congress of Mummy Studies. Many of the key players discussed by these authors are explored in more depth in several contributions in *The Global History of Paleopathology* (Buikstra and Roberts 2012).

Aufderheide (2003) links the earliest scientific investigation of mummies to advances in anatomical and pathological anatomy that began during the Renaissance. Although mummies were occasionally unwrapped, these were principally forms of entertainment and not truly scientific explorations. The first comprehensive scientific program of mummy research occurred in the context of Napoleon's invasion of Egypt in 1798 (Aufderheide 2003). The expedition included nearly 100 scientists who were tasked with detailing Egyptian society, natural history, and material culture.

It was not until the first decades of the twentieth century that the scientific study of mummies truly began to develop. Pivotal figures during this period include Grafton Elliot Smith, Frederic Wood Jones, Marc Armand Ruffer, Margaret Murray, and Warren R. Dawson. Although gross morphological examination was the primary means of investigations (it is estimated that Smith dissected 30,000 mummies), significant methodological advances were being made. Grafton Elliot Smith (1912) used newly developed X-ray technology to create an age estimate based on epiphyseal union for the mummy known as Tuthmosis IV. Marc Armand Ruffer, a bacteriologist by training, is remembered for developing a solution for rehydrating mummified tissue. Researchers applied advances in immunology in the attempt to identify human blood and hemoglobin (e.g., Schmidt 1908; cited by Aufderheide 2003), whereas Alfred Lucas (1932) identified the chemical makeup of natron.

Amongst this early, and primarily biomedical research, there were some glimmers of integrative bioarchaeological research. As noted by Baker and Judd (2012), the work by Grafton Elliot Smith and Frederic Wood Jones for the First Archaeo-logical Survey of Nubia (1907–1911) was groundbreaking in its integration of biological and archaeological data: "It is the first duty of the anatomist working in conjunction with the archaeologist to supply the latter with information, derived from the study of human remains, which is of essential importance in the interpre-tation of many of the results of the archaeological investigation" (Smith 1908: 25).

The field stagnated in the second quarter of the twentieth century due to eco-nomic depression and world wars (Aufderheide 2003). Although significant contri-butions occurred during this period (e.g., Boyd and Boyd's (1939) paleoserological research), the promise of the first quarter of the twentieth century was not realized. In contrast, Aufderheide (2003) characterizes the 1950s–1970s as a 'reawakening' in mummy studies. New technologies were facilitating expansion of the field, includ-ing electron microscopy (Leeson 1959; Lewin 1967), the modification of Ruffer's solution for rehydrating mummified tissues (Sandison 1955), and blood serology (e.g. Gilbey and Lubran 1952, 1953). As discussed earlier, this was also the period when key critiques of paleopathology—and by extension, mummy studies—were articulated.

The modern era of mummy studies began in the 1970s and is marked by sev-eral key publications and projects. Michael Zimmerman (1972) published his research on the histology of experimentally mummified tissues. Marvin Allison and Enrique Gerszten from the Medical College of Virginia began anatomical dis-section of Peruvian mummies and formed the Paleopathology Club, which held their thirty-eighth meeting in 2015.[1] Two key multidisciplinary mummy projects were initiated in 1973. The Manchester Mummy Project of Margaret Murray was reactivated (David 2008b), and Aidan and Eve Cockburn brought together seventy-five scientists to examine the mummy known as PUM II (Cockburn et al. 1975). The latter served as the basis for the formation of the Paleopathology Association, which held its first meeting in 1974 and continues to meet in conjunction with the American Association of Physical Anthropology meetings (Powell 2012) as well as hold biennial meetings in Europe and South America. These projects and their team approach represent a key development in mummy research, one that remains a hallmark of mummy research today.

Radiography has always been a central feature of mummy investigations. A key advance came in 1976 with the development of computer-assisted tomography (Hounsfield 1976), which was soon harnessed for mummy studies (Harwood-Nash 1979; Lewin and Harwood-Nash 1977). In the following decades, the field adopted other biomedical imaging technology and continues to test new applications.

Scholars from the biomedical fields have always heavily influenced the develop-ment of mummy studies. The pivotal pioneers in the scientific study of Egyptian mummies, such as Marc Armand Ruffer, Grafton Elliot Smith, and Thomas Joseph Pettigrew, had their initial training in the biomedical sciences (Aufderheide 2003; Baker and Judd 2012). It should be noted that Margaret Murray was an archaeolo-gist; the team she established included a physician, chemists, and textile experts (Aufderheide 2003). Many of the main architects of modern mummy studies are pathologists including Marvin Allison, Michael Zimmerman, Arthur Aufderheide, and Enrique Gertzen (Allison and Zimmerman also hold PhDs in anthropology). Aidan Cockburn, founder of the Paleopathology Association, was an epidemiologist (Roberts et al. 2012). The major methodological advances in the field also stem largely from the biomedical fields, and this is particularly evident in the application of imaging technology. Derek Harwood-Nash and Peter Lewin, the first researchers to utilize CT technology to scan mummies, were a radiologist and a pediatrician respectively.

Recent History

The recent history of mummy studies is dominated by two features: the World Congress on Mummy Studies and multidisciplinary mummy projects. Although there are indications that the number of academic meetings dedicated to mummy research is increasing[2] the World Congress on Mummy Studies remains the primary venue for mummy studies. Multidisciplinary research teams have been a key aspect of the field since the first Manchester Mummy Project in 1908, and they have become something of a staple in modern era of mummy studies.

World Mummy Congress

Lynnerup et al. (2012) provide a wonderful discussion of how the World Mummy Congress became the main international venue for the presentation of mummy research. The origin of the Mummy Congress lies in the research trips of Arthur and Mary Aufderheide, who visited the Canary Islands in 1988 as part of their worldwide search for mummies (Nystrom and Cartmell 2012; Lynnerup 2012). While in the Canary Islands, the Aufderheides, in collaboration with Rafael González Antón, Fernando Estévez González, and Conrado Rodríguez-Martín, organized a project on Guanche mummy paleopathology. This project, with the help of Miguel Zerolo, ultimately resulted in the First World Congress on Mummy Studies. Held in 1992 on the island of Tenerife, Canary Islands, the meetings were organized in parallel sessions that included sessions on Guanche mummies' bioanthropology, paleopathology, museology, and conservation (Lynnerup et al. 2012). Subsequent meetings have occurred every three years (except in 2011 and 2013, Table 2.1) and have had the same basic organization: parallel sessions that include both 'standard' topics (e.g., paleopathology, applied/research methods) but also sessions that reflect research efforts into specific groups of mummies or investigative trends.

These meetings are unique in several ways. They are held in locations that, to put it simply, have larger collections of mummies. The meetings are also an intimate affair with attendance generally around 200 to 300 participants, which facilitates a high degree of engagement while also affording the opportunity for discussion and collaboration. The research reported truly represents the state of the art in mummy studies.

TABLE 2.1 Year and location of the World Congress on Mummy Studies meetings.

Year	Location
1992	Santa Cruz, Tenerife, Canary Islands
1995	Cartagena, Columbia
1998	Arica, Chile
2001	Nuuk, Greenland
2004	Turin, Italy
2007	Teguise, Lanzarote, Canary Islands
2011	San Diego, California, USA
2013	Rio de Janeiro, Brazil
2016	Lima, Peru

They are also unique in that they are not the extension of a professional academic association comparable to the American Association of Physical Anthropology or the European Anthropological Association. As such, there are no membership dues and no standing executive committee, officers, by-laws, or journal. Thus, although organization committees are formed for each meeting, there is no overarching structure to the field.

Multidisciplinary Mummy Research

Conducting research on mummified remains encourages the formation of multidisciplinary teams. The presence of soft tissue draws in biomedical and imaging experts whereas skeletal biological anthropologists and archaeologists are key to reconstructing behavior. There are also unique curatorial and conservational demands given that mummification is really just the temporary halting of decomposition (Fernicola and Samadelli 2011; Klocke 2010; Klocke and Petersen 2010; Piñar et al. 2014). The birth of modern mummy studies is grounded in the team-based intensive examination of remains curated by museums. These collections are small and many consist of Egyptian remains that were dispersed across the world during the nineteenth and twentieth centuries and the height of 'Egyptomania.' The Egyptian mummies examined by the team put together by Dr. Margaret Murray were curated at the Manchester Museum. This work continued in The Manchester Egyptian Mummy Research Project with the appointment of Rosalie David as curator. The mummy known as PUM II was from the Philadelphia Art Museum (Cockburn et al. 1975) whereas ROM I was curated by the Royal Ontario Museum (Hart et al. 1977a). More recent examples of projects that looked at small collections of Egyptian remains include the Vatican Mummy Project (Amenta et al. 2013), the German Mummy Project (Bernschneider-Reif et al. 2010; Rosendahl et al. 2010), the Lisbon Mummy Project (Figueiredo et al. 2002), the Sulman Mummy Project (Gardner et al. 2004), and the Ankhpakhered Mummy Project (Malgora et al. 2014). This research has principally been descriptive, focusing on deriving demographic data (e.g., age/sex estimation, stature, biological affinity) and documenting any pathologies, most often based on CT scans. A primary limiting factor in the analysis of these types of collections is that the remains often lack provenience, and although it is still possible to extract a considerable amount of useful bioanthropological and biomedical data from such remains (e.g., Arriaza et al. 2008; Carminati et al. 2014) there is little chance of developing broader comparative studies.

There are of course examples of interdisciplinary projects that are initiated soon after the recovery of the remains (e.g., Grauballe Man, Asingh and Lynnerup 2007) or actually in their primary context (e.g., The Sicily Mummy Project, Piombino-Mascali et al. 2011, Figure 2.1; The Lithuanian Mummy Project, Piombino-Mascali et al. 2014).

The Swiss Mummy Project is distinct from the previously mentioned interdisciplinary projects in that it does not focus on a group of mummies from a single region or time period, nor does it have a research agenda focused on a single topic as we will see detailed later. The stated goals of the project are "to investigate ancient human mummies of multiple cultural and geographical backgrounds with state-of-the-art scientific methods. This allows gaining insights into the

FIGURE 2.1 Mummies from the Capuchin Catacombs, Palermo, Italy. Photo provided by Dario Piombino-Mascali.

evolution of disease, human variation but also socio-cultural aspects." (www. swissmummyproject.uzh.ch/index.html, accessed February 3, 2015). Many of the publications stemming from the Swiss Mummy project focus on exploring and extending the technical capabilities of mediconuclear technology (Münnemann et al. 2007; Öhrström et al. 2010, 2013; Rühli et al. 2002, 2004; Rühli et al. 2007a; Rühli et al. 2007b; Wanek et al. 2011), evaluating the impact of radiation exposure on DNA (Wanek et al. 2012), and disease diagnosis and the investigation of pathology (Rühli et al. 2004; Seiler et al. 2013). The focus on sociocultural aspects of mummified remains manifests principally as the reconstruction of mortuary behavior and mummification procedures (Papageorgopoulou et al. 2009; Rühli and Böni 2000a, b).

Interdisciplinary teams have also been established to address specific research goals and questions. A recent example in which a project was initiated in response to a specific research question is the Horus Mummy Group. Formed by cardiologists Gregory Thomas (UC Irvine and Mission Viejo, CA) and Adel Allam (Al Azhar University, Cairo, Egypt), the express purpose was to determine if ancient Egyptians suffered from atherosclerosis (Allam et al. 2010). In 2009, the team CT scanned twenty-two mummies from the Egyptian National Museum, sixteen of which had identifiable cardiovascular tissues (Allam et al. 2009). The researchers found that 31% of the mummies had definite signs of the condition (n = 5), and an additional 25% (n = 4) had probable atherosclerosis. The sample of mummies was subsequently expanded, resulting in a total sample of seventy-six Egyptian mummies, fifty-one Peruvian mummies, five Ancestral Puebloans from the American Southwest, and five Unangan mummies from the Aleutian Islands. The results were presented at the Eighth World Congress on Mummy Studies held in Rio de Janeiro, Brazil in 2013, and published in the *Lancet* (Thompson et al. 2013). In sum, the researchers identified forty-seven (34%) individuals as having either probable or definite atherosclerosis (Figure 2.2).

Although the focus of the original study was limited to atherosclerosis, the resulting CT scans have produced a significant database that is facilitating additional bioarchaeological research. Currently, the Andean Wing of the Horus group is cataloging and identifying (when possible) the artifacts contained within the collection of Peruvian mummy bundles. Future research questions are currently focused on documenting pathological conditions (e.g., dental health) and the reconstruction of mortuary behavior (e.g., textile analysis, arm and leg position, etc.).

As will be discussed in more depth in later sections of this book, several authors have raised concerns regarding standardizing methods used to study mummies, in particular paleoimaging. Although the Internet-based Mummy Picture Archive and Communication Technology (IMPACT) Radiological Mummy Database Project is not an interdisciplinary research project like those discussed earlier, it represents a significant data-sharing effort that seeks to address standardization. Launched in 2011 by Andrew Nelson and Andrew Wade at the University of Western Ontario, the aim of IMPACT is to "provide a basis for anthropological and paleopathological investigations, grounded in the most current technological imaging and

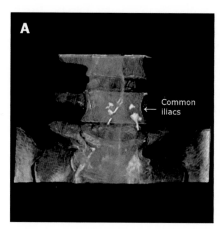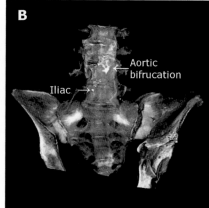

FIGURE 2.2 Evidence of atherosclerotic development in (A) a nineteenth-century middle-aged female (47–51 years) from the Aleutian Islands and (B) middle-aged female (41–44 years) from the Early Intermediate to Middle Horizon (200–900 AD) in Peru. The white arrows are pointing to areas of calcifications identified by the authors (Thompson et al. 2013).

communication standards" (Nelson and Wade 2015: 941). IMPACT consists of two linked databases: the radiographic data and the contextual data that goes along with a particular mummy. The former are held on a server running a mini-PACS (Picture Archiving and Communication System) that, while allowing researchers to access and examine the imaging data, prevents actual downloading of the images. This not only ensures the security of the images but also facilitates cross-study standardization as it relies upon the DICOM (Digital Imaging and COmmunications in Medicine) imaging standards established by the medical field.

The contextual data, which are accessible to the public, are contained in a Structured Query Language (SQL) database and will include information on "provenience, dating, mummification features, metric and non-metric observations, damage, restorations, and associated artifacts, as well as metadata on the imaging studies" (Nelson and Wade 2015: 944). Again, the construction of this database requires standardization in terms of data collection and reporting.

It is hoped that the availability of these data will facilitate the development of larger-scale comparative studies, moving beyond the case-study dominated nature of mummy studies (Nelson and Wade 2015). Examples include Wade and Nelson's recent diachronic study on Egyptian evisceration and excerebration (Wade et al. 2011; Wade and Nelson 2013a, 2013b).

Chapter Summary

With roots in the new physical anthropology and archaeology, bioarchaeological research in both the United Kingdom and the United States is an approach that melds archaeological and skeletal data in a biocultural, population-level, problem-orientated research design. The incorporation of the broader anthropological perspective into what was predominantly a descriptive, culture-historical, skeletal biology/paleopathology was critical for the development of a bioarchaeological approach to the interpretation of paleopathological data. It was the synthesis of two conflicting paradigms "(1) the determination of the chronology and geography of disease from a biomedical, even clinical, perspective and (2) the reconstruction of societal lifeways from an anthropological focus" that fostered the development of bioarchaeology (Armelagos 2003: 29).

Since its modern inception in the 1970s, mummy studies has been nearly synonymous with soft tissue paleopathology, with recent syntheses of the field (e.g., Aufderheide 2003; Lynnerup 2007; Monge and Rühli 2015; Zimmerman 2014) reinforcing this perception. As outlined earlier, the linked developmental histories of mummy studies and bioarchaeology raise several questions that pertain to its development, current state, and future. Was the examination of soft tissue paleopathology influenced by the same paradigmatic shifts associated with the new physical anthropology and archaeology experienced by skeletal paleopathology and bioarchaeology in the 1970s? Has it moved from a focus on cultural-historical explication to population-based, hypothesis-testing explanation? To what extent has mummy studies managed to successfully merge the biomedical and the anthropological paradigms? To try and provide answers to these questions, the next three chapters examine publication patterns in mummy studies and the degree to which the field has incorporated a contextualized, biocultural problem-oriented research perspective.

Notes

1. A recent publication (Gerszten et al. 2012) summarizes over forty years' worth of research on South American mummies.
2. The EURAC Institute for Mummies and the Iceman has held the Bolzano Mummy Congress in 2009, 2011, and 2016. The Roemer- und Pelizaeus-Museum in Hildesheim, Germany is hosting the International Conference on Comparative Mummy Studies in 2016.

3

PUBLICATION TRENDS AND CONTENT ANALYSIS

The field of mummy studies is expanding and entering a critical phase of its development. Investigators are starting to express concern about the structure and organization of the field as well as the ethical and methodological foundation of the discipline. Aufderheide (2013: 134) remarked that for mummy studies "to survive and flourish, the field will need to join a related discipline." He has also noted that one of the primary obstacles facing mummy studies is that it lacked a dedicated journal, a concern that was the primary motivation for the development and publication of the *Yearbook of Mummy Studies* (Gill-Frerking et al. 2011). Implied within these statements are (1) that mummy studies is not fully part of either of the disciplines that it principally draws from (i.e., biological anthropology and the biomedical fields) and (2) that the publication of mummy research is scattered. These statements likely ring true for most people in the field, though they have never been quantified.

I am advocating that mummy studies should strive to adopt a more holistic, anthropological perspective. Mummy studies draws heavily from the biomedical disciplines, and although I am not advocating for retrenchment of its influence, it is important that the field establish a balance where archaeological data and social theory are more deeply integrated into holistic research designs. Thus, it is necessary to consider the current state of the field and to identify areas where greater integration with anthropology and bioarchaeology may be possible and encouraged. The goal of the following analysis, therefore, is to document and discuss publication patterns in mummy research: What type of mummy research is being published and in what type of journals? These data will be discussed relative to current trends within bioarchaeology and the disciplinary divide between the anthropological and biomedical aspects of mummy studies. I hope that by taking a close look at trends in mummy research, the results will not only facilitate a critical evaluation of the current state of mummy studies but also stimulate greater integration into the broader bioarchaeological and anthropological fields.

Mummy Research in Edited Volumes

There has been a recent surge in the number of bioarchaeological volumes that focus on specific regions and archaeological contexts and themes or are exploring new theoretical perspectives. Springer recently launched a series edited by Debra L. Martin called *Bioarchaeology and Social Theory* that "highlights the application of social theories in the interpretation of data derived from bioarchaeological research" (www.springer.com/series/11976, accessed January 11, 2016). It is quickly accumulating titles (e.g., *The Bioarchaeology of Socio-Sexual Lives* by Pamela Geller) and promises to be a significant outlet for bioarchaeological publication.

The University Press of Florida's series *Bioarchaeological Interpretations of the Human Past: Local, Regional, and Global Perspectives,* edited by Clark Spencer Larsen, emphasizes the "integrative, interdisciplinary analysis of the links between biology and culture in past societies and the range of cultural, social, and economic conditions and circumstances that have shaped the human experience." (http:// upf.com/seriesresult.asp?ser=bioarc&indexnum=10, accessed January 11, 2016). As of 2016, this series has produced fifteen books, and though some of these volumes focus on specific contexts where mummified remains have not been recovered or are infrequent (e.g., *Bioarchaeology and Climate Change: A View from South Asian Prehistory,* Robbins Schug 2011; *Mission Cemeteries, Mission Peoples: Historical and Evolutionary Dimensions of Intracemetery Bioarchaeology in Spanish Florida,* Stojanowski 2013), many are more broadly thematic and thus could potentially include research on mummified remains. In this series, there are only two volumes, *Tracing Childhood: Bioarchaeological Investigations of Early Life in Antiquity* (Thompson et al. 2014) and *Bioarchaeology of Individuals* (Stodder and Palkovich 2012), that contain contributions that discuss mummified remains. Even my own chapter (Nystrom 2009) in the *Bioarchaeology and Identity in the Americas* (Knudson and Stojanowski 2009), in which I talk about the Chachapoya (where there are mummies), does not explicitly incorporate the analysis or discussion of mummified remains.

In the volume *Tracing Childhood,* Vivien Standen and colleagues (2014) discuss Chinchorro mortuary behavior as observed in children. As will be discussed in Chapter 5, the fact that such elaborate mortuary behavior is observed in a fisher-gatherer group runs counter to the general Binford-Saxe paradigm of the relationship between social complexity and mortuary complexity. As noted by the authors, however, the postmortem treatment of children is more informed by issues of grief, belief in a spiritual world, and the importance of children for group survival than the presence of social stratification and rank (Standen et al. 2014).

Contributions to the *Bioarchaeology of Individuals* focus on telling the stories of individuals, grounded and contextualized in the "populational framework of bioarchaeology" (Stodder and Palkovich 2012: 2). Indeed, the ability to produce such a detailed reconstruction of a single individual's life and death is predicated upon the detailed reconstruction of context. In the only chapter in this volume that deals with mummified remains, Maria Lozada Cerna and colleagues (2012) reconstruct the life and death of an individual from the site of El Yaral, part of the Chiribaya culture (AD 700–1350) from southern Peru. This individual was distinct from other burials from El Yaral and other Chiribaya sites in burial position (i.e., bound legs, flexed and on his left side) and grave accouterments (i.e., wooden spoon, tablet, and spatula made from nonlocal wood). Further, strontium isotope analysis of enamel indicates a nonlocal origin. Based on the unusual burial pattern, grave goods, and the stable isotope analyses, the authors suggest that the individual may have been a *curandero*, or healer.

I find the absence of additional chapters on mummies in the *Bioarchaeology of Individuals* volume to be interesting in that there are many examples of 'mummy-ographies' from the literature of historically known individuals: Rosalia Lombardo in the Capuchin Convent of Palermo (Panzer et al. 2010); Ferrante I (Fornaciari G. et al. 1999), Ferdinand II (Fornaciari G. et al. 2009), and Mary of Aragon (Fornaciari G. et al. 2003); Seqenenre Taa II (ten Berge and van de Goot 2002), Queen Tiye (Harris et al. 1978), Tutankhamen (e.g., Boyer et al. 2003; Hawass et al. 2010; Hawass 2013), Rameses II (Chhem et al. 2004), and Rameses III (Hawass et al. 2012). Further, there are many prehistoric mummies for which the osteobiographical approach has resulted in the detailed reconstruction of their life and death (e.g., Grauballe Man, Ötzi).

The general absence of mummy-related research in such volumes could be due to any number of reasons, from space constraints to the knowledge of the editors. An additional limiting factor may be the degree to which the previously described 'mummy-ographies' have been contextualized. As Stodder and Palkovich note, although the chapters in their volume begin with the study of a singular skeleton, the authors expand on "the analytical and interpretive scale from the grave outward to understand this person's context in life and in death" (2012: 1). As indicated previously in this book, one of the primary criticisms that may be leveled at mummy studies is the limited attention that has been paid to context. Much of the research on the historical mummies mentioned earlier has focused on paleopathology and is principally descriptive in nature. In his critical analysis of research conducted on Ötzi, John Robb (2009) argues that there has been little or no consideration of what the results obtained by these analyses mean in context. For example, the biological sex of Ötzi was established based upon the presence of intact external genitalia whereas the presence of the axe, knife, and bow and arrows, reinforced his fundamental 'maleness.' Although it could be argued that this association between material culture and gender is influenced by modern construction of gender-specific roles, Robb (2009: 113) acknowledges that archaeological evidence during the later European prehistory suggests that "there is strong evidence for dichotomized male and female genders." The point that Robb makes, however, is that there has been no discussion what maleness meant in Ötzi's world; that is, the biological sex of Ötzi has not been contextualized.

Of course, a balance must be struck and researchers must be cautious about overreaching and advancing interpretations that go beyond the data. Clearly, a single individual is not representative of a sample, let alone a population, and in the absence of a larger body of data that inform on the broader temporal or cultural context of the remains, discretion and interpretive restraint is to be recommended. Continuing with the example of Ötzi, although some authors have advanced the idea that he was deliberately buried (Carancini and Mattioli 2011; Vanzetti et al. 2010), their engagement and discussion of the ethnohistoric and archaeological data is thin and is not supported by the data (see Zink et al. 2011 for a refutation of these claims). This is in contrast to the richness of the ethnohistoric and archaeological evidence employed by Besom (2010, 2013) and Ceruti (2004, 2015) as they discuss isolated mountain-top sacrifices from the South American Andes.

There are also a number of other recent synthetic volumes on bioarchaeological research including:

- *Breathing New Life into the Evidence of Death* (Baadsgaard et al. 2011)
- *Social Bioarchaeology* (Argarwal and Glencross 2011a)
- *Social Archaeology of Funerary Remains* (Gowland and Knüsel 2006)
- *Interacting with the Dead: Perspectives on Mortuary Archaeology for the New Millennium* (Rakita et al. 2005)
- *The Routledge Handbook of the Bioarchaeology of Human Conflict* (Knüsel and Smith 2013)

In total, only three chapters from these volumes deal with mummies or mummification, and they are from the same volume edited by Rakita and colleagues (2005). Rakita and Buikstra (2005b) discuss Robert Hertz' (1907) explanatory model of secondary burial as it pertains to mummification; Guillén's (2005) chapter is a synthetic treatment of Andean mummification traditions; and Buikstra et al. (2005) discuss the results of stable isotopic analyses for a series of Chiribaya cemeteries along the south coast of Peru.

Mummy bioarchaeology has a much more obvious presence in the edited volume *Egyptian Bioarchaeology: Humans, Animals, and the Environment* (Ikram et al. 2015a). The volume considers a broad range of topics and chapters that examine skeletal material, human mummies, animal mummies, and plant material. Although the entire volume itself is a significant contribution given that skeletal, zooarchaeological, and archaeobotanical remains "have historically had a very marginal role in Egyptian archaeology" (Ikram et al. 2015b: 17), of particular interest for this volume are the chapters that discuss human mummies. Salima Ikram (2015) provides a general overview of the type of information that can be obtained from mummified remains as well as a detailed in-field guide for mummy examination. Although the focus of Tosha Dupras and colleagues' paper (2015) is really on the skeletal evidence of birth-related trauma, mummified remains were included in their analyses. Roger Lichtenberg (2015) summarizes his research on the frequency of Harris lines in skeletal and mummified remains recovered from three Ptolemaic and Roman period sites (Dush, Ain el-Lebekha, and el-Dier). Contributions by Dario Piombino-Mascali and colleagues (2015) and Bonnie Sampsell (2015) consider mummies acquired in the early twentieth century and currently held in museum collections. In both instances the researchers are evaluating the correspondence between what material artifacts (e.g., coffin style and decoration) and bioanthropological analyses (e.g., sex and age estimation, evidence of mummification processes) indicate regarding the identity and chronological age of the mummy. Both chapters are fundamentally about mortuary behavior because they focus on describing the evidence of mummification observed in the mummy (e.g., position of the arms, evidence of evisceration) and then compare this to the known historical development of Egyptian mortuary behavior.

There are of course many volumes dedicated explicitly to mummy-related research that target both general and specialized audiences:

- *The Man in the Ice* (Spindler 1994)
- *The World of Mummies: From Ötzi to Lenin* (Zink 2014)
- *Ancient Ice Mummies* (Dickson 2011)
- *Mummies of the World* (Wieczorek and Rosenthal 2010)
- *Grauballe Man: An Iron Age Bog Body Revisited* (Asingh and Lynnerup 2007)
- *The Mummies from Qilakitsoq-Eskimos in the 15th century* (Hart Hansen and Gulløv 1989)
- *Science in Egyptology* (David 1986)
- *Bog Bodies: New Discoveries and New Perspectives* (Turner and Scaife 1995)
- *Human Mummies: A Global Survey of Their Status and the Techniques of Conservation* (Spindler et al. 1996)
- *Lindow Man: The Body in the Bog* (Stead Bourke and Brothwell 1986)

These include both broad synthetic works (e.g., Wieczorek and Rosenthal 2010; Spindler et al. 1996; Turner and Scaife 1995) as well as those reporting research on specific mummified remains (e.g., Asingh and Lynnerup 2007; Hart Hansen and Gulløv 1989; Stead Bourke and Brothwell 1986). For example, the Asingh and Lynnerup (2007) volume reports the results of new investigations into the remains known as Grauballe Man in advance of the fiftieth anniversary of his discovery. Authors focus on a variety of issues including the state of conservation and preservation of the body (Frederiksen 2007), antemortem health (Ahrenholt-Bindslev et al. 2007; Boel and Dalstra 2007), biological anthropology (Lynnerup 2007), gut contents (Harild et al. 2007), and perimortem trauma (Gregersen et al. 2007).

The recent surge in the number of edited volumes on bioarchaeology in which the analysis of skeletal remains is contextualized with a broad corpus of social theory highlights a trend in the holistic integration of theoretical, cultural, and historical contexts in problem-orientated research (Buikstra et al. 2011). The production of more specialized volumes that report on mummy research is also robust, but it is noteworthy that so few mummy-related articles appear in these 'bioarchaeology' volumes.

Journal Content Analysis

This section explores trends in mummy-related research as represented by journal articles published between 1970 and 2015. The goal of this section is to examine where mummy-related research is being published and what type of research questions are being asked.

There are some necessary caveats and clarifications. Although I was able to collect 1063 articles from 367 different journals, except for a smattering of articles in Spanish, Italian, French, and German, these articles were published in English. Given this, in all likelihood I am sure articles have been overlooked. Still, I believe that this is a fairly representative sample of mummy research.

My choice of using 1970 as the cut-off point is because this represents the beginning of modern mummy research and is marked by the key events discussed in Chapter 2; Michael Zimmerman (1972) published his histological research on mummified tissue, the unwrapping and examination of PUM II in 1973 (Cockburn et al. 1975), the formation of the Paleopathology Association and its first official meeting in 1974 (Powell 2012), the introduction of the CT scanner in 1977, formation of the Manchester Mummy Project in 1973 (David 2008b), and the formation of the Paleopathology Club by Marvin Allison and Enrique Gerszten in 1978. This meant, however, that some significant pioneering work on mummies was not included (e.g., Sandison 1962; Wells and Maxwell 1962).

One difficulty I encountered during this process was determining whether or not to include articles that were initially presented at conferences. Ultimately, I *did not* consider conference proceedings that were published as isolated volumes, specifically the publication of the World Congress on Mummy Studies. Only one of these proceedings was published as a special issue of a journal (Fifth World Congress on Mummy Studies was published in the *Journal of Biological Research*), and generally the proceedings are not widely available. Nor did I count abstracts that were published in peer-reviewed journals. For instance, in 1987, 1992, and 1999 the *Journal of Paleopathology* published abstracts from the Seventh, Ninth, and Thirteenth European Meeting of the Paleopathology Association meetings, respectively.

I *did* include full-length articles that were published in special issues of peer-reviewed journals. The impact of these types of special publications can been seen in Figure 3.1. For instance, the early peak in publication rates in 1972 is due principally to papers published in the *Journal of Human Evolution* based on presentations at a 1969 Symposium on Population Biology of the Early Egyptians organized by Brunetto A. Chiarelli and Don Brothwell. Additionally, I counted articles published in *Chungara* based on presentations at the Third World Congress on Mummy studies and articles published in *Papers in Anthropology* from the Eighth World Congress on Mummy Studies. Alternatively, I choose *not* to include eighty-seven papers published in the *Journal of Biological Research* (published by the Italian Society for Experimental Biology) that were presented at the Fifth World Congress on Mummy Studies. I made this decision because, though they were published as a special issue of a peer-reviewed journal, they are qualitatively different than the previous examples.

Lastly, to be included, the article had to discuss research on the physical remains themselves including the analysis of soft tissue and/or hair. So, for example, I did not include an article by Charrié-Duhaut et al. (2007) in which the authors analyzed organic residuals on the interior of the canopic jars of Ramses II.

After the list of all the journals in which mummy research has been published since 1970 was compiled, I grouped them into the following categories based on journal type and target audience (as described by the journal's website):

- General Science (e.g., *Nature, Science, PLoS ONE*)
- Biology/Chemistry/Physics (e.g., *Analytical Chemistry, Annals of Anatomy, Free Radical Research, Radiation Physics and Chemistry, Journal of Mass Spectrometry*)
- Biological Anthropology (e.g., *American Journal of Physical Anthropology, International Journal of Osteoarchaeology, Anthropologischer Anzeiger*)
- Forensic (e.g. *Legal Medicine, Journal of Forensic and Legal Medicine, Forensic Science International, Journal of Forensic Science*)
- Anthropology (e.g., *Chungara, Current Anthropology, American Anthropologist, Arctic Anthropology*)
- Archaeology (e.g., *Journal of Archaeological Science, Journal of Egyptian Archaeology, Antiquity*)
- Radiography/Imaging (e.g., *Journal of Raman Spectroscopy, Journal of Roentgenology*)
- General Medical (e.g., *Journal of the American Medical Association, Journal of the Oklahoma State Medical Association*)
- Medical Specialties (e.g., *European Archives of Oto-Rhino-Laryngology, Bulletin of the History of Dentistry, Pathobiology, The Knee*)
- Parasitology (e.g., *Journal of Parasitology, Korean Journal of Parasitology*)
- Earth Sciences (e.g., *Palaeogeography, Palaeoclimatology, Palaeoecology, Quaternary International, The Holocene*)
- Humanities (e.g., *Journal of Applied Philosophy, Journal of Cultural Heritage, Journal of Humanistic Ideology, Mortality*)

Journals such as *Science* and *Nature* were categorized as General Science because they publish research from a wide variety of scientific disciplines. Biomedical journals were divided into those that report a broader range of research and clinical findings (e.g., *Journal of the American Medical Association, Minnesota Medicine*) and those that reflect a specific research or clinical focus (e.g., *Journal of the American Academy of Dermatology, Foot and Ankle Surgery*). Journals with a primary focus on radiography or imaging were put into a separate category even if they were biomedical or clinical in focus (e.g., *Journal of Medical Imaging and Radiation Oncology, Clinical Imaging*). The Biology/Chemistry/Physics category is something of a catch-all category, covering a large variety of topics (e.g., evolutionary biology, microbiology, mass/raman spectrometry, biochemistry). Although these topics are clearly related to both biomedical (e.g., *Radiation and Environmental Biophysics*) and bioanthropological research (e.g. *Current Biology*), these fields are not explicitly their target audiences.

To take a more detailed look, I considered those journals that published ten or more mummy-related articles as my working sample. I categorized articles published in these venues based on the primary research question being addressed:

General Descriptive: Articles in this category are broad in scope and are reporting preliminary results or synthetic summaries of interdisciplinary investigations. A good example of this type of research is Alt and colleagues' (2003) description of Nepalese mummies.

Health and Disease: This category includes any research where the reconstruction of health is the primary focus, irrespective of methodology. This therefore includes the examination of gross and microscopic morphological changes (e.g., Hershkovitz et al. 2014), DNA analysis (e.g., Lalremruata et al. 2013), biochemical signatures (e.g., Webb et al. 2010), and proteomics (e.g., Corthals et al. 2012). Additionally, this category would include parasitological analyses that identify ecto- and endoparasites based either on gross observation or DNA analyses.

Taphonomy: Research where the primary focus is investigation of post-depositional macro- and/or micro-level morphological and/or chemical changes in soft tissue, hard tissue, and their components (e.g., proteins, carbohydrates, lipids, DNA, etc.). Examples of research in this category would include the documentation of DNA degradation (e.g., Olivieri et al. 2010), postmortem diagenetic processes (e.g., Bertrand et al. 2014; Cervini-Silva et al. 2013) or postexcavation modification (e.g., Gill-Frerking 2014).

Methodological: This category includes research where the primary focus is on the application and feasibility of new investigative tools. This category would include the presentation of results associated with, for example, the application of new mediconuclear imaging modalities (e.g., Rühli et al. 2007a) and molecular techniques (Thèves et al. 2011).

Dietary Reconstruction: Research where the primary research question is the reconstruction of diet. The methods used could include stable isotopic and elemental analyses, palynology, and the microscopic examination of gut contents (e.g., Holden ad Núñez 1993; Reinhard et al. 2011).

Residential Mobility: Research where the primary research question is establishing residence patterns and/or mobility based on the analysis of stable isotopes (e.g., Turner et al. 2012).

Biochemical: Research in this category is investigating the biochemistry of mummified tissue and most commonly involves the detection of drugs (e.g., Ogalde et al. 2009) and alcohol (e.g., Musshoff et al. 2013).

Biodistance: Any research that considers group affiliation, including between-group comparisons and intracemetery kinship analysis. The range of data that could be utilized includes cranial/postcranial nonmetric or metric traits and molecular (e.g., Hart Hansen and Gürtler 1983; Sawyer et al. 1990).

Individual Identification: Research in this category focuses on specific aspects pertaining to an individual's identity. Examples of this type of research could include facial reconstruction, identification of historical personages, or the sex/age estimation of singular mummies. Importantly, this category *does not* include research that focuses on health and disease, mortuary behavior, or any of the other categories listed here. So for example, the reconstruction of Ötzi's last meals would *not* fall into this category. However, the Harris et al. (1978) article in which they identified an unknown mummy as Queen Tiye or Connolly and colleagues' (1976) attempt to establish the parentage of Tutankhanum are good examples of this type of article.

Mortuary Behavior: Research where the main focus is on the reconstruction and discussion of mortuary behavior, mummification procedure, or burial ritual, irrespective of method (e.g., Allison et al. 1984; Seiler and Rühli 2015).

Ethics and Conservation: Articles included in this category explicitly address the ethics of mummy research and the issues related to conservation (e.g., Lonfat et al. 2015).

Other: This category includes review articles (e.g., Lynnerup 2009) as well as topics that appeared very infrequently including research on weaning (Razmilic et al. 1987), paleodemography (Drusini et al. 2001; Masali and Chiarelli 1972), and activity patterns (Ruff et al. 2006).

Overall Results

In total, I collected references for 1063 articles from 367 different journals. As is clear from Figure 3.1, there has been steady increase in the number of articles published on mummified remains since 1970.

In Table 3.1, I provide the number and percentage of journals that published a single mummy-related article, those that published between two and nine articles,

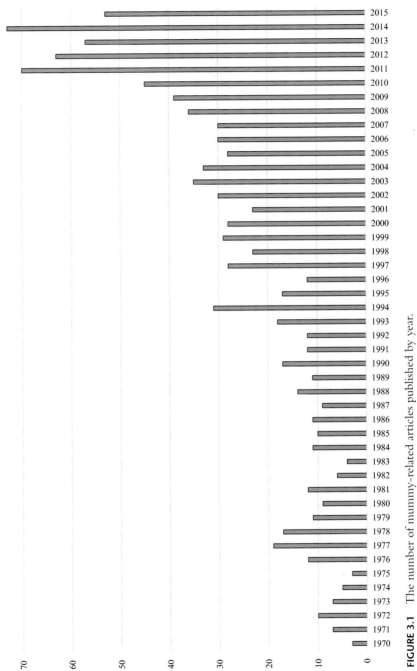

FIGURE 3.1 The number of mummy-related articles published by year.

TABLE 3.1 Journals with mummy-related research articles.

Category	Number of Journals (%)	Number of Articles (%)
Journals that published 1 article	254 (69.2)	254 (23.9)
Journals that published 2–9 articles	91 (24.8)	313 (29.4)
Journals that published > 10 articles	22 (6.0)	496 (46.7)
TOTAL	367	1063

TABLE 3.2 Journals that published ten or more mummy-related research articles.

Journal Name	Journal Category	N (%)[a]
American Journal of Physical Anthropology	Biological Anthropology	78 (7.3)
Journal of Archaeological Science	Archaeology	74 (7.0)
Yearbook of Mummy Studies	Biological Anthropology	45 (4.2)
Chungara	Anthropology	27 (2.5)
The Anatomical Record	Biology/Chemistry/Physics	25 (2.4)
Lancet	General Medical	25 (2.4)
International Journal of Osteoarchaeology	Biological Anthropology	21 (2.0)
PLoS ONE	General Science	21 (2.0)
Journal of Human Evolution	Biological Anthropology	19 (1.8)
Journal of Paleopathology	Biological Anthropology	17 (1.6)
Forensic Science International	Forensics	15 (1.4)
Journal of Parasitology	Parasitology	14 (1.3)
American Journal of Roentgenology	Radiographics/Imaging	13 (1.2)
Medicina nei Secoli	General Medical	13 (1.2)
Canadian Medical Association Journal	General Medical	12 (1.1)
Anthropologischer Anzeiger	Biological Anthropology	12 (1.1)
Bulletin of the New York Academy of Medicine	General Medical	12 (1.1)
Science	General Science	12 (1.1)
Papers on Anthropology	Biological Anthropology	11 (10)
Memórias do Instituto Oswaldo Cruz	General Medical	10 (0.9)
Journal of Egyptian Archaeology	Archaeology	10 (0.9)
Antiquity	Archaeology	10 (0.9)
	TOTAL	496 (46.7)[a]

a The percentage is relative to the total number of articles (n = 1063).

and finally those that published ten or more articles. The greatest percentage of journals published only one mummy-related article (n = 254, 69.2% of all journals). Ninety-one journals (24.8%) published between two and nine articles, accounting for 312 (29.4%) of the total number of articles. Finally, there were twenty-two that have published ten or more articles related to mummies (Table 3.2). These journals, which account for only 6% of the total number of journals, published a total of 496 articles, which represents 46.7% of the total number of articles.

Results Based on Journal Categories

The greatest number of mummy-related articles that have been published within a single journal are within Biological Anthropological and Archaeological categories, the *American Journal of Physical Anthropology* (n = 78) and the *Journal of Archaeological Science*, respectively (n = 74). Twelve different journals (3.3% of the total number of journals) were categorized as Biological Anthropology journals, publishing a total of 218 articles on mummies (20.5% of the total number of articles), whereas thirty-five (9.5%) journals were categorized as Archaeological and published a total of 154 articles (14.5%) (Figure 3.2). These 372 articles represent 35% of the total number of mummy articles. On the other hand, the number of journals in these two categories (n = 47) represent only 12.8% of the total number of journals that have published mummy research.

Mummy-related articles have not been a prominent feature of what we might consider broader anthropological journals. There were twenty-two different journals (6.0%) placed into the Anthropology category, publishing a total of sixty-nine mummy-related articles (6.5%). The largest contributor to this total is the journal *Chungara* with twenty-seven articles.

When I collapsed all of the anthropologically related journal categories together (Anthropology, Biological Anthropology, and Archaeology), a total of sixty-nine journals (18.8%) published 441 articles (41.4%). The remaining nonanthropology journals published a total of 622 (58.5%) articles and are distributed across 298 different journals.

The category with the greatest number of journals represented is the Medical Specialties category with ninety-nine different entries, which represents 27% of the total number of journals, and published 146 articles (13.7%) (Figure 3.2). General Medical journals (n = 36) accounted for 9.8% of all journals and 129 articles (12.1%). Together these two categories accounted for 36.8% of the total number of journals and published 275 articles, or 25.9% of the total number of articles.

Considering just those journals that have published ten or more articles, both the Biological Anthropology and the General Medical categories have five journals represented. The remaining journal categories are distributed as follows: Archaeology, n = 4; General Science, n = 2; Anthropology, n = 2; Radiography/Imaging, n = 1; Forensics, n = 1; Biology/Chemistry/Physics = 1; and Parasitology, n = 1.

There are three journal categories in which no journal published ten or more articles, and as such will not appear in the discussion below. There is, however, interesting research being published in these venues that is worth noting.

Medical Specialties—The majority of these journals (n = 78, 78.8%) in this category published only one mummy-related article. As one would expect, the primary focus of research published in these journals is health and disease, but many articles are also principally methodological. A small sampling of recent work includes research on atherosclerosis (e.g., Allam et al. 2014; Cheng 2012; Gaeta et al. 2013), congenital heart conditions (Séguéla et al. 2013; Zanatta et al. 2014), and the oral

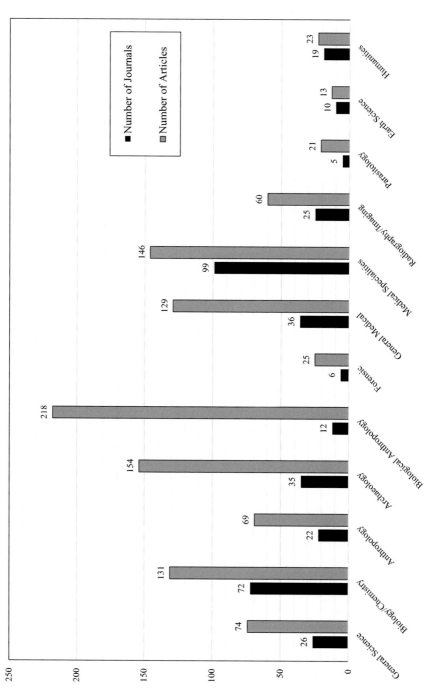

FIGURE 3.2 Number of articles and journals that published mummy articles by journal category.

health and chronic pain that Ötzi may have experienced (Kean et al. 2013). Recent methodologically oriented research explored the use of digital volume tomography (Schmidt et al. 2013) and computed tomography (Pelo et al. 2012) with an eye toward the feasibility of these methods for examining issues related to reconstructing health and disease.

Earth Sciences—There were ten journals that were classified as Earth Science, which accounted for 2.7% of the total number of journals and published thirteen (1.2%) articles. Based on the palynological analysis of sequential samples of gut contents, Oeggl et al. (2007) were able to reconstruct the last approximately thirty-three hours of Ötzi's life and itinerary. Several researchers effectively use human remains as biomonitors for tracking climatic change (Iacumin et al. 1996; Touzeau et al. 2013) or for documenting exposure to environmental toxins (Egeland et al. 2009).

Humanities—The Humanities category includes philosophy, religion, cultural heritage, and social science journals. These journals account for only a small percentage (n = 19, 5.2%) of the total number of journals and published twenty-three articles (2.2% of the total articles). The topics covered by these articles are eclectic, ranging from the ethics of research on human remains (Bahn 1994; Wilkinson 2002) to the examination of the creation of collective memory in respect to bog bodies (McLean 2008), the social meaning of tattoos in mummies from the Philippines (Salvador-Amores 2012), and the mummification of Chinese Ch'an priests (Sharf 1992). Despite the fact that they are not well represented, these articles bear directly on topics that will be discussed in Chapter 4.

Journal-Specific Results

I am going to limit the discussion of journal-specific results to the following journals in that they have the most distinct or noteworthy publication patterns over the time span covered by this research: *PLoS ONE, International Journal of Osteoarchaeology, Lancet, Chungara, The Anatomical Record, Yearbook of Mummy Studies, Journal of Archaeological Science*, and the *American Journal of Physical Anthropology*.

PLoS ONE

Since it was launched in 2006, the open-access online journal *PLoS ONE* has rapidly become one of the largest journals (in terms of the sheer number of articles published) in the world. Further, it seems to be rapidly becoming a significant venue for publishing mummy research. In the space of six years (the first mummy article I was able to locate was published in 2008), eighteen mummy-related articles were published in PLoS ONE, with six articles published in 2014.

All of the articles are decidedly laboratory-focused and present little or no archaeological data or demonstrate any engagement with social theory. In two cases, researchers were working with unprovenienced mummies from museums (Bianucci et al. 2008; Panzer et al. 2014). Six of the fifteen articles focused on some aspect of health, either detecting the presence of pathogenic DNA or based on gross morphological changes. Three of these health-related articles employed molecular/immunological methods. For example, Corthals et al. (2012) used shotgun proteomics to detect the presence of an immune response to tuberculosis in two Andean mummies. The articles by Théves et al. (2011) and Dabernat et al. (2014) both examine a large collection of frozen mummies from Yakutia in eastern Siberia that date to between the fifteenth and nineteenth centuries. Théves and colleagues were attempting to isolate and amplify bacterial DNA in individuals that exhibited no outward pathological conditions, whereas Dabernat and colleagues looked at the paleoepidemiology of tuberculosis.[1] The remaining health-related articles were based on 'traditional' radiographic or morphological (i.e., autopsy, histological) examination (Kim et al. 2014—congenital diaphragmatic hernia; Panzer et al. 2012—femoral herniation pits).

The increasing importance of considering the impact of the microbiome in the study of human health and evolution is reflected in three articles. Tito et al. (2012) sequenced bacterial DNA from a collection of coprolites and found distinct differences in composition between rural and urban groups. Maixner and colleagues (2014) used next-generation sequencing to identify the spirochete *Treponema denticola* in the metagenome of Ötzi whereas Swanston et al. (2011) amplified and identified *Helicobacter pylori* from the stomach of Kwäday Dän Ts'ìnchi.

International Journal of Osteoarchaeology

The stated aim of the *International Journal of Osteoarchaeology* is to publish research that addresses "all aspects of the study of human and animal bones from archaeological contexts" and that these "remains can be examined to provide detailed and nuanced information about the behaviour and ideology of past cultures" (http://onlinelibrary.wiley.com/journal/10.1002/(ISSN)1099-1212, accessed August 19, 2016). As such, it is the only journal considered in this research that is explicitly grounded in a bioarchaeological perspective.

Compared to the other major biological anthropology and archaeology journals, the *International Journal of Osteoarchaeology* has not been a common venue for mummy-related research, having published twenty-one mummy-related articles since its inception in 1991. As can be seen in Figure 3.3, the majority (48%) of mummy-related articles focus on health and disease (n = 10). Of these health-related articles, the majority (60%, n = 6) are based on morphological evidence. For instance, the earliest article that I was able to identify was Bellard and Cortés (1991) in which the authors discuss the presence of *Trichinella spiralis* in the remains of young female from nineteenth-century Spain. Other more recent examples include the examination of perimortem trauma in South America (Standen et al. 2010), examples of amputation from Egypt (Dupras et al. 2010), and evidence of embryotomy from ninetheeth-century Italy (Capasso et al. 2016).

The remaining articles cover a variety of topics including those focused on taphonomy (e.g, Chang et al. 2008), the reconstruction of mortuary behavior based

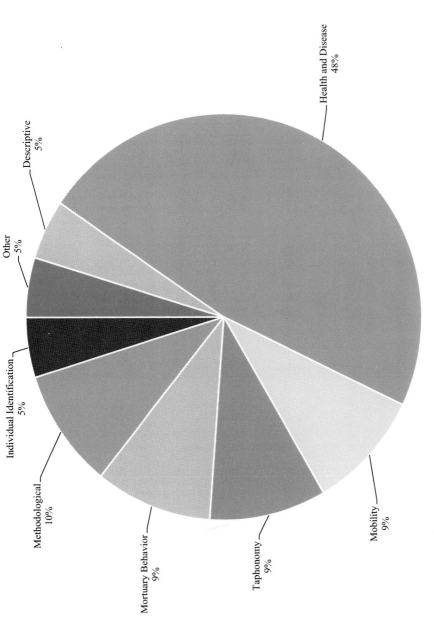

FIGURE 3.3   Categories of mummy-related articles published in *International Journal of Osteoarchaeology.*

on insect remains (Nystrom et al. 2005), and mobility based on stable isotopic analyses (Knudson et al. 2012).

The Lancet

The Lancet is "an international general medical journal" (www.thelancet.com/lancet/ information-for-authors, accessed September 5, 2016), and, therefore, it should not come as a surprise that nearly all of the articles focus on health and disease (nineteen out of twenty-five articles, 76%, Figure 3.4). The remaining articles were classified as Biochemical (Parsche et al.1993) and Methodological (Appelboom and Struyven 1999), while reviews or short comments were categorized as Other.

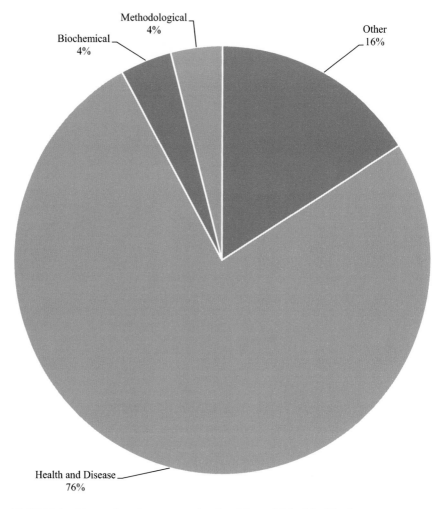

FIGURE 3.4 Categories of mummy-related articles published in *The Lancet*.

The first mummy-related articles that I was able to locate both dealt with the documentation of smallpox in Italian mummies (Field 1986; Fornaciari G. and Marchetti 1986). This was followed by the description of other infectious diseases such as syphilis (Fornaciari G. et al. 1989), Chagas disease (Fornaciari G. et al. 1992; Guhl et al. 1997), tuberculosis (Nerlich et al. 1997a), and viral skin papillomas (Fornaciari G. et al. 2003). There was a small surge in the number of articles during the late 1990s, with seven articles that focused on Ötzi, though not all were original research. In 1998, Capasso (1998) proposed that Ötzi was self-medicating using the fungus *Piptoporus betulinus* to combat intestinal parasites, which elicited two responses (Pöder and Peintner 1999, Tunón and Svanberg 1999). In 1999, Dorfer and colleagues advanced the hypothesis that Ötzi's tattoos were therapeutic in nature (published in *Science* the preceding year as well), which in turn has stimulated further research that was published in other venues (e.g., Kean and Kean 2014; Kean et al. 2013; Renaut 2004). After a surge in the late 1990s and early 2000s, mummy research has appeared only infrequently in the *Lancet*.

Although based on limited data, there may be two trends to note. First, whereas the earlier research was principally based on morphological examination (Fornaciari G. and Marchetti 1986; Capasso et al. 1999) and immunochemistry (Fornaciari G. et al. 1989), the more recent research utilizes advances in CT imaging technology. Secondly, contrary to the earlier research, which focused on infectious diseases, the most recent articles in the *Lancet* focus on atherosclerosis, the greatest risk factors of which are considered to be diet, lifestyle, and environment. Thompson and colleagues (2013) present additional data based on whole-body CT scans of 137 mummies from Egypt, Peru, and North America, expanding on previous results reported by Allam and colleagues (2009, 2011) in the *Journal of the American Medical Association* and *JACC: Cardiovascular Imaging*. Based on these scans, the Thompson et al. identified forty-seven (34%) individuals as having probable or definite atherosclerosis (though see Charlier and Huynh (2010) for a critique of the original findings by Allam and colleagues). Contrary to the association between atherosclerosis and our modern lifestyle, the high frequency of the condition in these groups, which exhibit a wide range of diet, environmental contexts, and social complexity, led the authors to conclude that atherosclerosis is an "inherent component of human ageing and not characteristic of any specific diet or lifestyle" (Thompson et al. 2013: 1221).

Chungara Revista de Antropología Chilena

Chungara is published by the Departamento de Antropología, Universidad de Tarapacá, Arica, Chile. The journal publishes "original articles in the different fields of anthropology and other associated sciences that include cultural or social anthropology, archaeology, bioarchaeology, ethnobotany, ethnohistory, geography, geology, geoarchaeology, history, linguistics, paleoecology, semiotics, zooarchaeology, conservation of cultural materials, and museology" (www.chungara.cl/index.php/en/our-journal, accessed June 21, 2014). Given its broad scope *Chungara* was categorized as an Anthropology journal for the purposes of this analysis.

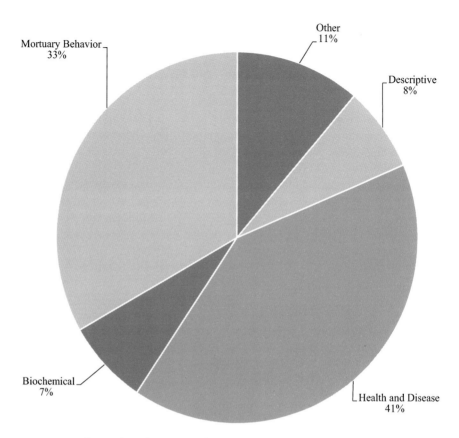

FIGURE 3.5 Categories of mummy-related articles published in *Chungara*.

A total of twenty-seven mummy-related articles were published in *Chungara* with the majority focused on health and disease (41%, n = 11) and mortuary behavior (33%, n = 9) (Figure 3.5). Although officially the geographic scope of the journal is not limited to the Andes, twenty-two of the articles reported on mummies from South America including: Chiribaya mummies (Aufderheide et al. 2005), the Late Horizon mountain-top sacrifice from Cerro El Plomo (Rodríguez et al. 2011), and Chachapoya mummies from the Laguna Huayabamba (Nystrom et al. 2010). The majority of articles in *Chungara*, however, focus on the Chinchorro; fifteen out of the total of twenty-six articles focus exclusively, or incorporate samples from, Chinchorro mummies. These articles have examined a wide range of topics, including skeletal pathologies (Arriaza et al. 1984; Standen et al. 1984), age at weaning (Razmilic et al. 1987), coca-chewing (Cartmell et al. 1994), exposure to environmental toxins (Figueroa et al. 1988), and endoparasitic infestation (Rivera et al. 2008).

Several articles examine Chinchorro mummification, including primarily descriptive analyses of the mummification styles (Allison et al. 1984), analyses of hairstyles (Arriaza et al. 1986), and archaeological funerary material (Standen 2003).

Sepúlveda et al. (2015) discuss evidence for the repainting of the surfaces of the mummies. Several articles have also explored some broader questions related to Chinchorro mummification. Arriaza (2005) suggest that naturally occurring arsenic levels in the Camarones valley may have resulted in elevated infant mortality rates and may have been one of the motivating factors behind the development of the complex mummification processes. This work spurred a number of other publications that report additional data and tested this hypothesis (Arriaza et al. 2010; Byrne et al. 2010; Madden and Arriaza 2014; Silva-Pinto et al. 2010). Santoro and colleagues (2012: 648) also examine the relationship between the natural environment and how the Chinchorro "were able to support the leisure time needed for the creativity, experimentation and transmission involved in creating a unique cultural landscape," which included artificial mummification. Along similar lines, (though in a different journal), Marquet et al. (2012) discuss the relationship between environmental factors, the emergence of social complexity, and the complex mortuary behavior of the Chinchorro.

The Anatomical Record: Advances in Integrative Anatomy and Evolutionary Biology

The Anatomical Record is the official journal of the American Association of Anatomists and "publishes new discoveries in the morphological aspects of molecular, cellular, systems, and evolutionary biology" (http://onlinelibrary.wiley.com/journal/10.1002/(ISSN)1932-8494accessed September 9, 2015). In 2015 a special issue of the journal published twenty-five articles devoted to mummy research; prior to this I was unable to locate any mummy-related research.

The most frequent type of article (n = 8, 32%) discussed the application and limitations of various imaging modalities, including CT scanning (Conlogue 2015; Cox 2015), terahertz imaging (Öhrström et al. 2015), magnetic resonance imaging (Posh 2015; Rühli 2015), and endoscopy (Beckett 2015). The next most frequent article type were descriptive articles (n = 6, 24%) that included synthetic summaries of research on groups of mummies (e.g., the Thule Inuit, Lynnerup 2015), prospective summaries of preliminary research (e.g., the Tres Ventanas mummies, Wann et al. 2015), and the reanalysis of previously examined mummies. Zimmerman and Gleeson (2015) provided a retrospective look at the autopsy of PUM I and how the examination itself might have proceeded differently, given technological advances since 1972. Wade and colleagues (2015) discuss the 2010 radiological examination of the body artificially mummified by Bob Brier and Ronald Wade in 1994 (MUMAB).

Yearbook of Mummy Studies

The *Yearbook of Mummy Studies* is the only journal dedicated exclusively to the publication of mummy-related research. It was developed because it was considered necessary for the field to form a strong and independent discipline (Aufderheide 2013; Gill-Frerking et al. 2011), a point I will return to later on in this work.

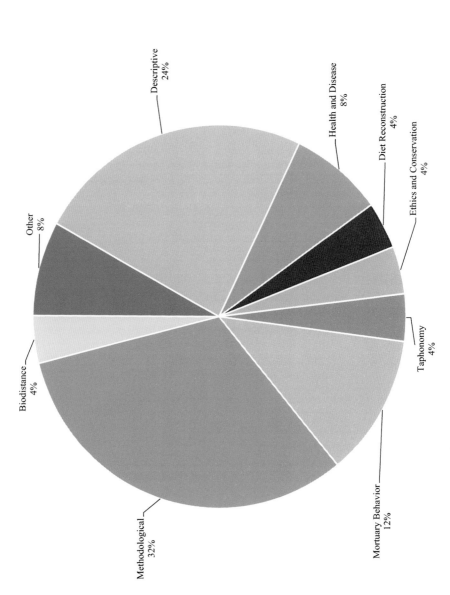

FIGURE 3.6 Categories of mummy-related articles published in the *Anatomical Record*.

The journal has two issues (2011 and 2014) and has published forty-five articles. Topical diversity is broader relative to the other journals (Figure 3.7), with the highest frequency in the Descriptive (20%), Mortuary Behavior (18%), and Health and Disease (15%) categories.

The majority of articles in the *Yearbook* are principally 'descriptive' in that the initial research goal is not centered on a specific research question or hypothesis (e.g., Gaudio et al. 2014; Meier et al. 2011). For instance, the goal of Meier and colleagues examination (2011: 99–100) of a mummified body from Brazil is to "revisit" the remains as new technology offers the opportunity for "discovering greater details" and "more detailed description of the remains."

Alternatively, the contribution by Madden and Arriaza (2014) offers one of the clearest examples of hypothesis-driven research. The Chinchorro mummification traditions are unique for being based on its antiquity, complexity, and variability. The number of children that have been mummified is unusual, given the association between ascribed status (and thus reflective of the presence of social stratification) and social complexity. This has led Arriaza (2005) to suggest that the Chinchorro mummified their children as an expression of grief. Previous geochemical analyses (Arriaza et al. 2010; Byrne et al. 2010) have demonstrated that the Chinchorro were exposed to extremely high levels of naturally occurring arsenic. Madden and Arriaza (2014) test this hypothesis by examining the radiographs of thirty-one mummies/mummy bundles for the presence of birth defects clinically associated with arsenic exposure.

Many of the articles employ some form of mediconuclear imaging technology (2011: seven of twenty-six articles; 2014: twelve of twenty-four articles), with some focusing on testing new modalities (e.g., Friedman et al. 2011) or are primarily reporting descriptive results (Belén Daizo et al. 2014). The most common application of mediconuclear technology is the reconstruction of mortuary behavior (Belén Daizo et al. 2014; Davey et al. 2014; Elias et al. 2014, Malgora et al. 2014;; Wade et al. 2014; Wisseman and Hunt 2014) and documenting pathology (Harris 2014; Kean and Kean 2014; Kustár et al. 2011; Madden and Arriaza 2014).

Engagement with mortuary *theory*, that is, discussions of the social significance and cultural context of the observed mortuary behavior, is limited. There are no articles in the 2011 volume that I would characterize as engaging with theory. Beckett et al. (2011a: 12) briefly discuss the potential function of mummification in modern Papua New Guinea: "The purpose of the mummification appears to be for the maintenance of a line of political power" and also place their project within what is known about mummification in Oceania more broadly. The bulk of their paper, however, focuses on reconstructing the steps in the mummification procedure.

In the 2014 volume, Wade et al. (2014: 107) discuss cultural impact on changes in mortuary behavior, and in particular suggest that the inclusion of an abdominal incision plate in a mummy, for example, that had no such incision, represents an attempt by the embalmers to symbolically ensure "a more favorable afterlife." Castilla Ramírez (2014) uses taphonomic evidence and body position to suggest the

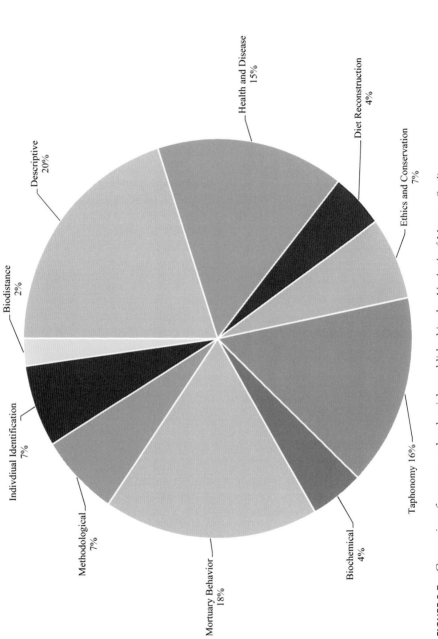

FIGURE 3.7 Categories of mummy-related articles published in the *Yearbook of Mummy Studies*.

presence of 'premature' burial of individuals from Mexico. The author also suggests that use of ferns from the genus *Selaginalla* in some of the burials, and the use of panniers, may be associated with rebirth or resurrection (2014: 138).

Journal of Archaeological Science

The *Journal of Archaeological Science* publishes research "aimed at archaeologists and scientists with particular interests in advancing the development and application of scientific techniques and methodologies to all areas of archaeology" (www.journals. elsevier.com/journal-of-archaeological-science/, accessed September 7, 2016). In the last decade the *JAS* has become one of the principal journals for the publication of bioarchaeological research. A search of the journal's website using the term "bioarchaeology" returned 192 hits.[2] Since 2006, the number of bioarchaeology articles published per year has consistently increased (2006, n = 11; 2013, n = 31).

A total of seventy-four mummy-related articles have been published in the journal, and as can be seen in Figure 3.8, the numbers have been increasing for the last ten years. When these data are compared to number of articles published in the *American Journal of Physical Anthropology* and the *International Journal of Osteoarchaeology* over the last decade, it is clear that *JAS* is becoming one of the main venues for publishing mummy research.

Similar to the *Yearbook of Mummy Studies*, there is a relatively high topical diversity (Figure 3.9). For the first time, we see Dietary Reconstruction being the most commonly encountered type of research (n = 18, 24.7%). This is largely due to the number of articles that were using stable isotopic analyses (n = 15). It is interesting to note that the most commonly sampled tissues for analysis are bone, tooth enamel, and hair. Four studies sampled skin (Corr et al. 2008; Finucane 2007; Iacumin et al. 1998; Thompson et al. 2005), and only two studies took muscle samples (Aufderheide et al. 1994; Finucane 2007). As will be discussed in Chapter 5, these tissues have unique turnover rates and therefore could potentially be utilized to address different aspects of diet. Several of these articles consider shorter-term variability in diet through sequential sampling of hair (and, in one instance, fingernails), including Webb et al. (2013), White et al. (2009), Schwarcz and White (2004), and Williams and Katzenberg (2012).

The *Journal of Archaeological Science* is also unique in that it published the greatest number of articles that were classified as taphonomic (n = 14). A recent example is Prats-Muñoz and colleagues' (2013) discussion of the environmental conditions that facilitated soft tissue preservation at the site of Cova des Pas, a Bronze Age site in Minorca.

American Journal of Physical Anthropology

Since the inception of the *American Journal of Physical Anthropology*, and despite the thousands of articles published in its pages, only seventy-eight articles deal with mummified remains. In and of itself this is an interesting fact and would

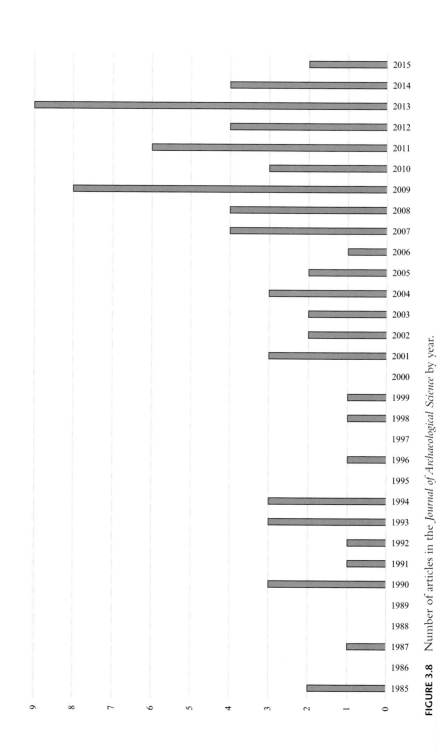

FIGURE 3.8 Number of articles in the *Journal of Archaeological Science* by year.

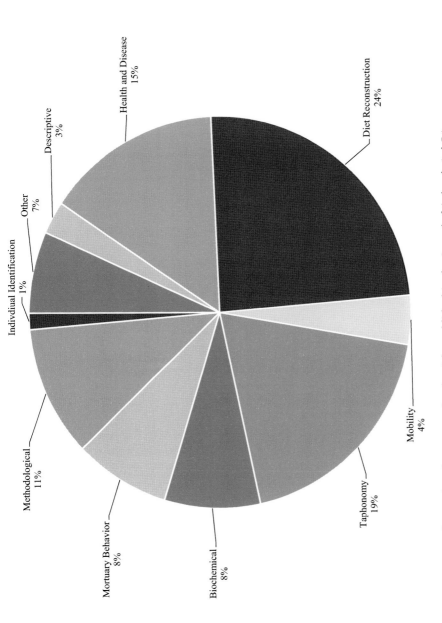

FIGURE 3.9 Categories of mummy-related articles published in the *Journal of Archaeological Science*.

seem to suggest that the flagship journal of the largest academic association of physical anthropologists (over 1700 members; http://physanth.org/; in comparison the British Association for Biological Anthropology and Osteoarchaeology has approximately 500 members) in the world is not generally considered as a venue for publishing mummy-related research. Indeed, based on the data presented in Figure 3.10, there has been a slow but steady decline in the number of mummy-related articles published in the *AJPA*. Topical diversity if relatively rich (Figure 3.11) but follows the same general pattern observed in the other journals with Health and Disease articles predominating. Given that the position of the journal in biological anthropology, I take a somewhat deeper look at the history of mummy research in the AJPA. Although the following pre-1970 references are obviously included in the bibliography, they *are not* included in any of the figures or calculations.

From the 1930s to the early 1960s, the research focus in mummy-related articles was dominated by paleoserology and histology. A series of articles were published by Pompeo Benjamin Candela (1939a, b, 1943), a physician and surgeon, based on the Aleutian mummies originally obtained by Aleš Hrdlička in 1937 and the Paracas mummies examined by T. Dale Stewart. Mildred Trotter (1943) also examined the same Paracas mummies, describing the morphology of hair from ten individuals. Lyle G. Boyd and William C. Boyd conducted paleoserological studies on Egyptian mummies (1939). Although this type of research continues to be present in the pages of the *AJPA* (e.g., Georges et al. 2012), it began decreasing in visibility beginning in the 1960s (Allison et al. 1976, 1978; Lippold 1971; Llop and Rothhammer 1988; Otten and Flory 1963; Paoli et al. 1993).

As the field of mummy studies underwent a revitalization beginning in the 1960s and 1970s led by figures such as Arthur Aufderheide, Michael Zimmerman, Don Brothwell, Marvin Allison, Rosalie David, and Enrique Gertzen, soft tissue paleopathology articles begin to appear in the journal. In the early 1970s, this research was principally morphological and based on the gross examination of mummies (e.g., Allison et al. 1973; Allison et al. 1974b; Ashworth et al. 1976; El Najjar et al. 1980; Munizaga et al. 1978a, 1978b; Post and Donner 1972), or alternatively on the microscopic examination of tissue samples obtained during autopsy (e.g., Allison et al. 1974c; Weinstein et al. 1981). At the same time, Sawyer, using the South American mummies autopsied by Allison and Gertzen, produced a series of anatomical studies (Sawyer et al. 1978, 1979, 1982, 1990).

The presence of paleopathological articles begins to decline in the 1980s, and during the last decade there have been no mummy-based paleopathological articles published in the *AJPA*. The absence of such articles is likely due at least in part to the appearance of journals such as the *International Journal of Osteoarchaeology* and the *Journal of Paleopathology* (not to be confused with the more recent *International Journal of Paleopathology*), which have the more general reputation as being appropriate venues for such research.

There is a distinct shift in the 1990s toward the analysis of molecular data. Again, as noted previously this shift in methodological emphasis has been driven by changing perspectives on the balance between destructive and nondestructive research

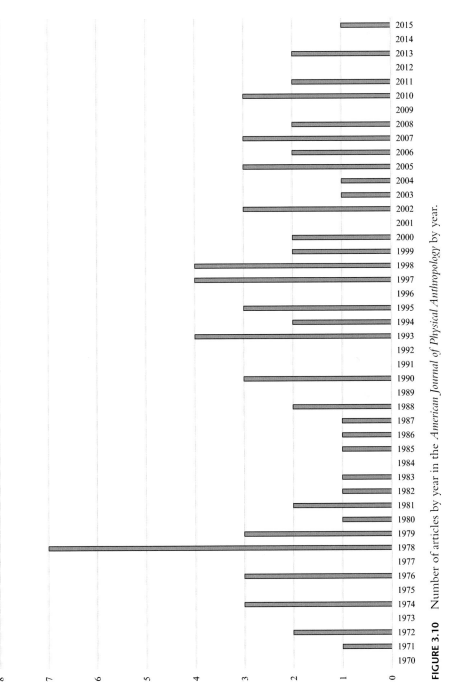

FIGURE 3.10 Number of articles by year in the *American Journal of Physical Anthropology* by year.

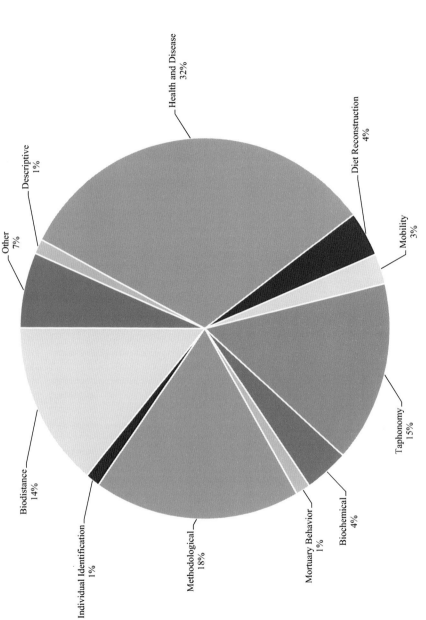

FIGURE 3.11 Categories of mummy-related articles published in the *American Journal of Physical Anthropology*.

methods (Lynnerup 2007). There is a distinct lag time, however, in when this type of research appears in the *American Journal of Physical Anthropology*. Five years after Svante Pääbo published his results on Egyptian DNA in *Nature* (1985a) and subsequently in the *Journal of Archaeological Science* (1985b), Rogan and Salvo (1990) publish a synthetic article in the *Yearbook of Physical Anthropology*. The first article that reports novel molecular data obtained from mummified remains is the Arriaza et al. (1995) analysis of South American mummies for the presence of *Mycobacterim tuberculosis* DNA. This status as the *first* molecular work conducted on mummified needs to be a bit qualified; the authors amplified *M. tuberculosis* DNA from bone samples that came from a mummy. It really was not until that late 1990s that we see articles appear in the *AJPA* in which soft tissue is being sampled. Ubaldi et al. (1998) took samples from multiple internal organs of an Andean mummy, followed closely by Guhl and colleagues' (1999) isolation of DNA from *Trypanosoma cruzi* from heart, esophagus, and colon samples collected from Chilean mummies. Again, this is when this type of research appears in the *American Journal of Physical Anthropology*; both of Pääbo's 1985 articles sampled soft tissue (e.g., cartilage, epidermis).

The number of molecular-based articles begins to increase in 2000. A series of articles were published focusing on Ötzi, including research based on DNA extracted from the stomach and colon contents (Cano et al. 2000), skin, and muscle (Rollo et al. 2000). Many of these articles were ultimately taphonomic in focus and attempted to reconstruct the series of environmental events that led to Ötzi's mummification (Rollo et al. 2000). A series of articles and responses also discussed the preservation of DNA from Egyptian remains (Gilbert et al. 2005; Marota et al. 2002; Zink and Nerlich 2003, 2005).

Despite the long history of the utilization of X-ray technology to examine mummified remains (Chhem and Brothwell 2010; Böni et al. 2004), the explicit use of mediconuclear technology as a research tool does not appear in the *American Journal of Physical Anthropology* until the mid-1970s with Marvin Allison and colleagues' (1974a) analysis of Harris lines in skeletal and mummified remains from South America. In the 1980s we can observe a slight uptick in frequency, but when compared to the number of publications in other journals, this type of research remains very underrepresented (n = 7) in the journal. These articles are principally methodological in orientation, exploring the application of other modalities such as nuclear magnetic resonance imaging (Piepenbrink et al. 1986), computed tomography (Melcher et al. 1997; Pickering et al. 1990; Rühli et al. 2002), and terahertz imaging (Öhrström et al. 2010).

Results Based on Article Type

It should be clear from the preceding discussion that a wide range of mummy research is produced in a number of different venues. As mentioned at the beginning of the previous section, clearly the nature of the journal itself is going to influence the type of research that is published in its pages. To examine what impact this may have on the type of research that is being published, I placed all of the articles (n = 496) that were published in these top journals into categories based on the primary research question as described above (e.g., General Descriptive, Health and Disease, Taphonomy, etc).

The frequency of each article type across all of the top journals is presented in Figure 3.12. Articles in the Health and Disease category are the most frequent (33%), with a total 163 articles. Taphonomy, Descriptive, Methodological, and Mortuary Behavior articles round out the top five. Topics that are otherwise common in skeletal bioarchaeology such as diet, paleodemography, and biological distance, are not commonly encountered in mummy studies.

Health and Disease Articles

As should be clear from the previous journal-specific discussions and from Figure 3.12, health and disease-related articles are the most commonly encountered type of mummy research. Several factors contribute to paleopathology being a dominant focus in mummy studies. From goiter to atherosclerosis to human papillomavirus, at the most basic level, the preservation of soft tissue opens up the possibility of identifying a much wider range of pathological conditions that have little or no impact on skeletal tissue. This potential is of course balanced by the fact that some soft tissues decompose rapidly and are inherently more susceptible to postmortem taphonomic alteration and/or loss.

Another factor that likely drives the focus on paleopathology is the disciplinary background of many mummy researchers. The retention of soft tissue opens up many research possibilities, but it also means that certain educational backgrounds become more important. Although many biological anthropologists have taken (or teach) gross anatomy courses, our background in pathophysiology and histopathology is not as great as professionals in the biomedical fields. Mummy studies has always had a more distinct biomedical flavor, with some of the most prominent early (e.g., Grafton Elliot Smith, neuroanatomist; Thomas Pettigrew, anatomist; Augustus Bozzi Granville, gynecological surgeon) and modern practitioners (Aidan Cockburn, epidemiologist; Enrique Gerszten, physician; Arthur Aufderheide, pathologist) coming from medical fields.

The frequencies reported in Figure 3.13 are based on the total number of articles placed into this category (n = 163). What these numbers indicate is that despite any disciplinary emphasis that may exist, health and disease articles account for the majority of mummy-related research irrespective of journal type. That is, articles that focus on paleopathology are the most frequent in both major bioanthropology (e.g., *American Journal of Physical Anthropology*), archaeology journals (e.g., *Journal of Archaeological Science*), and biomedical journals (e.g., *The Lancet*). The journals publishing the greatest number of health and disease-related articles are listed in Table 3.3. For comparison, I included the journals identified by Zweifel et al. (2009) and Dageförde et al. (2014) in their meta-analyses of published soft tissue paleopathology.

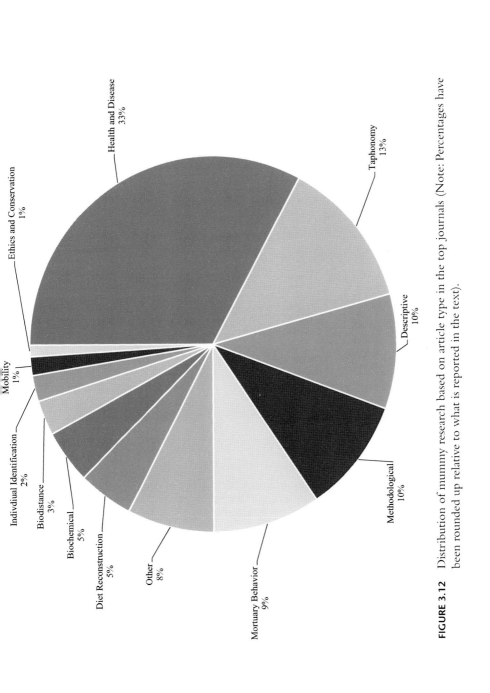

FIGURE 3.12 Distribution of mummy research based on article type in the top journals (Note: Percentages have been rounded up relative to what is reported in the text).

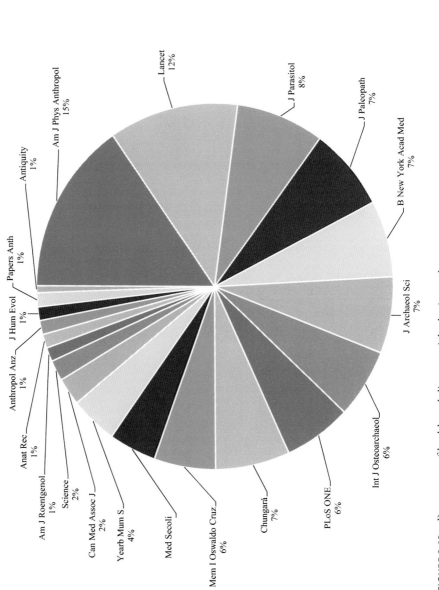

FIGURE 3.13 Percentage of health and disease articles by journal.[a]

TABLE 3.3 Journals with the highest number of paleopathology articles.[a]

Rank	South American (Dageförde et al. 2014)		Egyptian (Zweifel et al. (2009)		All Regions Current Study	
	Journal	N	Journal	N	Journal	N
1	Am J Phys Anth	18	Can Med Assoc J	12	Am J Phys Anth	25
2	B NY Acad Med	4	Am J Phys Anth	10	Lancet	19
3	J of Neurosurg	3	Am J Roentgenol	6	J Parasitol	13
4	Annals of Human Genetics	2	Paleopathol Newsl	4	J Paleopathol	12
5	Mem Inst Oswaldo Cruz	2	Nature	3	J Arch Sci	11
6	J Parasitol	2	Lancet	3	B NY Acad Med	11
7	Lancet	2	J Am Med Assoc	3	Int J Osteoarch	10
8	Proc Natl Acad Sci U.S.A.	2	Science	2	PLoS ONE	10

a It is important to note the differences in how the data were collected. First, I am reporting numbers only from journals that have published 10 or more mummy-related articles and so some of the journals (e.g., Journal of Neurosurgery) included by these authors are not considered in my results. Additionally, my analysis covers articles published between 1970 and 2015. There are also some difference in how some articles were categorized. For example, Zweifel et al. (2009) classified Barraco (1977) and Horne and Lewin (1977) as paleopathological in focus, whereas I classified them as taphonomic in focus.

There are several things to consider regarding these data and the presence of paleopathological research in mummy studies. The *American Journal of Physical Anthropology* has the highest number of health and disease-related articles, accounting for 15% (n = 25) (Figure 3.13). There is a near-even split between the number of articles published in anthropology-related journals and the more biomedical/general science journals (n = 82 and n = 80, respectively).

It is possible to observe two different features of health and disease articles based on the data presented in Figure 3.14. First, there is a steady increase in the number of health and disease articles through time. The early peak in 1977 is largely due to the publications in the *Canadian Medical Association Journal* of the investigation of ROM I (Hart et al. 1977). The number of paleopathological articles begins to increase in the early 1990s, with a very recent spike in publication in 2014.

I also classified these articles based on the primary method in which the paleopathological data were derived—based on morphological (i.e., gross, histological, or radiographic examination), immunological, biochemical, or molecular evidence (Figure 3.14). The 'Other' consists of articles that are not reporting primary data but are syntheses (Dageförde et al. 2014) or replies/comments to primary research (e.g., Tunón and Svanberg 1999). Articles in the 'Multiple' category utilized two or more of the methods.

The 1970s and 1980s were dominated by morphological examinations. Beginning in the 1990s there is an increase in the number of studies that use immunological (e.g., Deelder et al. 1990; Fornaciari G. et al. 1992) and molecular evidence (e.g., Guhl et al. 1997; Nerlich et al. 1997a). This is not unexpected given the

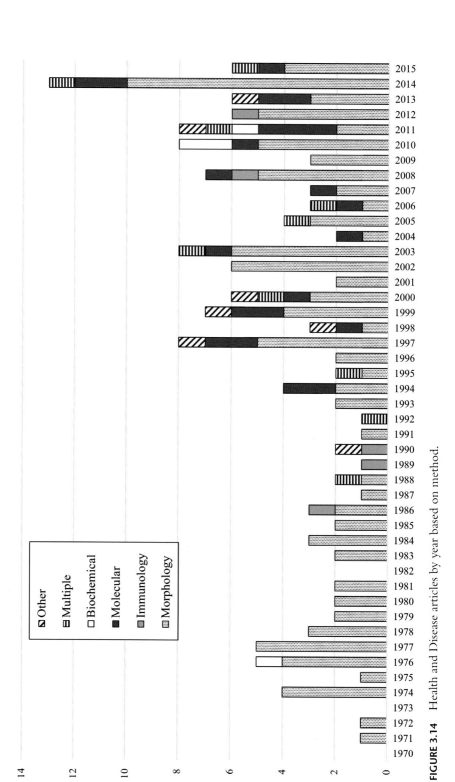

FIGURE 3.14 Health and Disease articles by year based on method.

general movement away from destructive analyses, such as autopsy (Lynnerup 2007), and the expanding array of minimally destructive/invasive biomolecular methods. Morphologically based articles continue to be frequent, but these include radiography (e.g., Haas et al. 2015), histology (e.g., Rodríguez et al. 2011), and the microscopic observation of parasites (e.g., Nezamabadi et al. 2013a, b). This reflects that fact that morphological observations will likely always be a principal means of conducting paleopathological investigations (Aufderheide 2003).

It is useful to consider an additional factor against this backdrop of shifting methodological approaches, and that is the balance between case study–based and epidemiological research. The birth of modern mummy studies is really grounded in multidisciplinary examinations of single bodies (e.g., PUM II, Cockburn et al. 1975; ROM I, Hart et al. 1977). Case studies are an important aspect of paleopathology because they document the presence of conditions in the past, yet they are also limited in their significance in that they do not provide information on the incidence and distribution of diseases. Nelson and Wade (2015: 941–942) note that the IMPACT project "is intended to provide researchers with large-scale primary data samples for anthropological and palaeopathological investigations that will move mummy studies from a case-study approach" to one that is "more in tune with epidemiological paradigms . . ." Implied in this statement is the perception that soft tissue paleopathology tends to be case-study driven.

In their meta-analyses of published paleopathological research on Egyptian and South American mummies Zweifel et al. (2009) and Dageförde et al. (2014) considered the distribution of case-study versus epidemiological studies. Both articles are important syntheses and provide valuable diachronic perspectives on this aspect of mummy studies as well as providing suggestions for improvement. The authors consider many different variables in their analyses, including those associated with the publication venue and authorship (e.g., journal, country of workplace for the first author), demographic of the mummy/mummies (e.g., sex, individual age, historical age, cultural background), methodology, and paleopathological diagnoses.

The authors defined case studies as involving one or two mummies, whereas epidemiological studies reported on three or more mummies. Zweifel et al. (2009) report that 131 articles on Egyptian mummies were published between 1977 and 2005. Dageförde et al. (2014) found sixty-one articles on South American mummies from the same time period. The former identified forty-six (35%) epidemiological studies and eighty-five (65%) case reports in the Egyptian literature, while Dageförde et al. (2014) classified thirty-seven (61%) as being epidemiological and twenty-four (39%) as case studies. Chi-square analyses of these count data indicate that there are significantly more case studies published on Egyptian mummies than South American mummies ($X^2 = 11.06$, p-value < 0.001) and significantly more epidemiological studies based on South American material than on Egyptian remains ($X^2 = 34.41$, p-value < 0.001).

Employing the same criteria, and using the articles I classified as Health and Disease (n = 163), I counted 102 articles (65.6%) as case studies and fifty-six (35.4%) as epidemiological.[3] Qualitatively, there might be some support to the notion that mummy research is heavily case-study oriented. As can be seen in Figure 3.15, mummy research was predominantly case study–based between 1970 and 1990, with what looks like a distinct increase in epidemiological studies in the latter two decades. However, chi-square analysis indicates that there has not been a significant increase. Comparing counts of epidemiological papers from 1970 to 1990 and from 1991 to 2015, there is no significant increase ($X^2 = 1774$, p-value $= 0.1828$). On the other hand, there has been a significant increase in the number of published case studies ($X^2 = 15.12$, p-value < 0.001). When the data from Zweifel et al. (2009) and Dageförde et al. (2014) are pooled, there is no significant difference between the frequency in epidemiological and case-study research when compared to my data.

Descriptive Articles

As defined earlier, articles were put in the Descriptive category if they were broad in scope and were not addressing a specific problem-orientated research question. The articles published on the autopsy of ROM I are examples of descriptive research from the early 1970s. More recent examples include McKnight et al. (2014) and Previgliano et al. (2003). Although these articles are significant in that they are contributing to the body of knowledge, these were classified as 'descriptive' because there was not a clear problem-orientated research statement. As can be observed in Figure 3.16, descriptive articles have been a regular feature of mummy research published in the top journals. There has been a very recent spike in frequency, in large part based on articles published in *Papers in Anthropology, Anatomical Record*, and *Yearbook of Mummy Studies* (Figure 3.17).

Taphonomy Articles

The impact of postmortem taphonomic processes can be much more profound in soft tissue, impacting the ability to identify and diagnose pathological conditions at several levels. The loss of color, texture, and even location of internal organs can hamper identification whereas changes can also occur at the tissue, cellular, and chemical levels. Despite the potential impact of postmortem diagenetic processes on soft tissue preservation, the "infrastructure database for soft tissue taphonomy is alarmingly small" (Aufderheide 2011: 79). Based on my analysis, the top journals for mummy research published sixty-four (13% of 496) articles that I would character-ize as dealing with taphonomy (Figure 3.18).

The highest percentage of taphonomy articles are present in the *Journal of Archaeological Science* (n $= 14$), *American Journal of Physical Anthropology* (n $= 12$), and the *Yearbook of Mummy Studies* (n $= 7$). They are less frequent (or absent) in the biomedical journals (e.g., *Canadian Medical Association Journal, Journal of Parasitology*, and *The Lancet*). This is not to say that an individual article within one of these later journals does not discuss the potential impact of taphonomy, just that examining taphonomy was not the primary focus of the research.

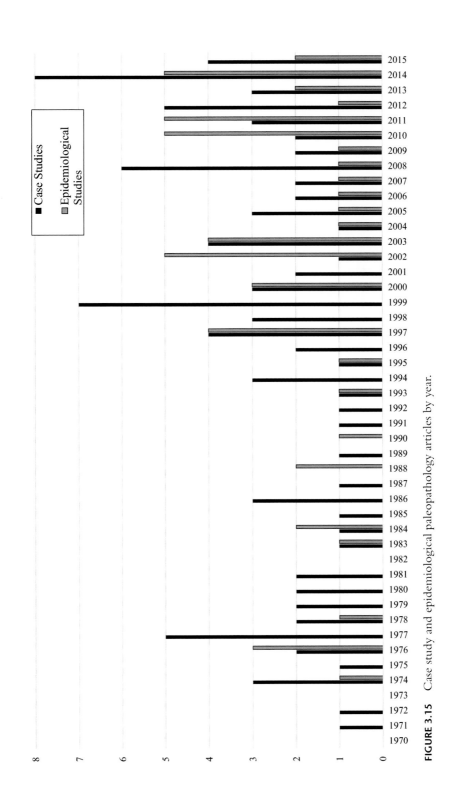

FIGURE 3.15 Case study and epidemiological paleopathology articles by year.

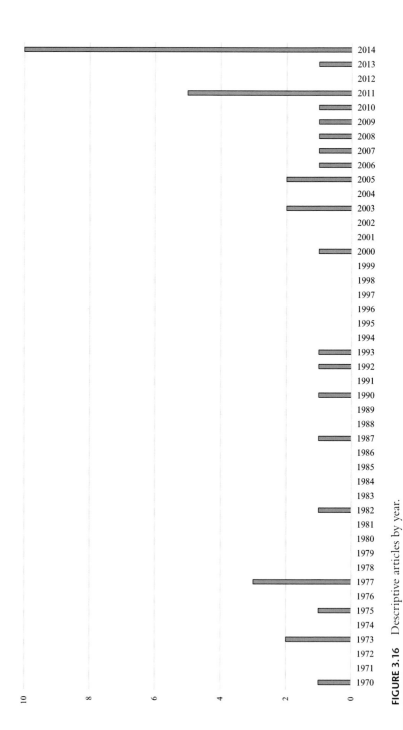

FIGURE 3.16 Descriptive articles by year.

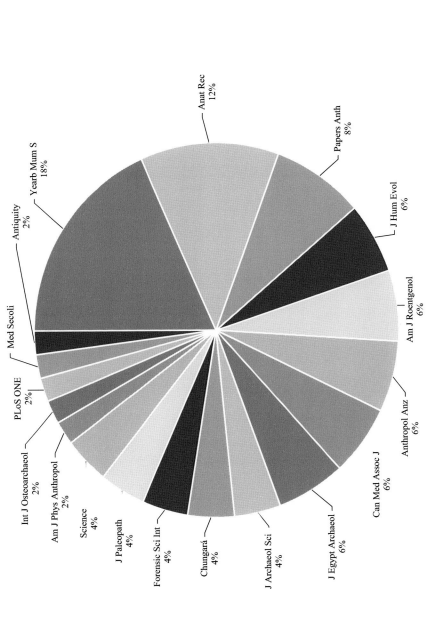

FIGURE 3.17 Percentage of Descriptive articles by journal.[a]

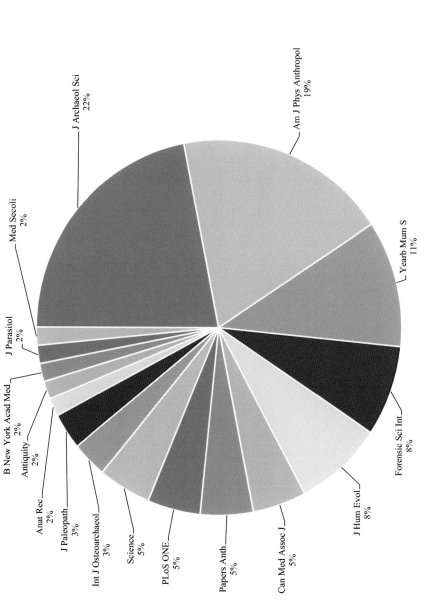

FIGURE 3.18 Percentage of taphonomy articles by journal.

To get a better sense of the type of taphonomic research that is being conducted, I placed each of the articles into one of the following categories by year (Figure 3.19):

Descriptive: Research where the primary focus is on the description of postdepositional macro- and/or micro-level morphological and/or chemical changes in soft tissue, hard tissue, and their components (e.g., proteins, carbohydrates, lipids, DNA, etc.).

Mummification/Preservation Process: Research where the primary focus is the discussion of the taphonomic processes that led to soft tissue preservation.

Mortuary Behavior: The category includes articles where description of the taphonomic changes is used to discuss mortuary behavior. This category is distinct from the previous in that this research explicitly addresses the anthropogenic impact on the decomposition process.

Other: This would include review articles (e.g., Ubelaker and Zarenko 2011) as well as articles that considered post-excavation modifications (e.g., Carminati et al. 2014; Gill-Frerking 2014).

As can be seen in Figure 3.19, taphonomic research during the 1970s, 1980s, and 1990s, although relatively stable, is infrequent. Additionally, the majority of this research is descriptive in nature (56%). Beginning in 2005, however, the number of articles begins to increase and also increasingly begins to address a broader range of research questions.

Methodological Articles

Forty-nine articles (9.9%) published in the top journals were categorized as being primarily methodological in focus (Figure 3.20). The most common venue for methodological papers is in the *American Journal of Physical Anthropology* (34%), *Journal of Archaeological Sciences* (19.5%), and the *American Journal of Roentgenology* (9.5%).

To see where the focus on methodological advancement has been, I placed each of the articles into one of the following categories and then graphed them by year (Figure 3.21):

Molecular: These papers focus on the molecular methods that involve the identification, extraction, and/or amplification of DNA (e.g., Amory et al. 2007; Woide et al. 2010).

Immunological: All of the articles that fall into this category are examples of paleoserological research (e.g., Paoli et al. 1993).

Radiography/Imaging: This is research that explores the feasibility of different modalities of paleoimaging technology (e.g., CT scan, terahertz imaging).

Stable Isotopes: Research that is improving or testing current isotopic methodologies (e.g., Williams et al. 2011) or are considering the application of novel isotopes (e.g., Sharp et al. 2003).

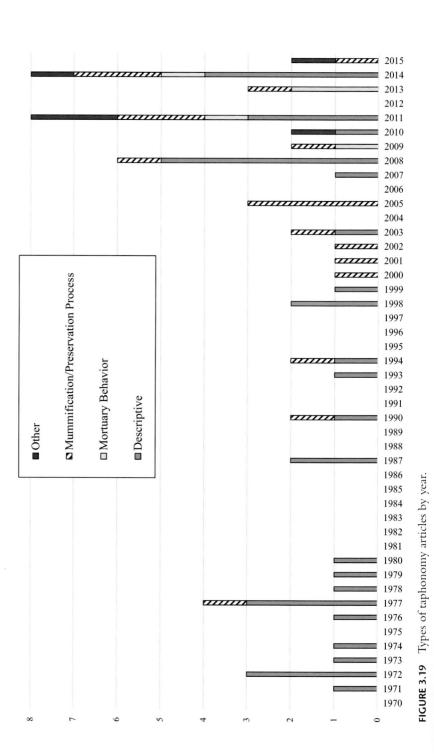

FIGURE 3.19 Types of taphonomy articles by year.

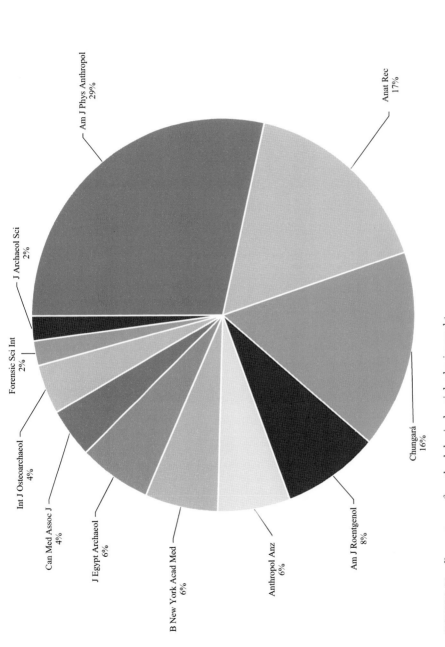

FIGURE 3.20 Percentage of methodological articles by journal.[a]

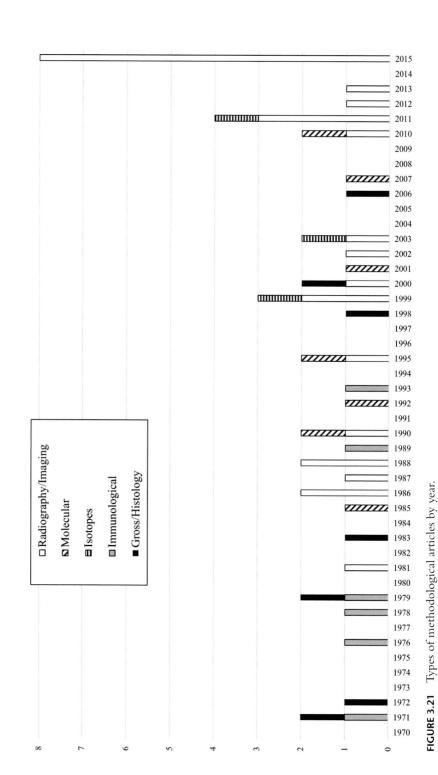

FIGURE 3.21 Types of methodological articles by year.

Gross/Histology: These papers focus on the gross identification of tissue (Zimmerman 1972) or specimens (e.g., Argüello 2006).

Articles that are exploring the application of mediconuclear imaging technology make up the majority of articles in this category (n = 27, 65.9%), followed by molecular methodologies (n = 7, 17.1%), immunological and gross/histology (both n = 6, 14.6%), and finally isotopic methods (n = 4, 9.8%).

Mortuary Behavior

As discussed previously, mortuary behavior is a topic that can include the examination of the steps and procedures taken that results in mummification (i.e., the *how*) as well as the broader social context in which these steps occur (i.e., the *why*). If we want to frame these different aspects relative to the trends in bioarchaeological research noted by Buikstra et al. (2011), increasing methodological sophistication is facilitating a closer examination of the processes associated with anthropogenic mummification, whereas the integration of theory encourages the more holistic discussion of mummification practices in their social contexts. A good example of this is the work of the Cladh Hallan 'mummies' discussed in Chapter 1. On the one hand, methodological advances have let researchers determine that the remains from Cladh Hallan exhibit evidence that decomposition was halted (Parker Pearson et al. 2005) and that the 'individuals' recovered during excavation were in fact composed of skeletal elements derived from multiple individuals (Hanna et al. 2012). On the other hand, Parker Pearson et al. (2005) discuss the implications of such treatment for the changing perceptions of individuality after death during the British Middle Bronze Age.

The discussion of mortuary behavior has not been featured prominently in the top journals, with only 9.5% (n = 47) focusing on this topic. The frequency of this type of article has remained consistently low throughout much of the time period included in this analysis. Beginning in the mid- to late-2000, there is a slight increase in frequency (Figure 3.22). The majority of these articles appear in the anthropological or archaeological journals, including *Chungara, Yearbook of Mummy Studies, Antiquity,* and *Journal of Archaeological Sciences* (Figure 3.23). Articles discussing aspects of Egyptian mummification focus on reconstructing the process itself (e.g., McCreesh et al. 2011; Saleem and Hawass 2013; Seiler and Rühli 2015). It is in *Chungara* where we observe articles that are not only addressing *how* the mummies were made (e.g., Arriaza 1994) but *why* as well (e.g., Nystrom et al. 2010; Santoro et al. 2012).

It is noteworthy that I classified only a single article as dealing explicitly with mortuary behavior within the *American Journal of Physical Anthropology*, the largest and presumably most influential journal in biological anthropology. This was Aufderheide and colleagues' (1993) discussion of the mummification methods observed in seven Chinchorro mummies. The discussion is principally descriptive and does not explore any broader issues related to mortuary behavior.

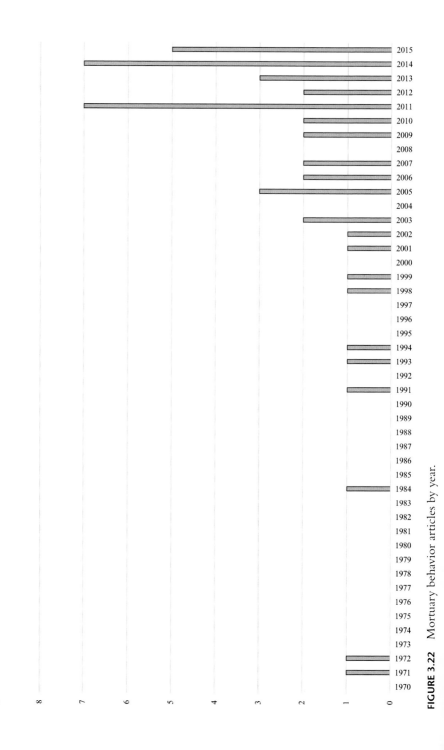

FIGURE 3.22 Mortuary behavior articles by year.

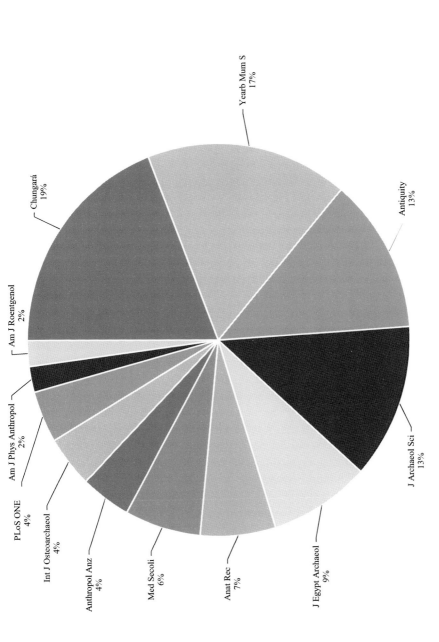

FIGURE 3.23 Percentage of mortuary behavior articles by journal.[a]

Chapter Summary

The data presented in this chapter clearly indicate that mummy-related research is on the rise; nearly as many articles have been published in just the last ten years as in the preceding thirty-five years combined. This growth reflects the rich research potential represented by mummified remains and has recently stimulated the field to assess its current methodological standards and ethical practices.

Whereas an increase in the number of articles reflects the promise of the field, the number and diversity of journals in which this research has been published highlights a fundamental division. The number of biomedical journals in which mummy research has been published (n = 135), far exceeds the number of anthropology-related journals (n = 69) in which this type of research appears. Thus, although the interdisciplinary nature of mummy studies is one of the field's strengths, it may also reflect a significant hurdle to its development and expansion. Based on the previously described data, it is clear that a shift is occurring in where mummy research is being published.

During the 1970s and 1980s the *American Journal of Physical Anthropology* was one of the main journals for mummy-related publications. Although mummy research is still being published there (e.g., Turner et al. 2013), the number of articles has remained consistently low for the last twenty years (Figure 3.24). The situation is similar for *Chungara, Anthropologischer Anzeiger*, and *International Journal of Osteoarchaeology* as well as for journals in the general medical, medical specialty, and forensic categories (Figures 3.24 and 3.25). There are two journals, however, in which it is possible to observe an increase in publications over the last decade, *Journal of Archaeological Science* and *PLoS ONE* (Figure 3.24).

With a quick turn-around time and an open access policy, *PLoS ONE* quickly became the largest journal in the world. Anthropology does not have a very significant presence in the 'pages' of *PLoS ONE*. Anthropology and Archaeology are sub-categories of the Social Science subject area in *PLoS ONE*, which includes other disciplines such as Economics, Linguistics, Human Geography, Law and Legal Sciences, Political Science, Psychology, and Sociology.

As noted by Goldstein (2006) and Knüsel (2010), some research programs in bioarchaeology have fostered a much closer connection with the natural sciences and do not engage as deeply with archaeological data or social theory. The majority of mummy-related articles published in *PLoS ONE* reflect this emphasis. This is not to say that this research is somehow flawed or not significant. Prime examples include work of Corthals et al. (2012), Lalremruata et al. (2013), Thèves et al. (2011), and Maixner et al. (2014). The work is significant and provides fascinating results; it is just not as deeply connected to archaeological context.

Journal of Archaeological Science has a longer history in terms of publishing mummy-related articles and is the second most common venue for publishing mummy articles. It is also clear that the frequency of mummy-related articles in *JAS* has increased over the last ten years. Additionally, the diversity of topics within *JAS* is greater than in most of the other venues; indeed, *JAS* is one of the few journals

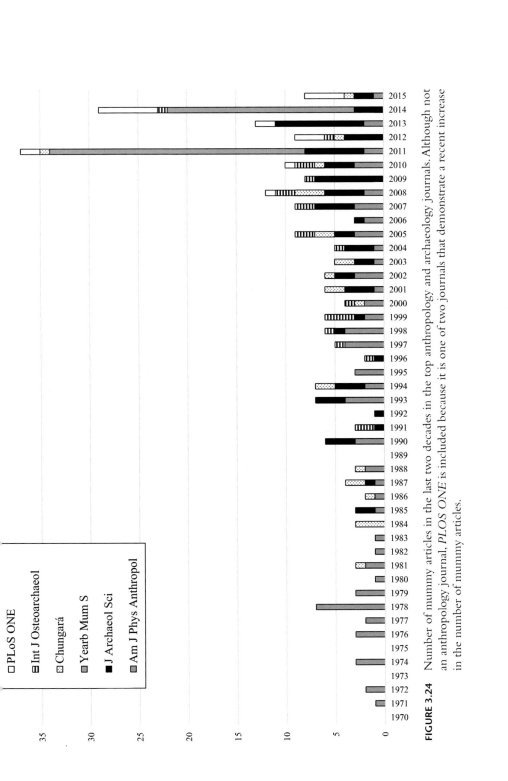

FIGURE 3.24 Number of mummy articles in the last two decades in the top anthropology and archaeology journals. Although not an anthropology journal, *PLOS ONE* is included because it is one of two journals that demonstrate a recent increase in the number of mummy articles.

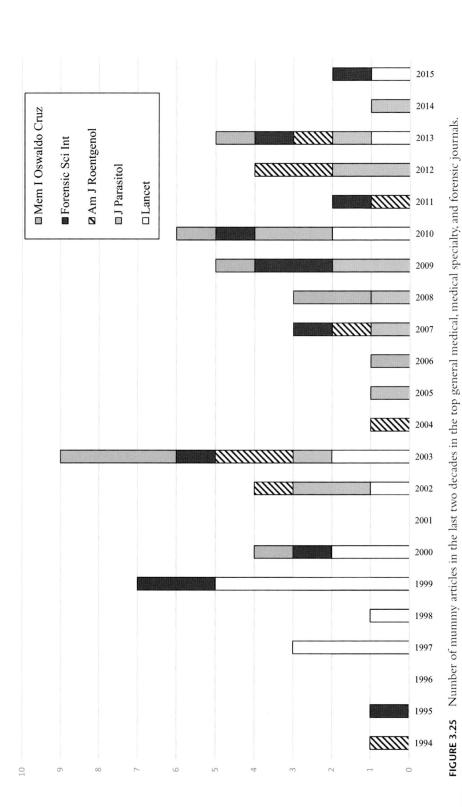

FIGURE 3.25 Number of mummy articles in the last two decades in the top general medical, medical specialty, and forensic journals.

discussed earlier in which Health and Disease articles are *not* the most frequent. This diversity also reflects a greater emphasis on the archaeology (and anthropology) side of bioarchaeology. Hypothesis-driven research questions and development of the archaeological context tend to be more common in *JAS*. For example, White and colleagues (2009) derive $\delta^{13}C$ and $\delta^{15}N$ values from hair to reconstruct short-term dietary changes, which are then used to discuss possible functions of the site of Pacatnamu on Peru's northern coast. Wade and Nelson (2013b) test the association between excerebration and evisceration and sociopolitical factors in Egyptian mummies. Touzeau and collegues (2013) examined how diet changed from the Predynastic period (ca. 5500 B.P.) to Byzantine period (ca. 1500 B.P.) in Egypt

Since its inception, bioarchaeology was explicitly articulated as a collaborative endeavor, providing equal weight to both archaeology and bioanthropology. This not only entails the 'in-the-dirt' aspects of archaeology but also the integration of archaeological and social theory. The next chapter discusses publication patterns in mummy studies relative to the field's engagement with social theory.

Notes

1. Other publications from this same collection include Dedouit et al. (2010), who conducted a morphological examination of a young adult female; Biagini et al. (2012), which identified variola viral DNA (the virus that causes smallpox); and Crubézy et al. (2010), which examined population genetics. Additionally, modern Yakuts have been the focus of several genetic analyses (e.g., Pakendorf et al. 2006).
2. As discussed in Chapter 2, in some countries bioarchaeological research includes the analysis of faunal material. Given that JAS is a large international journal, these search results included both what New World bioarchaeologists would consider to be zooarchaeology as well as research on human skeletal material. The earlier publications are generally split between faunal and human bioarchaeological work. Beginning in the mid-2000s the latter begin to significantly increase in frequency.
3. Five articles were not included because they were synthetic review articles and were not reporting original results.

4

MUMMY STUDIES AND SOCIAL THEORY

The biocultural model has proven very useful within skeletal bioarchaeology and a considerable amount of research is grounded in this perspective. The inclusion of different ecological, cultural, and biological variables (i.e., the context) in the examination of human adaptation, however, is not the same thing as the integration of theory. The contextualized analysis of human remains refers not only to the incorporation and consideration of these different variables but also to the integration of social theory in the formulation of a problem-orientated research design. In this chapter, social theory is defined as "Bodies of general knowledge about sociocultural phenomena expressed in postulates, premises, assumptions, principles, and models" that "ostensibly answer *how* and *why* questions about human behavior and societies" (Schiffer 2000: 1, emphasis in original). The incorporation of theory expands the interpretive power of any results, moving research from a limited case study to something that speaks more broadly to human behavior and adaptation. Debra Martin and colleagues (2013) provide a discussion of some of the main theories that have been employed by bioarchaeologists including evolutionary theory, human ecology, human body and identity, sex and gender, human violence, inequality, and colonization and imperialism. To this, I would add the corpus of literature on mortuary archaeology and theory. Grounded in these theories, recent bioarchaeological work has considered the embodied experiences of death (Baadsgaard 2011), fragmentation and the *dividual* body (e.g., Duncan and Schwarz 2014; Geller 2012; Hodge 2013), and structural violence (e.g., de la Cova 2012; Klaus 2012; Nystrom 2014; Stone 2012).

It is possible to observe the influence of the biocultural model on mummy research, yet it is in the integration of theory where we can observe the greatest division between the biomedical and anthropological treatments of mummies. In the following discussion, I will highlight areas where mummy researchers have a longer tradition of engaging with theory: evolutionary theory and mortuary theory.

The discussion will then shift to topics where there is room for elaboration and new areas that may prove productive avenues. For the field to move forward, there needs to be greater integration between the theoretical approaches currently being employed in skeletal bioarchaeology and the biomedical side of the discipline.

Evolutionary Theory

Evolutionary theory has long been central to anthropological research and in particular biological anthropology in the examination of human behavior. Although the reliance upon and inclusion of evolutionary theory within anthropology has shifted through time, Zuckerman and colleagues (2012) recently argued for the fuller integration of evolutionary theory into paleopathology.

One of the most oft-cited goals of mummy research is reconstructing the evolution of disease. Zimmerman (2014: 120–121) states that "The examination of mummies has two goals: fitting the diagnosis of diseases in individual mummies into a picture of the health status of a given ancient population; and providing information on the evolution of disease." There are several examples where the examination of mummies have contributed significantly to the reconstruction of the evolutionary history of a disease.

The goal of Dabernat and colleagues' (2014: e89877) research on tuberculosis in sixteenth- to nineteenth-century mummies from the Yakutia region in Eastern Siberia is to "elucidate the natural history and host-pathogen coevolution of human tuberculosis." Skeletal changes associated with tuberculosis were observed in 13 of the 140 individuals included in the study; in four of these individuals researchers were able to successfully amplify the IS*6110* sequence unique to *Mycobacterium tuberculosis*. Further, the sequence belongs to the PGG-2 genetic group and is distinct from the PGG-1 strain that afflicts modern Russia and Siberia. Ultimately, the authors suggest that "this strain might have exerted some selective pressure on a small population that was subsequently hit by epidemics caused by other MTB strains centuries later" and "favored the evolution of TB" (Dabernat et al. 2014: e89877).

Over ten million people in Central and South American are infected with the parasite *Trypanosoma cruzi*, which causes Chagas disease. The natural sylvatic cycle of the parasite involves transmission via members of the Reduviidae insect family to over 100 different mammalian species. The goal of Aufderheide and colleagues' (2004b) research was to reconstruct the evolution of the domestic cycle of the disease. Based on the extraction and amplification of *T. cruzi* DNA from 300 Andean mummies, the authors (2004b: 2038) conclude that "Upon settlement of this coastal segment ≈9500 years ago, humans intruded upon and became participants in this sylvatic cycle, perhaps augmented by various forms of trypanosome ingestion, including consumption of infected food. Gradually, the domestic cycle evolved, leading to its current status today."

Molecular analyses are also providing insight into the evolutionary history of other conditions including atherosclerosis and cardiovascular disease (Zink et al.

2014), hepatitis (Kahila Bar-Gal et al. 2012; Marota et al. 1998), human lympho-tropic virus-1 (Li et al. 1999; Sonoda et al. 2000), and human papillomavirus (Fornaciari G. et al. 2003). Although this research provides insight into the evolutionary history of a pathogen, or the presence of genetic predisposition in antiquity, it also demonstrates the importance of the biocultural perspective in that it reveals the central role that cultural environments have in the manifestation of disease.

Mortuary Theory and Archaeology

Although death and burial have long been of anthropological interest, the development and elaboration of modern mortuary archaeology began in the 1970s and is marked by several key publications including Arthur Saxe's (1970) dissertation, *Social Dimensions of Mortuary Practices*, and James Brown's (1971a) edited *Approaches to the Social Dimensions of Mortuary Practices*. Using ethnographic data drawn from three groups, Saxe developed and tested eight hypotheses that examined the degree to which a deceased social persona or a society's sociopolitical organization may manifest in mortuary practices. Though Saxe's dissertation was hugely influential on the development of mortuary archaeology, it was his Hypothesis 8 concerning the relationship between the presence of a bounded disposal area and group territoriality and resource control that subsequently attracted the most attention (Goldstein 1980; Charles and Buikstra 1983).

The most influential papers in Brown's (1971a) edited volume were his own examination of mortuary practices at the Mississippian period site of Spiro, and Lewis Binford's (1971) analysis of the relationship between social and mortuary ritual complexity. Brown's research would later be used to support the correlation between the presence of rare grave goods and high social status (e.g., Tainter 1978). Binford considered the correspondence between social complexity, measured based on subsistence strategy, and the complexity of mortuary ritual. He concluded that as societies transition from food-foraging to food-production, and as the number of social roles that an individual may have during life increases, that mortuary rituals became more complex. As noted by Rakita and Buikstra (2005a: 4), the work of these researchers "are often summarized to justify the assumption that there is a direct relationship between the social status of the deceased and the relative amount of treatments, grave goods, or energy expended in the burial of the individual." Dubbed the 'Saxe–Binford approach,' this perspective on the relationship between mortuary behavior and social structure remains the dominant interpretive paradigm in much of American archaeology (Rakita and Buikstra 2005a).

The 1980s witnessed two key publications in mortuary archaeology, Goldstein's (1980) reformulation of Saxe's Hypothesis 8 and the *Archaeology of Death* volume edited by Chapman and colleagues (1981). At the same time, a number of important critiques of the Saxe-Binford approach, and processual archaeology in general (e.g., Hodder 1980; Parker Pearson 1982; Shanks and Tilley 1982), were published. Out of this period, several important themes continue to influence mortuary bio/archaeology, including acknowledgment of regional diachronic variability in mortuary behavior and the important role of the landscape (Rakita and Buikstra 2005a). What comes out of this literature is the appreciation of a much more dynamic interaction between the dead and the living. Indeed, this perspective is being taken even further in recent discussions on postmortem agency and the manner in which the dead may retain the ability to influence social processes (e.g., Arnold 2014; Crandall and Martin 2014; Tung 2014).

The reconstruction of mortuary behavior has long been a central feature of mummy research, no doubt related to the first scientific investigations of Egyptian mummification during the late 1900s. There are two aspects to the investigation of mortuary behavior: the reconstruction of the mummification process itself (e.g., Buckley et al. 1999; Jones et al. 2014; Maurer et al. 2002; Seiler and Rühli 2015) and the ideological or cultural significance of the process (e.g., Arriaza et al. 2005; Nystrom et al. 2010; Sepúlveda et al. 2015). It is in the latter where we can witness the most explicit incorporation of theory.

One region where mortuary theory has been frequently integrated in the analysis of mummified remains is in the South American Andes. In both prehistoric and contemporary settings, the physical remains of the ancestors play a pivotal social function in Andean communities and social reproduction, agricultural fertility, and group identity (DeLeonardis and Lau 2004; Dillehay 1995; Gose 1994; Salomon 1995). The corporeal remains of the ancestors were avenues through which group rights and responsibilities could be established and reinforced, thus the manipulation of ancestors or the spaces they occupied were powerful means of establishing and signaling control over resources, production, and sociopolitical affiliations (Buikstra 1995). In this manner, mortuary theory has informed on the investigation of the Chinchorro (Arriaza 1995a; Arriaza et al. 2005; Marquet et al. 2012), the Chachapoya (Buikstra and Nystrom 2015; Nystrom et al. 2010), the Chiribaya (Guillén 2012), and Inca mountain-top sacrifices (Ceruti 2004).

The integration of mortuary theory can also be observed in the discussion of mummification in Egypt mummification (Wade et al. 2011; Wade and Nelson 2013a, b), Bronze Age Britain (Parker Pearson et al. 2005), and Sicily (Piombino-Mascali et al. 2010, 2011, 2012). Despite these examples, the majority of articles I classified as 'mortuary behavior' in Chapter 3, were focused on reconstructing the process of mummification and did not explicitly discuss its connection to theory.

Identity and the Body

Although the body is *the* source of data for bioarchaeologists, it is only recently that the discipline has begun to explicitly ground discussion within social theory of the body; the body has always been there, but it has been something assumed rather than interrogated. The body and its constituent parts are acknowledged as not only responding to social, political, and economic factors in the environment but actively structuring society as well (Gowland and Thompson 2013). Scheper-Hughes and Lock's (1987) discussion of three interrelated bodies—the body as individual experience, the social body, and the body politic—serves as a productive foundation for the bioarchaeological investigations of the body (Gowland 2006; Knüsel 2011; Marsteller et al. 2011; Roberts 2011; Torres-Rouff 2011; Sofaer 2011).

The Individual Body

Bioarchaeologists reconstruct the lived experiences of an individual or group by examining the physiological consequences of behavior based on a wide variety of evidence including disease and nonspecific indicators of stress, activity patterns, trauma, diet, and mobility. Much as in skeletal bioarchaeology, examples abound in mummy studies that examine the lived experiences of individuals including:

- Exposure to environmental (Arriaza 2005; Arriaza et al. 2010; Madden and Arriaza 2014) or anthropogenic toxins (Kowal et al. 1989)
- Parasitic infection (Arriaza et al. 2012; Arriaza Standen and Nuñez et al. 2013; Arriaza Standen and Reinhard et al. 2013; Ferreira et al. 2000; Reinhard and Buikstra 2003; Reinhard and Urban 2003; Reinhard et al. 2003; Searcey et al. 2013; Shin et al. 2011; Madden et al. 2001; Martinson et al. 2003)
- Dental health (Gerloni et al. 2009; Seiler et al. 2013)
- Trauma (Lee et al. 2009; Nerlich et al. 2005, 2009; Zimmerman et al. 1981),
- Alcohol and stimulant use (Báez et al. 2000; Cartmell et al. 2005; Rivera et al. 2005; Wilson et al. 2007, 2013)
- Developmental anomalies (Boano et al. 2009; Carod-Artal and Vázquez-Cabrera 2006)
- Diet (Webb et al. 2013; White et al. 1999; Williams and Katzenberg 2012)

Many of the earliest examples of modern mummy research (post-1970) reflect this focus on the individual, and in particular on reconstructing health. The primary foci of seventeen of the ninety-four articles published between 1970 and 1979 was on pathology and involved the analysis of a single (e.g. Cockburn et al. 1975; Tapp et al. 1975) or a small handful of mummies (e.g., Zimmerman 1977). Though these case studies are informative, they are inherently limited when attempting to discuss population-level epidemiology. More recent investigations (e.g., Aufderheide et al. 2004b; Contis and David 1996; Ege et al. 2005; Kloos and David 2002), using the individual lived experience as a basis, have explored how larger-scale cultural (e.g., occupation, age, sex, social status, housing) and environmental conditions (e.g., modification of the landscape through irrigation) contribute to and influence health. In this sense, these larger-scale epidemiological approaches to health begin to explore the social body and body politic.

The Social Body

Paleoepidemiological approaches offer insight into the social influences on the lived experience of health, and thus broadly touch on the social body, but there are limitations. First, this perspective relegates the body to a passive role in that it can respond only to external stimuli or stress. Nor does it address the social experiences of an illness (e.g., Marsteller et al. 2011), a point that I will return to later in this chapter. Skeletal bioarchaeologists investigate how manipulation of the body and how modification of its surfaces reflect "the representational uses of the body as a natural symbol with which to think about nature, society, and culture" (Scheper-Hughes and Lock 1987: 7). Cranial and dental modification have been used to discuss social status and ethnicity (Blom 2005; Tiesler 2012; Williams and White 2006), the identity of enslaved Africans in Campeche, Mexico (Price et al. 2006), and the highland-coastal political affiliations in Chile (Torres-Rouff 2003, 2008).

Tattooing represents one of the most visible ways mummy researchers have engaged with the social body. Modern anthropological and sociological literature on tattoos clearly indicates the personal and social significance often associated with tattoos (e.g., Rubin 1988; Sanders 1989). Because skin is the first and most immediate boundary, things that transgress that boundary are particularly powerful and dangerous (Douglas 1966). From this perspective, skin becomes a potent site for displaying, creating, and transmitting information and representing a manifestation of the 'social body.'

Tattoos have been observed on mummified remains from Alaska (Smith and Zimmerman 1975; Figure 4.1), Peru (Allison et al. 1981; Cagigao et al. 2013;

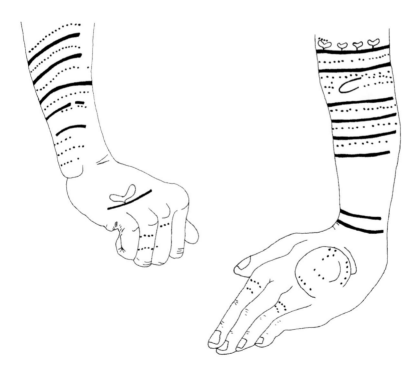

FIGURE 4.1   Tattoos on the right and left forearm of a 1600-year-old frozen mummy from Alaska (Smith and Zimmerman 1975).

Gill-Frerking et al. 2013; Pabst et al. 2010; Vásquez Sánchez et al. 2013; Figure 4.2), Sudanese Nubia (Alvrus et al. 2001), Egypt (Bianchi 1988; Tassie 2003), Greenland (Kromann et al. 1989), Bronze Age Alps (Figure 4.3), East-Central Asia (Rudenko 1970; Yetsenko 2013; Figure 4.4), and the Philippines (Salvador-Amores 2012). Research on mummified tattoos have focused on establishing the material used to make them (e.g., Pabst et al. 2010; Vásquez Sánchez et al. 2013), their potential therapeutic function (e.g., Kean et al. 2013), and their cultural or symbolic meaning.

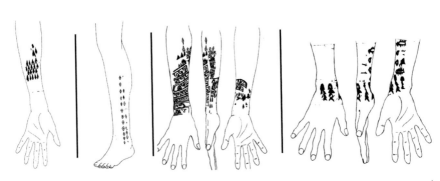

FIGURE 4.2 A selection of the tattoos documented by Allison et al. (1980) from coastal Peru and Chile.

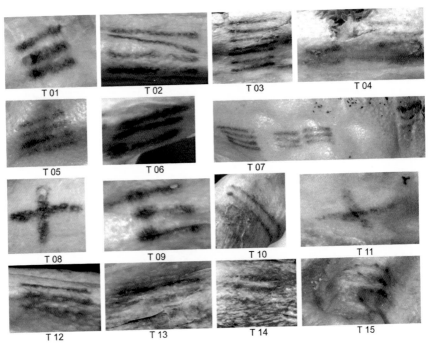

FIGURE 4.3 Examples of the tattoos documented by Samadelli et al. (2015).

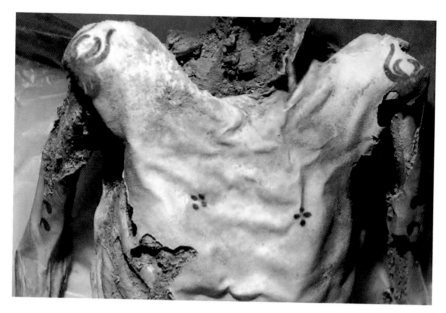

FIGURE 4.4 An infrared photo of tattoos on the shoulders, arms, and chest of a mummy from the Central Asia/Southern Siberia site of Oglakhty (Pankova 2013).

It is this latter portion where we can observe the most explicit engagement with the social body in mummy studies.

Interpreting what tattoos *mean*, particularly when observed on prehistoric remains, is difficult to say the least. As will be discussed further, tattoos are often divided into two categories: communicative/symbolic tattoos and therapeutic tattoos. Commonly, the communicative function of a tattoo is discussed as marking a transition in social identity or status (e.g., Cagigao et al. 2013; Gill-Frerking et al. 2013). For example, tattoos observed on Pazyryk mummies from southern Siberia have generated considerable interest based on their complexity and beauty (Figure 4.4) and their possible ideological and social significance (Cheremisin 2007; Polosmak 2000). Rudenko (1970: 113) suggests that the tattoos on the Pazyryk male from barrow 2 (see Figure 4.7) most likely indicates an elite social status and/or the "mark of manhood." He goes on to suggest that "these figures all had some kind of magical significance not yet understood; they were perhaps protective (apotropaic) signs" though he acknowledges that "tattooing could be used purely decoratively" without any associated symbolic or magical significance.

Yatsenko (2013) contends that there are status and gender differences in the type and location of tattoos. In lower-status individuals, tattoos were isolated to the hands or shoulders, whereas higher-status individuals had tattoos in areas that were not exposed. Further, females have tattoos that depict predator-prey interactions of local animals, whereas males generally depict animals from the steppe. This has been suggested to reflect the composition of Pazyryk society, with men being connected to the "Saka-Tigrahauda groups of the Lower Syrdarya Basin, Southwest Kazakhstan near the Aral Sea in the desert-steppe zone; most of the women, however, were similar to the 'Scythoid groups' of Western Mongolia in the mountain steppe-forest zone." (Yatsenko 2013: 99).

Argent (2013) approaches the Pazyryk tattoos from a different perspective, one that attempts to move away from solely human-generated meaning. Specifically, Argent (2013: 178) suggests that "horse tattoos are presented as polysemic materializations of the bonds between particular Pazyryk horses and people, of blended identities, and of cosmological values related to time, memory, and belonging." She notes that as one moves up the arm, the level of detail and ornamentation increases, which Argent (2013) interprets not only as the transformation of a green horse to seasoned 'schoolmaster' horse but as directly linked to the similarly adorned sacrificial horses found in Pazyryk burials. These sacrificed horses, decorated with horn headdresses, were considered to transport the human soul to the otherworld (Argent 2013).

The Body Politic

The body is a site where social power and control can manifest. Connecting data from skeletal remains to the body politic is challenging (Martin et al. 2013), but it is possible to evaluate the impacts of institutionalized forms of socioeconomic and political power on individual bodies. Fundamentally, we can approach investigating the body politic in two ways: in the living or the dead body. In the living, it is possible to reconstruct the impact of institutionalized domination and control as it manifests on the bones. Examples of this type of research in skeletal bioarchaeology consider the impact on health and diet (e.g., Andrushko et al. 2006; Buzon and Richman 2007; Harrod et al. 2012; Hastorf 1990; Klaus and Tam 2008). The bodies of the dead are also controlled and manipulated to serve sociopolitical ends, in what Verdery (1999) calls dead-body politics. At the most basic level, dead bodies can be moved around and displayed, marshaled at specific times and places to support whatever message a political body may want to convey. Numerous examples from the mummy literature speaks to the body politic including the manipulation of Vladimir Ilych Lenin's body (Quigley 1998), the postmortem history of Oliver Cromwell's head (Tarlow 2008), and Kelly's (2013) interpretation of Irish Iron Age bog bodies.

The following examples are both derived from the Late Horizon (AD 1470–1532) of the South American Andes and demonstrate how the Inca Empire regulated and controlled both living and dead bodies. The bodies of ancestors occupied a fundamental sociopolitical role in many prehistoric Andean groups, being associated with agricultural production, regenerative cycles, and group identity (Bastien 1995; DeLeonardis and Lau 2004; Dillehay 1995; Gose 1994). These bodies, in addition to the ritual and physical structures (e.g., burial towers) that comprise mortuary behavior, were means through which corporate group rights and responsibilities could be established and reinforced (Bloch and Parry 1982). In the Andes, the body was mapped onto the landscape, and in death the vital water of the living human was extracted and reintroduced into the agricultural cycle (Gose 1994). From this brief discussion, it is possible to see how the control of bodies could be equated with socioeconomic control and legitimation of access to resources; if you control the bodies of the ancestors, you are controlling the water and hence a group's agricultural production. Within many Andean groups, access to land within the *ayllu* (the basic socioeconomic unit among indigenous groups) was based upon kinship, and lineages were traced to actual or fictive progenitors (Salomon 1995: 321). Therefore, the manipulation of ancestors or the spaces they occupied could be powerful means of establishing and signaling control over resources and production (Buikstra 1995).

One manifestation of Inca imperial control of bodies was in the selection of young children from conquered territories to be part of *capacocha*. A multistage ritual that transformed them into divine intermediaries, the selected children traveled to the Inca capital and then to important mountain tops to be sacrificed. The mummified remains of *capacocha* have been documented at a number of sites in the Argentinian and Peruvian Andes (Ceruti 2004). Bioarchaeologial analyses clearly document the extent to which the Inca appropriated and controlled the bodies of these individuals, and by extension the body politic of conquered territories, represented by alteration in diet (Fernández et al. 1999; Wilson et al. 2007), drug and alcohol consumption (Bárcena 1989; Wilson et al. 2013), and trauma (Schobinger 2012).

In a series of well-contextualized and data-rich articles, Wilson and colleagues (2007, 2013) reconstructed the dietary and locational history of the Llullaillaco mummies utilizing hair and a suite of stable isotopes analyses (i.e., carbon, nitrogen, sulfur, hydrogen, and oxygen) and chemical analyses. In particular, the impact of Inca control of the body is exemplified by the analysis of hair from the mummy known as the Maiden. Stable carbon and nitrogen isotopic data indicate that the Maiden's diet became significantly richer in animal protein and C_4 plants approximately one year before her death, perhaps marking her new social status as *capacocha*. Increasingly positive C_4 values during the final four-and-a-half months of her life most likely indicate increased maize consumption. Liquid chromatography–mass spectrometry (LC-MS/MS) analysis of the Maiden's hair also reveals a significant and prolonged increase in coca and alcohol consumption, beginning approximately twelve months before her death (Wilson et al. 2013).[1]

Another example of Inca control of the body comes from the Chachapoya region of northern Peru (Schjellerup 1997; von Hagen 2002). The region was incorporated by the Inca emperor Huayna Capac in approximately AD 1470. Similar to other regions, Chachapoya sociopolitical infrastructure, economics, production, and demographics were altered under imperial rule. Within the past decade, several new Chachapoya mortuary sites have been discovered with evidence suggesting that the Inca also significantly influenced Chachapoya mortuary behavior. The most dramatic of these are the Laguna de los Cóndores (Guillén 1998; von Hagen 2002) and Los Pinchudos (Morales Gamarra 2002; Morales Gamarra et al. 2002), components of which date to the Late Intermediate Period (AD 1000–1470) and Late Horizon (AD 1470–1532). In particular, remains from the Laguna de los Cóndores have structured current interpretations of Chachapoya mortuary behavior and how it may have been influenced by Inca conquest.

Similar to other Chachapoya mortuary sites, the Laguna de los Cóndores consists of a series of *chullpas*, or burial towers, set within a rock overhang. Two-hundred and nineteen mummy bundles and the skeletonized remains of approximately 1000 individuals were recovered in 1997 (Guillén 2003). The mummies have been described as anthropogenic because there is evidence that the internal organs were removed through the rectum or the vagina as well as the potential use of some form of natural antiseptic (Guillén 2004). The skeletonized remains, some of which were secondarily wrapped into textile bundles (Figure 4.5) and externally look like

FIGURE 4.5   A 'bone' bundle recovered from the Laguna de los Condores (Wild et al. 2007).

mummy bundles, are thought to belong a Chachapoya ethnic group known as the Chilchos (von Hagen 2002).

Radiocarbon dates (Wild et al. 2007) for these secondary skeletal bundles place them in the Late Intermediate Period (AD 1000–1470), whereas samples from the mummified remains are from the Late Horizon (AD 1470–1532). Based on these results, it has been suggested that pre-conquest Chachapoya mortuary behavior consisted of secondarily interred skeletal material and that anthropogenic mummification was introduced into the region by the Inca (Guillén 2003, 2004; von Hagen 2002; Wild et al. 2007). According to the researchers, following Inca conquest the skeletal remains of the Chachapoya were removed from their original enclosures and were replaced by the mummy bundles of foreign administrators, *mitimae* (tributary laborers) groups brought into the region, as well as local lords and kin (Guillén 2005; von Hagen 2002). The connection to the regulation and control over the bodies of the conquered is clearly expressed in the following quote from Guillén (2004: 153): "The use of the funerary rooms is a clear statement on domination as the conquering group replaced the old ancestors who were pushed to a less important place and the new group took over the sacred funerary site." Although alternative explanations for the divergent mortuary traditions observed in Chachapoya region have been suggested (Nystrom et al. 2010), this remains a fascinating possibility because other sources clearly indicate that the Inca regulated and controlled the body of conquered groups in a variety of ways, including the forced relocation of thousands of individuals and the reorganization and state control of labor and production (D'Altroy et al. 2000; Hastorf 1990).

Sex and Gender

The estimation of sex is one of the first steps in any bioarchaeological analysis, because it is considered a fundamental component of an individual's 'identity' and thus a parameter that structured aspects of the individual's life and experiences (e.g., activity patterns, diet, occupation, exposure to trauma). Pamela Geller (2008: 115) questions this fundamental structuring influence of sex, however, highlighting the impact of the biomedical representation and perception of sex and gender and how bioarchaeologists tend to "import universalizing narratives about sex and gender that distort the past and ultimately reify the modern sex/gender system." Bioarchaeologists need to be cognizant of how they may contribute to the perpetuation of modern constructs and perceptions of gender roles and sexuality, to avoid the naturalization of "cultural values that are in fact modern constructs" and that "often situate modern (hetero)sexist ideas deep within antiquity" (Geller 2009: 504). Despite the elaboration and development of lesbian and gay anthropology (Lewin and Leap 2002), feminist-bioarchaeology (Geller 2008), and gender archaeology (Joyce 2008; Nelson 2006), bioarchaeologists have generally not engaged with this perspective (Geller 2009).

The term 'gender' was introduced in the 1970s in response to the feminist critique of the biological determinism that was common in scientific literature

(Krieger 2003). The term was deployed to account for "culture-bound conventions about norms for—and relationships between—women, men, girls, and boys" (Krieger 2003: 652), thus acting as a balance to the presumably innate biological differences between women and men. Sex became "natural, bodily, and ahistorical" and something that "could be 'read' directly off the body" (Gowland and Thompson 2013: 19), whereas gender was fluid and historical. Further, the investigation of sex became the domain of science, and gender was studied by the social sciences.

It is probably safe to say that for most people (and most bioarchaeologists), the distinction between sex and gender is that the former is determined by biology/genetics, whereas the latter is a social construct. This simple dichotomization, however, is more reflective of our often-unquestioned intellectual heritage. Although we categorize individuals as either female or male, in reality there is a continuum: "there is no unambiguous dividing line between the two sexes, and every criterion of differentiation that might be invoked, from genitalia to hormones to chromosomes, fails to perform a strict demarcating function" (Epstein 2004: 192). In biological anthropology, this is evident by the simple fact that when we produce a sex estimate based on cranial or pelvic morphology, there is a range of possible categories between hypermasculine and hyperfeminine. Even when an individual skeleton is categorized as 'possible female' or 'possible male' or even 'indeterminate,' we still assume deep down that if it were not for the imprecision of the methodology itself, that if we could actually see the fleshed person, they would fall out into one of the two fundamental categories: male or female. In this dichotomy, the biomedical/scientific analysis of both skeletal and mummified remains leads to the detemporalization of the material, where "analysts move from present to past (and back again) without reflecting on bodily differences as made meaningful within specific environmental, historical, or socioeconomic settings." (Geller 2009: 505). Sex is a fluid category, however, and thus the dichotomization of sex into male and female itself is a cultural construct (Joyce 2000; Sofaer 2006). To date, the engagement with sex and gender in mummy research mimics that of skeletal bioarchaeology: there are examples where the researchers demonstrate an appreciation and understanding of the differences between sex and gender (e.g., Wade and Nelson 2013b) as well as research when the terms are conflated (e.g., Dedouit et al. 2010; Pabst et al. 2010; Woide et al. 2010).

From a methodological point of view, the presence of mummified soft tissue presents both limitations and possibilities from the perspective of sex estimation. From the osteological point of view, mummified soft tissue is really just an impediment, obscuring the morphological characteristics we so commonly rely upon. From this perspective, the development of computed tomography and computer software that allows 3-D reconstruction of the pelvis and cranium bodes well for the noninvasive estimation of sex and age from mummified material (e.g., Davey et al. 2013; Decker et al. 2011; Grabherr et al. 2009; Selma Uysal et al. 2005; Villa et al. 2011; 2013; Wink 2014). Alternatively, the presence of soft tissue external genitalia are taken as the ultimate form of sex verification: "A significant effort should be made to identify the presence of breasts. Sex prediction from skeletal tissue alone is not invariably accurate and degenerative perineal changes often destroy the female external genitalia. Hence, unequivocal identification of the presence of breast tissue can make an independent and valuable contribution to sex *determination.*" (Aufderheide 2003: 345, emphasis added).

I want to briefly explore three examples where researchers did not fully delve into the complex relationship between sex and gender, yet where such an approach could prove to be a productive means of exploring questions of broader anthropological significance. In all three examples, although sex is estimated based on the presence of external genitalia, it is possible to observe the structuring influence of the modern biomedical perception of sex coupled with an incomplete exploration of the social constructive nature of gender.

Post and Donner (1972) discuss a mummy from the site of Quitor 1 near San Pedro de Atacama, Chile. There is evidence for bilateral antemortem amputation of the toes, which the authors suggest was in response to the onset of gangrene stemming from frostbite. Regardless of the veracity of their diagnosis, these antemortem changes are explicitly identified as deformities, and when considered by the authors in relation to mortuary behavior, clearly demonstrate the imposition of modern constructs regarding sexuality:

> Of the hundreds of mummies excavated around San Pedro de Atacama, this is the only case of a male . . . buried with arms extended, the hands covering the genitals—a position otherwise found only among females. All other males were buried with hands folded across the chest. There may, of course, be no causal connection between the burial position and the frostbite injuries. The possibility, however, exists that this individual was, because of his deformities, treated as a female during his lifetime, and hence buried as female after death. An alternative explanation is that the injuries were received during exposure as punishment either for homosexual tendencies or some other reason.
>
> *(Post and Donner 1972: 191)*

There are (at least) two ways in which the authors perpetuate stereotypical gender roles. In their first statement, the authors equate deformation of the body with femininity. In doing so, the authors reinforce the biomedical bodyscape discussed by Geller (2009), where the male body is fundamentally a productive body; the implication being that his deformity prevented him from fulfilling his gender-specific roles of being a producer, thus the default position for such an individual must be female. Their alternative explanation further reveals the modern heteronormative framework; homosexuality is characterized as deviant social behavior and deserving of punishment.

A productive alternative explanation could be that this burial represents the presence of a third- or transgender individual. Hollimon (2001, 2006, 2011) and Kirkpatrick (2000) have both suggested that nonbinary genders may have been present in groups that colonized the New World. To my knowledge, however, such a queered perspective has never been integrated into South American bioarchaeological research (see Ardren (2008) for a discussion of gender studies in pre-Hispanic Americas and Ebert and Patterson (2006) for a synthetic discussion of gender in South American archaeology).

The second example comes from the Chinchorro region of Chile. There is some evidence that during the production of the complex anthropogenic mummies discussed in Chapter 2, that some external features, including genitalia, were modeled (Arriaza 1995a; Standen 1997). In their discussion of mortuary behavior and diet in mummies from the site of Camarones-17, Aufderheide et al. (1993: 195) conclude that a neonate (ca. six months old) was male based on the presence of a "hide-modelled penis." This is fascinating on several levels and is ripe for a discussion of the relationship between gender, sex, and mortuary behavior. What could these examples mean in terms of Chinchorro perception of biological differences between the sexes? Perhaps we could speculate that these differences were noted as somehow being socially important as an effort was made to model them, but we have no real basis for concluding how these morphological differences were culturally interpreted.

The last example stems from the research conducted on the frozen remains of Ötzi. In their analysis of Ötzi's mtDNA genome, Rollo and colleagues (2006) observed two substitutions that are associated with reduced sperm mobility. The authors are careful to note, however, that there is no way to actually determine if these substitutions resulted in sterility:

> While the idea that Ötzi suffered from sterility is intriguing, for possible social implications and, in particular, as a clue to the so-called "disaster" into which he seems to have incurred (Spindler 1994), the presence of the two substitutions (9055 and 11719) in the mummy's DNA cannot be taken as evidence that the Iceman actually suffered from this kind of pathology.
>
> *(Rollo et al. 2006: 563)*

These results made it into the popular press with headlines like "Ötzi the Iceman May Have Been Infertile."[2] In that news article, the following quote is attributed to the South Tyrol Museum of Archaeology: "This not improbable hypothesis raises new questions concerning his social rank within his society,' it adds, arguing that the new evidence supports a theory that views the man as a social outcast." Even if, for the sake of argument, we accept that Ötzi was sterile, what 'social implications' this raises and why being sterile would make him a 'social outcast' is unclear.

The other narrative that took shape soon after the recovery of the remains was that semen was found in Ötzi's anus, which would make him the first documented homosexual man (Schmidt 2002). At the time, Spindler (1994) responded to these reports by stating that the anal canal was not identifiable and thus has not been examined, and further that the anal region of the corpse was damaged during the recovery of the corpse and so made any such claims impossible. Schmidt's (2002: 165) characterization of the reaction to these claims is that they are indicative of "heterosexual tunnel vision" through which Spindler and most archaeologists interpret the past.

Robb (2009) contends that Ötzi's social persona has been reconstructed to fit within the modern constructs of maleness and sex roles. The biological sex of Ötzi was established based on the presence of intact external genitalia. The presence of the axe, knife, and bow and arrows, reinforced his fundamental 'maleness.' Robb (2009: 113) acknowledges that while archaeological evidence during the later European prehistory suggests that "there is strong evidence for dichotomized male and female genders," there has been no discussion what maleness meant in Ötzi's world. By questioning our basic assumptions regarding the connection between sex and gender and acknowledging the culturally dynamic nature of these concepts, a bioculturally informed mummy studies can begin to address new questions: was Ötzi's maleness predicated upon fathering children (as implied by the suggestion that because he was sterile he was a social outcast)? What is heteronormative?

Bioarchaeology of Care

The bioarchaeology of care framework developed by Tilley and Oxenham (Tilley and Cameron 2014; Tilley and Oxenham 2011; Tilley 2015) may not be, strictly speaking, 'social theory' and so may seem out of place in this chapter. However, as a group's "response to the health care requirements of its members is shaped by a combination of cultural beliefs and values; collective knowledge, skills and experience; social and economic organization; and access to resources" (Tilley and Oxenham 2011: 35), the framework provides a holistic approach that expands the interpretive significance of paleopathological data. Although a considerable amount of mummy research focuses on the reconstruction of health, disease diagnosis, and epidemiology, the discussion of health care and the culturally contingent individual experience of disease has until recently been very limited. I believe the bioarchaeology of care framework can be valuable for mummy researchers, drawing the field closer to bioarchaeology (Nystrom and Piombino-Mascali 2017; Nystrom and Tilley 2018).

Tilley and Oxenham (2011: 36) discuss two broad areas in which skeletal and/or mummified remains could provide evidence of care: (1) long-term survival with disability "rendering functional independence impossible" and (2) healed/healing trauma or illness that would have necessitated intervention or care to ensure recovery and survival. These reflect relatively serious and potentially disabling circumstances and thus would present the greatest potential for inferring the provisioning of care. As the diagnosis of pathological conditions based on skeletal material is hampered by bone's limited ability to respond to pathogens, mummified soft tissue, as well as other sources of data such as coprolites and intestinal contents, may provide additional opportunities to observe or infer care. This is tempered by the fact that soft tissues are in general much more susceptible to postmortem taphonomic changes than osseous tissue. As the rate of decomposition is influenced by level of metabolic activity, tissues composed of cells that have a significant role in secretion and absorption, such as epithelial and heart muscle, decay more quickly than connective tissues such as collagen and cartilage. Organs such as the liver and kidneys decay rapidly, whereas seemingly delicate structures as the lungs are commonly well preserved (Aufderheide 2003). Therefore, while the preservation of soft tissue offers the promise of identifying a wider range of pathological conditions, the postmortem morphological changes that they have undergone may make identification of pathological conditions impossible. The following discussion will focus on two areas where mummy researchers have most explicitly engaged with the concept of care: the use of medicinal plants and therapeutic tattooing. Still, engagement with the broader social context of these examples of 'care' is limited and could be expanded upon.

Medicinal Plants

The following examples of the medicinal use of plants come from a range of time periods and cultural contexts. The data are derived from both gross observation (i.e., archaeopalynology) and biochemical analyses (e.g., gas chromatography, mass spectrometry, radioimmunoassay), and from a variety of sources including coprolites, intestinal contents, hair, and soft tissue. The use of medicinal plants has been implicated in the management of pain to the treatment of parasitic infection. Some authors are able to document paleopathological conditions, whereas in other cases there is no evidence of soft or hard tissue pathologies. All of the authors explicitly articulate the presence of plant material or its metabolites as 'medicine' or 'therapy' and are therefore, at least implicitly, suggesting that the administration of these plants represents some sort of health care.

In the early 1990s, researchers began to work on methodologies to detect the presence of psychoactive substances such as nicotine, cocaine, tetrahydrocannabinol (THC), and tryptamine from hair or soft tissue (e.g., Balabanova et al. 1992, 1994; Cartmell et al. 1991a, 1991b; Parsche et al. 1993; Parsche and Nerlich 1995). This research was ultimately used to consider 'recreational' or ritual 'drug' use within a society (Bárcena 1989; Cartmell et al. 1994; Echeverría and Niemeyer 2013; Wilson et al. 2007). Many of these drugs also have therapeutic or medicinal properties (e.g., cocaine was originally isolated from coca leaves in 1860 and was used as an anesthesia in 1884; Martin 1970) referred to in contemporaneous texts, ethnohistorical documents, or based on modern pharmacology. Therefore, the detection and identification of these substances or their metabolites can provide some insight into the presence of care.

Archaeological evidence indicates that the leaves of the coca shrub (*Erythroxylum sp.*) have been used in South America for thousands of years in ritual contexts and as a symbol of sociopolitical power (Ceruti 2004; Dillehay et al. 2010). Most readers are familiar with the modern derivative of coca (i.e., cocaine) and in the form of coca tea for treating altitude sickness. The medicinal use of coca leaves is also attested to by ethnohistoric and modern accounts, being used to treat various gastrointestinal problems (e.g., dysentery, indigestion, cramps, diarrhea, and stomach ulcers), toothaches, and rheumatism (Martin 1970; Plowman 1986).

In one of the earliest examples of this type of research, Cartmell and colleagues (1991a) analyzed hair from 163 individuals from a number of different cultural phases in northern Chile (spanning some 4500 years' worth of time) for the presence of cocaine or its metabolite, benzoylecgonine. When cocaine/benzoylecgonine was detected in adults, the researchers focused their interpretation on what this may indicate about highland-coast connections. It is when positive results were observed in tissues from subadults that coca use is characterized as medicinal in nature: "Alternatively, medicinal cocaine administration (as tea?) to at least some of these ailing infants cannot be excluded, assuming they survived at least 10 days after such assumed treatment" (Cartmell et al. 1991a: 266–267). In another study a decade later, Cartmell and colleagues (2001) explicitly link high levels of cocaine or its metabolites in subadults with a therapeutic function: "it is inviting to speculate that this child suffered from a chronic illness that may have been eased by coca leaf chewing or medicinal coca tea for a period of months before death." Similarly, Rivera and colleagues (2005: 458) suggest that the detection of cocaine metabolites in the hair of a three- to four-year-old child from the site of Pisagua-7 (2900–2700 BP) from northern Chile is most likely due to "coca leaf tea administered as a therapeutic agent to combat what proved to be her terminal illness."

Material artifacts associated with the inhalation of psychoactive drugs (e.g., snuff trays, spoons, and spatulas) have been recovered from archaeological contexts and have tested positive for the presence of drugs (Torres et al. 1991). Yet psychoactive beverages that are imbibed do not require such specific paraphernalia and so are archaeologically less visible (Torres 1995). One such hallucinogenic drink, known is ayahuasca, is derived from the mixture of the plant of the same name (scientific name *Banisteriopsis caapi*) and *Psychotria viridis*. *Banisteriopsis* contains harmine, which inhibits enzymatic action in the stomach that would normally block the metabolism of the main psychoactive component of *Psychotria*, *N*, *N*-dimethyltryptamine (DMT). Ogalde et al. (2009) analyzed hair samples from thirty-two mummies from the Azapa Valley of Chile dating to the middle Tiwanaku period, testing for evidence of *Banisteriopsis caapi* consumption. The authors detected the presence of harmine, but not DMT, leading them to conclude that "the consumption of *Banisteriopsis* was part of a medicinal practice, perhaps as Ayahuasca infusion" (Ogalde et al. 2009: 471).

At this point, it is important to note that the authors of these South American studies do not link the evidence of therapeutic drug use with any evidence of gross skeletal or soft tissue pathology. It is certainly possible that whatever disease processes these individuals may have experienced didn't leave a mark on the bones or weren't preserved in soft tissue. Still, the presence of these drugs is tantalizing evidence for care and deserves further investigation and elaboration.

One of the most interesting aspects of reconstructing health care in ancient Egypt is that there are documents that describe surgical and medical practices, pharmacology, and herbal medicine (Aboelsoud 2010; Campbell 2008). David (2008d) notes that one of the aims of the Manchester Mummy Project is to "identify scientifically any traces of therapeutic treatments that may remain in mummified tissue." Although several authors (Aboelsoud 2010; Campbell 2008; Counsell 2008) discuss the documentary and archaeological evidence for drugs and pharmacology in Egypt, very little direct evidence from human remains speaks to the therapeutic use of these substances.

Nerlich and colleagues (1995) report histochemical findings that document extensive depositions of hemosiderin within the collapsed, but otherwise normal, lung tissue in a Twenty-First Dynasty Egyptian mummy. The authors conclude the "patient suffered from possibly recurrent pulmonary bleeding during life" (Nerlich et al. 1995: 427). Further, they documented the presence of nicotine, cocaine, and THC and/or its metabolites in several organs including the lungs, stomach, and intestines. Based on the differential concentration levels in these organs, the authors suggest that the nicotine and cocaine had been ingested, while the THC was inhaled. The authors conclude that the existence of these various drugs "provides evidence that multidrug therapy was given to relieve his pain" (Nerlich et al. 1995: 428). Given that coca (*Erythroxylum coca*) and tobacco (*Nicotiana tabacum*) are exclusively New World plants, these results may reflect postmortem contamination rather than treatment (Buckland and Panagiotakopulu 2001; Counsell 2008).

Paleoparasitological research on mummies has clearly and convincingly demonstrated that we have a long history with a variety of ecto- (Fornaciari G. et al. 2011; Reinhard and Buikstra 2003; Rick et al. 2002) and endoparasites (Lee et al. 2011; Reinhard and Urban 2003; Searcey et al. 2013; Shin et al. 2011). In this section I will present two examples that involve the use of plants to treat endoparasitic infestations.

As has been noted in other places within this book, the ailments suffered by Ötzi the Tyrolean Iceman have been studied in great detail. Specifically, Aspöck and colleagues (1996) identified the eggs of the whipworm *Trichuris trichiura* in samples taken from Ötzi's colon.[3]

Although these results are not unexpected, this connects to the reconstruction of health care because among Ötzi possessions were the fruit of the bracket fungus *Piptoporus betulinus*. Capasso (1998: 1864) describes the biochemical components and therapeutic characteristics of the fungus as follows: "*Piptoporus betulinus* contains toxic resins and an active compound, agaric acid, which are powerful purgatives and result in strong though short-lived bouts of diarrhea. *Piptoporus betulinus* also contains oils that are toxic to metazoans and have antibiotic properties, acting against mycobacteria." Based on this, Capasso suggested that Ötzi was carrying the fungus to combat a nasty case of intestinal parasites. Several authors (Peintner et al. 1998; Pöder 2005; Pöder and Peintner 1999; Tunón and Svanberg 1999) were quick to point out that Capasso was incorrect in his description of *P. betulinus*'s medicinal properties. In sum, Pöder (2005: 358) concluded this regarding why Ötzi had these fungi: "Consequently, we have to admit that we simply do not know the Ice Man's intentions concerning these mushrooms."

The story of Ötzi's gastrointestinal problems and his attempts at self-medication, however, does not stop here. Microbotanical analysis of sequential gut samples (small intestine, near the iliocaecal valve, the transverse colon, the colon sigmoideum, and the rectum) indicates the intentional consumption of bracken (*Pteridium aquilinum*) (Oeggl et al. 2005). Oeggl and colleagues (2005) conclude that the bracken was likely used as an anthelmintic given the presence of human whipworm eggs in Ötzi's colon.

As part of the Sicily Mummy Project, Piombino-Mascali and colleagues (Kumm et al. 2010; Piombino-Mascali et al. 2013b) examined the mummified remains known as Piraino 1 from the Piraino Mother Church, in the province of Messina, Sicily (Figure 4.6). Paleopathological examination of Piraino 1 indicated several conditions including degenerative joint disease in the spine and pleural adhesions possibly stemming from pneumonia. Radiographic analysis documented multiple small, osteolytic lesions in several ribs, right and left humeri, right pubic bone, and skull, Piraino 1 may have suffered from multiple myeloma (Piombino-Mascali et al. 2013b). Additionally, coprolite analysis revealed very high concentrations of *Trichuris trichiura* eggs (Kumm et al. 2010). Palynological analysis of the coprolite indicated the presence of several plant residues, which Piombino-Mascali and colleagues (2013b) suggest may have had medicinal functions. Remnants of genus *Prunus sp.* (e.g., peaches, apricots, cherries) were detected, one member of which, the dried plum fruit, is a laxative. The most common pollen detected was from *Polygala vulgaris*, which may have been imbibed as part of a tea (Piombino-Mascali et al. 2013b). Traditionally, *P. vulgaris* has been used as an expectorant, to treat lung disease and skeletal pain and has been demonstrated to have antitumor compounds. Given the range of observed pathological conditions in Piraino 1, the authors conclude that it is likely that the individual was intentionally ingesting *P. vulgaris* as a form of medicinal treatment (Kumm et al. 2010; Piombino-Mascali et al. 2013b).

FIGURE 4.6   Piraino Mother Church in the 'Sepulcher of the Priests'. Pictured are Arthur Aufderheide (left) and Dario Piombino-Mascali (right) examining the mummy Piraino 1 (Piombino-Mascali et al. 2013b).

Therapeutic Tattooing

The documentation of tattoos observed on mummified remains has been structured by a fundamental division, based on complexity and location, between communicative/symbolic tattoos and therapeutic tattoos. Communicative or symbolic tattoos are composed of representational or abstract designs (e.g., animals, geometric shapes) whereas therapeutic tattoos consists of dots and/or dashes. Function is also inferred based on visibility; those tattoos that are thought to be visible during life are characterized as decorative/communicative; those that would be hidden tend to be considered as *non*-decorative and, almost as a default position, as therapeutic (a twist on the archaeological adage that if we cannot figure out a function for an artifact it must be related to ritual).

This distinction was established early on in mummy research. In his publication on the Pazyryk mummies from Siberia, Rudenko (1970) differentiates between the elaborate animal tattooing on the arms and legs of the Pazyryk individual from barrow two (Figure 4.7) and the two rows of "disks" that run parallel to the vertebral column. Rudenko concludes, citing ethnographic data and personal observation, that the parallel rows of disks "were probably put there with a therapeutic aim" (Rudenko 1970: 112).

This established an interpretive paradigm that has influenced research up to the present. In 1993, Capasso (179–180) described the tattoos observed on Ötzi as follows: "In the Val Senales mummy, the pigmented marks are located in regions of

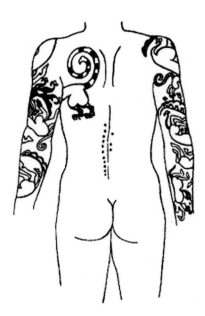

FIGURE 4.7   Posterior view of the tattoos observed on the Pazyryk male mummy from barrow 2 (Iwe 2013).

the body that would normally have been covered (back, knee, ankle). This would exclude a 'communicative' function for these tattoos. . . . In our case, the pigmented marks on the skin are geometric, without curved segments, are simple, and contain neither anthropomorphic nor zoomorphic motifs. This allows us to rule out an ornamental function for the tattoos found on the Val Senales mummy." Similarly, Dorfer and colleagues (1999: 1023) conclude that Ötzi's tattoos "do not seem to have decorative importance because they have a simple linear geometric shape and are located on the less visible parts of the body."

In their description of a Chiribaya mummy, Pabst and colleagues (2010: 3257) differentiate between two different types of tattoos: ornamental tattoos that are "representing birds, apes, reptiles, and symbols" and a series of overlapping circles on the neck that are potentially therapeutic in function (Figure 4.8). The circles are located on the posterior of the neck and thus "would have been hidden by the neck hairs and the clothing during the lifetime of the bearer" (Pabst et al. 2010: 3257), whereas the representational tattoos would have been fully visible.[4]

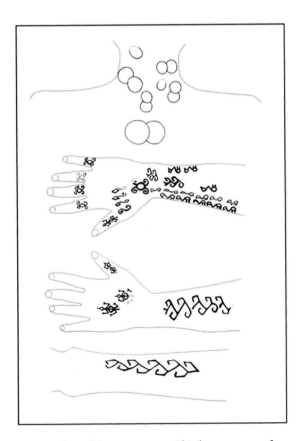

FIGURE 4.8   Representation of the tattoos on a Chiribaya mummy from southern Peru (Pabst et al., 2010).

Pabst and colleagues (2010) concluded that the therapeutic and ornamental tattoos on the Peruvian mummy were created using two different substances. Although this is interesting and suggests the possibility greater internal variability (e.g., different tattoo artists, temporal differentiation, divergent cultural/social significance of the tattoos), Pabst and colleagues rally no evidence to support their contentions that some of the tattoos are therapeutic. They do note that the location of the tattoos on the neck correspond to meridians identified in Chinese acupuncture, an argument that has been advanced to explain the location of the tattoos observed on Ötzi as well (Dorfer et al. 1998, 1999): "the possible medical intention lying behind the circle tattoos, we assume local problems of the upper spine or headaches as possible reasons for treatment by the tattooing" (Pabst et al. 2010: 3262). There is, however, no CT or X-ray data presented that would indicate the presence of any pathological or degenerative process in the neck region that may have necessitated the application of a therapeutic tattoo.

As noted previously, very early in the research on Ötzi, the presence of tattoos was linked to a noncommunicative, therapeutic function: "Among the motivations that have emerged from the search for the reasons behind the application of these most singular tattoos, one hypothesis is especially intriguing: they could be traces of treatments for articular pathologies" (Capasso 1993: 180). This assumption has structured nearly all of the subsequent work on Ötzi's tattoos (e.g., Pabst et al. 2009). Most recently, Samadelli et al. (2015) identified new tattoos whose location (Figure 4.9), at first, "seems to contradict the theory" that the tattoos had a therapeutic function. Ultimately, the authors conclude that additional studies on "the location of the new tattoos and its relation to acupuncture points and/or meridians should be further explored and discussed" (Samadelli et al. 2015: 5).

Fundamentally, the argument that Ötzi's tattoos are therapeutic is predicated upon the following: "In previous work on the tattoos of the iceman it was mainly believed that their application was done as a kind of treatment or diagnosis of health problems, in particular lower back pain and degenerative joint disease of his knees, ankle and wrist. The conclusion was drawn because *basically* all tattoos were located in morphological areas *close to* the underlying spine and joints where degenerations have been identified based on earlier radiological studies" (Samadelli et al. 2015: 4–5; emphasis added).

Utilizing X-ray and CT imaging, Murphy et al. (2003) identified areas of degenerative arthritic development in Ötzi, including the cervical and lumbar vertebra, right sacroiliac joint, and pubic symphysis. They also identified healed antemortem fractures of the fifth through the ninth left ribs; frostbite to the left fifth toe; and some vascular calcifications. Further, it was determined that Ötzi only had eleven rib-bearing thoracic vertebra and that T12 was lumbarized (Murphy et al. 2003). Kean et al. (2013) also note that the L5 vertebra was in a transitional, abnormal shape, with a narrowing of the L4/L5 disc space and right sacroiliac joint.

As can be seen in Figure 4.9, Ötzi's tattoos are found on the lower back, right medial knee, left and right lower legs, right lateral ankle, left lateral wrist, and lower right thorax. Therefore, except for the lumbar area, none of these tattoos correspond

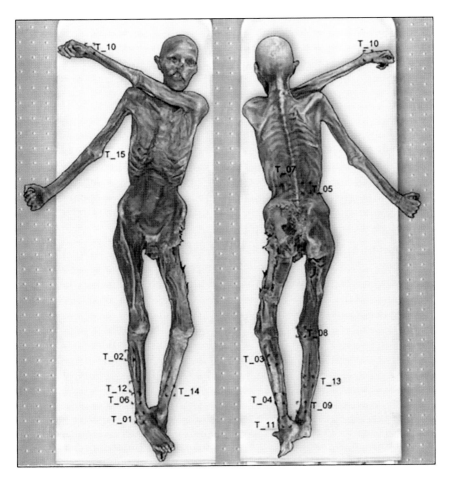

FIGURE 4.9   The location of all of the tattoos identified by Samadelli et al. (2015).

to the areas of osteoarthritic development noted by Murphy and colleagues (Kean et al. 2013; Kean and Kean 2014). Kean and Kean (2014) suggest that these other location may not have resulted in significant pain or may have been asymptomatic. Kean and colleagues, citing clinical data, point to "an association between transitional vertebrae and episodes of spinal pain and referred pain to the legs" (2013: 16). The authors conclude that there is a general correspondence between tattoo location and clinically known areas of musculoskeletal pain: "The tattoos in the left thoracolumbar area correspond to sites of mechanical back pain. The right and left lower lumbar tattoos correspond to the problem of lower lumbar mechanical back pain. . . . The bilateral lower leg tattoos in the calf muscle area correspond to possible sites of sciatic nerve referred pain in an individual with mechanical back pain who had episodes of sciatica. In addition, the right ankle tattoos also correspond to sites of referred sciatic nerve pain" (Kean and Kean 2014: 13).

Ultimately, however, as noted by the authors themselves, their conclusions are not based on any physical evidence from Ötzi himself: "Although we have no histological nor other evidence for diagnostic support, we believe based on clinical experience that it is possible that the ankle tattoos mark the site of right ankle retinacular injury, calcaneo fibular ligament injury, or more likely anterior talofibular ligament injury, which had resulted from a foot/ankle inversion injury" (Kean et al. 2013: 15–16).

I am not arguing that tattoos cannot be therapeutic in nature nor that this could explain some tattoos observed on mummies. In fact, Lars Krutak has documented therapeutic tattoos among modern groups, including the St. Lawrence Island Yupiget, native Greenlanders, the Ainu, Aleuts/Unangan in Alaska, and Chippewa of the Great Lakes area in North America (Krutak 2013), noting similarities in location (often at major joints) and form (small series of dots, incised lines) between these modern examples and those observed on some mummies (Figures 4.4 and 4.9). What I am suggesting is that the categorization of tattoos as either decorative *or* therapeutic has been fairly simplistic and based on culturally laden concepts of what constitutes decorative and communicative versus nondecorative. Further, this research has not engaged with pain as a biopsychosocial phenomenon (see Callister 2003; Lasch 2000; Lovering 2006 for a discussion of the cultural influence on pain and pain management from the perspective of nursing).

Notes

1. Panzer and colleagues (2012) present some interesting evidence that an unprovenienced female mummy currently housed in the Bavarian State Archeological Collection may have been a *capacocha* sacrifice. Several pieces of evidence point to a New World/South America origin including the recovery of nonhuman hair consistent with New World camelids and the immunohistochemical, histological, and molecular identification of *Trypanosoma cruzi*. Radiocarbon dating would place the individual in the Late Horizon and Early Colonial (AD 1451–1642) periods, and stable isotopic analysis of her hair indicated a radical change in diet approximately three months before her death from one composed principally of marine resources to terrestrial resources. Finally, the authors draw a comparison between the massive craniofacial trauma observed in this mummy with that observed in other *capacocha* mummies, though they acknowledge that this is "highly speculative" (Panzer et al. 2012: 9).
2. www.abc.net.au/science/articles/2006/02/06/1562968.htm; accessed September 26, 2014. This is how the research of Rollo et al. (2006) is summarized at the South Tyrol Museum of Archaeology: "the Iceman belongs to the European genetic haplogroup K and was probably infertile" (www.archaeologiemuseum.it/en/milestones, accessed September 4, 2014).
3. Capasso (1994) describes the presence of Beau's lines (growth arrest lines in fingernails analogous to linear enamel hypoplasias) on one of Ötzi's recovered fingernails as indicating that he experienced recurring systemic and severe physiological stress for several months before he died and, in his 1998 article, explicitly links these Beau's lines with the evidence of parasitic infection.
4. Pabst et al. (2010) offer no supporting evidence regarding the nature of Chiribaya clothing or hairstyles to support their claim that some tattoos would be hidden and some would be visible. Reinhard and Buikstra (2003) provide some insight into Chiribaya hairstyles, with men more commonly having complex braids, whereas women and children had straight, unbraided hair. Reycraft (2005) and Minkes (2008) discuss Chiribaya clothing, though only the latter provides a visual representation of what it may have looked like while actually being worn. While Arriaza et al. (1986) were discussing Chinchorro mummies from Arica, they too provide some insight into hairstyles.

5

METHODS IN MUMMY RESEARCH

Methods employed in mummy research range from the 'traditional' autopsy (e.g., Oh et al. 2011; Dedouit et al. 2010; Hershkovitz et al. 2014) to quite specialized biochemical and spectrographic analytical tools such as scanning electron microscopy with energy dispersive X-ray spectrometer (Degano and Colombini 2009), optical interferometry (Vargiolu et al. 2013), and atomic force microscopy (Maixner et al. 2013). Because several recent publications provide excellent reviews of current laboratory methods (Aufderheide 2003; Lynnerup 2007, 2009) I will focus on three methodological advances that have stimulated mummy research: biogeochemistry and isotope analyses, paleoimaging, and paleogenetics. This then provides the foundation for discussing whether or not these methodological advances are facilitating the development and exploration of new research questions (Armelagos and Van Gerven 2003; Zuckerman and Armelagos 2011).

Biogeochemical Methods and Isotopic Analyses

The analysis and interpretation of isotopic ratios have become a fairly standard tool in bioarchaeology. The development and refinement of these methods over the last several decades has resulted in a substantial amount of literature that addresses a wide range of topics in a multitude of temporal and geographical contexts. Isotopic analyses are commonly employed in the reconstruction of mobility and residence and diet-related behaviors. In both areas, researchers are exploring questions of broader anthropological significance including migration and ethnicity (White et al. 2004b), gender- and status-based differences in consumption patterns (Ambrose et al. 2003; Barrett and Richards 2004), exposure to environmental and anthropogenic pollutants (Bower et al. 2007; Schroeder et al. 2013), the impact of imperialism (Tung and Knudson 2011), breastfeeding and weaning (Jay et al. 2008), and the onset of animal husbandry and milk consumption (Lösch et al. 2006; Reynard et al. 2011). Despite this, based on the publication data generated for this study, stable isotopic analyses of mummified remains are not common. Out of the total sample of 1063 articles, 41 articles utilized isotopic analyses in some manner. Although isotopic analyses may not be common, the types of research questions being addressed are quite broad.

The earliest example of stable isotopic analyses of mummified material is Walter Kowal and colleagues' (1991) analysis of remains from the ill-fated Franklin Expedition in which all 129 crew members died. Previous gross examinations had yielded evidence regarding cause of death in several of the recovered crewmen (e.g., Amy et al. 1986; Notman et al. 1987), but the question as to why the whole expedition failed remained open. Elemental analysis of bone samples indicated abnormally high levels of lead. Based on results of isotopic analyses, Kowal and colleagues (1991) concluded that the skeletal lead had the same isotopic profile as the lead used to solder the canned food carried by the expedition. This led the researchers to suggest that lead poisoning "was a major contributing factor to the loss of the expedition" (Kowal et al. 1991: 201).

The earliest published efforts to reconstruct diet based on stable isotopic analyses of mummified remains looked at seasonality of diet and death in Nubian mummified remains (White 1993; White and Schwarcz 1994) and at highland-coastal dietary shifts at a coastal site in northern Chile (Aufderheide et al. 1994). Fernández et al. (1999) used stable isotopes of carbon, nitrogen, and sulfur to reconstruct the diet of the Inca period mummy recovered from Mount Aconagua in Argentina but also used this data to discuss the geographical origin of the individual. The first example where researchers utilized strontium and oxygen isotopes to reconstruct mobility was in an effort to determine the geographical origin of Ötzi the Tyrolean Iceman (Hoogewerff et al. 2001).

Researchers have also employed isotopes in paleoenvironmental reconstruction. Sharp et al. (2003: 1715) employed hydrogen isotope ratios because they provide "a

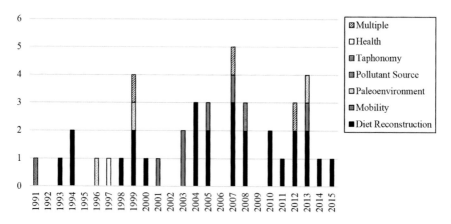

FIGURE 5.1   The year of publication of isotopic studies that samples from mummified remains.

link to paleoenvironmental and paleodietary conditions." Alexandra Touzeau and colleagues (2013: 92) used oxygen isotopes derived from bone and enamel samples taken from Egyptian mummies "to track the $\delta^{18}O$ evolution of the Nile from 5500 to 1500 B.P." Similarly, Iacumin et al. (1996: 28) derived $\delta^{18}O$ values from skin, hair, and bone samples from Egyptian mummies, noting that the "changes of palaeo-Nile water which may reflect either temperature changes or meteorological and environmental changes."

Several authors are reconstructing diet to examine a variety of larger-scale research questions including seasonal changes in diet (Williams and Katzenberg 2012), migration and mobility (Thompson et al. 2008; Webb et al. 2013; White et al. 2009), the impact of imperialism (Turner et al. 2013; Williams and Murphy 2013; Wilson et al. 2007, 2013), and larger-scale political economics (Knudson et al. 2005; Turner et al. 2013).

The tissues most commonly used in stable isotopic research on mummified remains are bones, teeth, and hair (Lynnerup 2007), with only a few studies actually using soft tissue for stable isotopic analyses. Soft tissues that have been sampled include skin, muscle, dura mater, dermis (Aufderheide et al. 1993; Finucane 2007; White and Schwarcz 1994), 'soft tissue,' 'blood,' 'chest tissue,' and 'underarm tissue' (Ramaroli et al. 2010).[1] Because these tissues have different turnover rates, they could provide distinctively different interpretations. Collagen is the most ubiquitous protein in body tissues, constituting approximately 30% of total body protein (Di Lullo et al. 2002), so tissue-specific turnover rates could influence interpretation. In bone, 2–10% of collagen is replaced annually, whereas animal model studies have reported a wide range of turnover rates in different organs: 5–9%/day in the heart, 4–10%/day in the lung, and 3%/day in skeletal muscle (Laurent 1982; McAnulty and Laurent 1987). Collagen turnover in the skin is slower, observed in rats to be less than 1–4%/day (Laurent 1982; Nissen et al. 1978) and approximately 0.076 ± 0.063%/hr in humans (El-Harake et al. 1998), which produces a turnover rate of approximately two to four months. Therefore, when compared to bone collagen, collagen derived from the dermis (or other soft tissues) may provide finer temporal resolution for dietary or mobility studies.

Paleoimaging

Paleoimaging technologies are commonly used tools in mummy studies. The history of major advances in paleoimaging and its application within mummy studies has been previously summarized by several authors (Böni et al. 2004; Lynnerup 2009). I therefore present here a brief summary that should provide the reader with a basic understanding of the technology as well as the pros and cons of different modalities. Although it is clear that a significant amount of research has been dedicated to determining the feasibility and applicability of paleoimaging technology to the investigation of mummified remains, much of it is not problem-oriented, hypothesis-driven research (Cox 2015; O'Brien et al. 2009).

Radiography

Shortly after their discovery by William Röntgen in 1895, X-ray imaging was used to examine mummified remains (Böni et al. 2004; Chhem and Brothwell 2010). In 1896, Walter Koenig published a monographed titled "14 Photographs with X-rays Taken by the Physical Society of Frankfurt am Main" with images of the mummified remains of a young child and a cat from Egypt. This was soon followed by several other researchers (e.g., Alexander Dedekind, Albert Londe, Heinrich Ernst Albers-Schoenberg), who utilized X-rays primarily as means of estimating skeletal age and as an aid in identifying fake mummies (Böni et al. 2004). Although conventional radiography is limited (e.g., though good at visualizing skeletal tissue, it has a limited ability to differentiate between soft tissues; Lynnerup 2009; Rühli et al. 2004) and has been superseded by other modalities, X-rays remain an important component of both skeletal and mummy research (Beckett and Conlogue 2010; Harris 2014).

The first major advance in radiographic technology came with the introduction of computed tomography, which uses X-rays to produce two-dimensional cross-sectional images (aka slices), which are then be reassembled to produce three-dimensional reconstructions. The first generation of CT scanners consisted of a single X-ray source and detector on a C-arm with the patient secured on a movable table. Second-generation CT scanners increased the number of detectors and used a fan-shaped X-ray beam. Both first- and second-generation CT scanners operated on a linear translate and rotate system in which the source and detector, moving in tandem, would scan and then rotate around the object from one side to the other. In addition to more detectors and wider fan-shape beam, third-generation CT units were a rotate-rotate system: the detectors (n = 250–750) are arranged in an arc opposite the X-ray tub with both rotating 360° around the patient. In fourth-generation units, anywhere between 600 and 2000 stationary detectors are arranged in a complete circle in the gantry while the tube rotates 360° (Carlton and Adler 2012). Additional advances include helical, multislice, and dual-source CT units, which produce a continuous helical pattern of scans from multiple sets of tubes and detectors.

CT scanners were first used in the investigation of mummies in 1977 by Derek Harwood-Nash and Peter Lewin (Harwood-Nash 1979; Lewin and Harwood-Nash 1977) who scanned two Egyptian mummies: Djedmaatesankh, an intact mummy from the Twenty-Second Dynasty and the brain of Eleventh Dynasty mummy known as Nakht-ROM I. These studies were followed by a report by Marx and d'Auria (1986) on eleven Egyptian mummies housed at the Museum of Fine Arts in Boston. Computed tomography quickly became a central feature in mummy studies, and the data are used in a wide variety of ways, including paleopathological diagnosis (e.g., Allam et al. 2011; Kim et al. 2014; Saleem and Hawass 2014; Sutherland et al. 2014), reconstruction of mortuary behavior and mummification process (e.g., Dazio et al. 2014; Meier et al. 2011; Friedrich et al. 2010; Panzer et al. 2013b;

Saleem and Hawass 2013), facial reconstruction (e.g., Bou et al. 1998; Cesarani et al. 2004; Hill et al. 1993), and the production of age and sex estimates (Villa et al. 2011, 2013). The technology and its application to mummy research continues to be explored (e.g., Friedman et al. 2012; Villa and Lynnerup 2012)

The advantages of computed tomography includes higher spatial contrast, high resolution, rapid scanning, and 3-D reconstruction with appropriate software. With succeeding generations, the machines have also become increasingly available. Additionally, and perhaps more importantly, computed tomography is minimally invasive and nondestructive. However, several variables limit its applicability and must be accounted for during analysis.

The process of mummification, be it anthropogenic or natural, can lead to density changes in soft tissues; desiccation makes soft tissues more radio-opaque due to a decrease in cell volume, increased intracellular salt content (Kanias and Acker 2006), and collagen fibers and organelles becoming more densely packed (Rylander et al. 2006). Anatomical changes stemming from the environmental factor or burial position may make it difficult to visualize anatomical structures, such as in the case of the nearly flat Damendorf Man, and can lead to the creation of pseudopathologies and misdiagnoses (Gregersen et al. 2007).

Mortuary ritual and processes associated with mummification may introduce imaging artifacts as well. For example, the dehydration and the application of resin characteristic of Egyptian mummification led to the misdiagnosis of alkaptonuria (Wallgren et al. 1986; Wells and Maxwell 1962) whereas the copious amounts of resin applied to Tutankhamen has hampered reliable identification of pathologies (Rühli and Ikram 2014). The thin layers of lead in the sealed coffin of Rosalia Lombardo resulted in reduced image quality as well as the creation of numerous imaging artifacts (Panzer et al. 2013b; Figure 5.2). Thick layers of textiles wrapping the body may not only make it difficult to get a mummy bundle into the gantry of a CT machine but may adhere to the body itself making it more difficult it will be to digitally 'remove' these layers to visualize the mummy.

As investigators move away from more invasive methods, they are increasingly reliant upon imaging for any number of research agendas, from taphonomy, paleopathology, and reconstruction of mortuary behavior to virtual autopsies and facial reconstruction (Figures 5.3 and 5.4). The success of these research topics, however, is influenced by the researchers' ability to differentiate between different types of tissues, between tissues and material artifacts, and between different types of material artifacts. Although diagenesis can negatively impact the gross morphological appearance of soft tissue, it can also influence tissue identification and discrimination in radiography (Wanek et al. 2011). As mentioned earlier, soft tissues tend to increase in density when dehydrated, whereas in some environmental contexts such as bogs, bones and teeth are decalcified. In living individuals, tissue discrimination is based on Hounsfield Units (HU), a measure of the attenuation of the X-ray beam; experience and algorithms are used in medical contexts to differentiate between tissues based on their Hounsfield density. These clinically derived

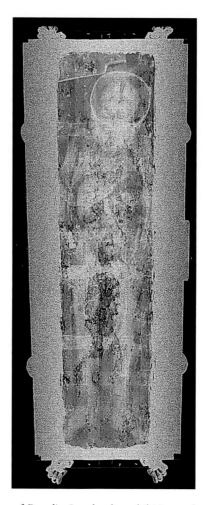

FIGURE 5.2 CT image of Rosalie Lombardo exhibiting reduced image quality and imaging artifacts due to the presence of metal in the coffin (Panzer et al. 2013b).

parameters, however, cannot be directly applied to mummified remains (Adams and Alsop 2008). Given this, documentation and standardization of HU values for different material is a vital area of research and several projects have begun developing these data.

Wanek et al. (2011) assessed tissue differentiation based on dual-energy computed tomography and micro-CT scans of the head and neck of a single Egyptian mummy. Villa and Lynnerup (2012) published a much broader set of HU values derived from mummified remains from a range of different environmental contexts including bogs, cold-dry, and hot-dry conditions. Additionally, the researchers scanned archaeological bone, cremated bone, fossils animal bones, and lastly bone

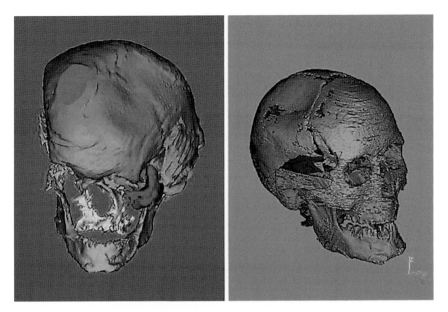

FIGURE 5.3   Reconstructed image of the skulls of Grauballe Man (left) and Tollund Man (right). The different bones in Grauballe Man's skull are color coded to aid in identification. This type of reconstruction can be used to differentiate between trauma and pseudopathology (Lynnerup 2009).

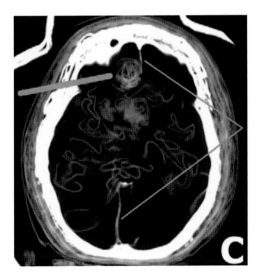

FIGURE 5.4   Example of CT scanning where differentiation between linen and tissue is relevant for reconstructing mortuary behavior. In this instance, in a scan of the cranial cavity of Djedmaatesankh, a Twenty-Second-Dynasty Egyptian mummy, the thick line points to an intranasal tampon and the thin lines indicate the falx cerebri. The thin lines within the cavity are linen. Adapted from Wade et al. 2011.

from forensic cases to serve as modern comparisons. The researchers were able to identify patterns of both within- and between-tissue differences in HU values based on environmental contexts. For instance, compact bone density was lowest in bog bodies, followed by cold-dry environment and hot-dry mummies, all of which are lower than modern comparative samples. Within-tissue density variability tended to be greater than observed in modern cases, though this is due in part to the collapsing of different subsamples. The authors noted largely homogenous results between three frozen Inca mummies with differentiation between calcified and soft tissues, whereas in bog bodies the samples were homogenous across tissue type.

Panzer et al. (2013c) conducted a systematic study of changes in soft tissue HU values based on CT scans of a modern experimentally mummified lower limb. The researchers replicated one aspect of Egyptian mummification by burying the limb in "artificial natron" composed of sodium chloride, sodium sulfate, sodium carbonate, and sodium bicarbonate. The limb was then imaged with both CT and MRI at regular intervals over a 160-day period. The authors found that although morphologically the tissues were very well preserved with limited evidence of putrefaction, there was an overall increase in HU density in the four different classes of soft tissue they considered (cutis, subcutis, muscle, and cartilage) and bone.

Gostner et al. (2013) reported HU values of material artifacts that may be encountered within a mummy bundle. The researchers scanned fifty-two objects, including many different types of gemstones and minerals (e.g., lapis lazuli, topaz, jade, obsidian, chert, agate), metals (e.g., iron, gold, silver), and a range of other material such as fired clay, wood, bitumen, amber, and calcified tissues (e.g., cow horn and bone, ivory).

Beyond issues associated with taphonomic changes, however, lies another, potentially more worrisome problem associated with the use of X-rays. Because X-rays are a form of ionizing radiation, it is possible that high radiation doses are damaging already fragmentary ancient DNA. Götherström et al. (1995) and Grieshaber et al. (2008) both examined the impact of X-ray exposure on DNA fragmentation and amplification using bones samples from modern pigs. Götherström and colleagues tested three samples; one served as a control and the remaining received either a 'small' or a 'large' dose of radiation. Grieshaber and colleagues increased the sample size using four bones from nine different pigs in the following experimental groups: control, low dose from conventional radiography, high dose from conventional radiography based on repeated exposure, low dose from single CT scan, and high dose from repeated CT scans. Both projects assessed the impact of X-ray induced DNA fragmentation by determining the efficiency of polymerase chain reaction (PCR) amplification and produced similar results. Götherström et al. (1995) concluded that DNA damage increased with radiation dose, though the study was limited to two treatment groups. Grieshaber et al. (2008: 686) concluded that "Despite the fact that none of the treatment groups differed significantly from the control" in the amount of amplifiable DNA, "most of the treatment groups took longer to amplify than the respective control groups, suggesting that radiation exposure is further fragmenting the DNA."

Paredes et al. (2012: 248) raise a number of issues that call into question these results. They note the small sample sizes and the qualitative assessment of PCR amplified fragments brightness. Further, both projects "failed to accurately measure or control for input DNA into the PCR; this being [sic] most important factor determining the number of cycles required to produce detectable levels of amplified DNA fragments in PCR or RT-PCR." (Paredes et al. 2012: 249). To address this shortcoming, Paredes et al. (2012) collected samples of skin from birds curated at the Natural History Museum in London and characterized the degree of pre- and post-CT DNA fragmentation. Ultimately the authors conclude that there was no significant difference in the quality of the DNA based on that "the most common strand length with respect to mass, revealed no significant difference pre- and post-CT" (Paredes et al. 2012: 249). They note that preservation method may have had a more significant impact on DNA preservation than exposure to X-ray radiation.

Wanek et al. (2012) ran simulations to determine if cell shrinkage and desiccation associated with mummification impacted the radiosensitivity of cells and the probability of DNA damage. They found that "mummified and shrunken cells are more radioresistant than normal cells" and that the probability "for the damage of ancient and highly fragmented DNA in a cell is 3 powers of 10 below the unfragmented DNA" (Wanek et al. 2012: 11). Essentially, given that mummified/shrunken cells are more radioresistant and the fact that DNA occupies only 2% of the nucleus, the odds of directly or indirectly hitting DNA with ionizing radiation is quite small.

Thus, although the results of more recent research seem to indicate that we are not damaging aDNA by conducting multiple full-body CT scans, researchers have also been investigating other imaging modalities including magnetic resonance imaging and terahertz imaging. Both modalities are nonionizing and, therefore, there is no concern about radiation dose. However, both are more limited in their capabilities when applied to mummified remains.

Nuclear Magnetic Resonance Imaging

Nuclear magnetic resonance imaging (NMRI) uses very strong magnetic fields that cause realignment of hydrogen protons in water. When the magnetic field is manipulated, protons shift back and forth from their realigned state and emit a radio frequency that is converted into an image. Different tissues can be identified based the rate they return to their realigned state, known as their relaxation times. The main limiting factor in the analysis of mummified remains is the absence of mobile protons (i.e., water) resulting in very short relaxation times relative to living tissue (less than 1 millisecond, Rühli et al. 2007b). The first study that used NMRI on mummified remains was Piepenbrink and colleagues' (1986) examination of a rehydrated foot and hand from an eleventh- to thirteenth-century AD Peruvian mummy. Though the authors were able to produce usable images in the rehydrated samples, they note that "experiments performed on the natural mummified tissue failed" (Piepenbrink et al. 1986: 27). Similarly, Notman et al. (1986: 95) concluded that NMRI "does not seem to be applicable to the investigation of desiccated human remains."

In light of this early research, the applicability of MRI to mummy studies seemed limited except in relatively rare instances of 'wet' mummies (e.g., Shin et al. 2010). More recently, however, several studies have had more success using MRI in paleoimaging.

Rühli and colleagues (2007b) used a three-dimensional ultra-short-echo time (UTE) sequence in their examination of an Egyptian mummified head. This sequence allowed the detection of very short relaxation times characteristics of desiccated tissue and produces images that allowed some tissue differentiation (Rühli et al. 2007b). Panzer et al. (2013a) also used the UTE sequence and compared CT and NMR images. The focus of Münnemann and colleagues' (2007) research was to explore the feasibility of nuclear magnetic resonance for imaging of ^{1}H and ^{23}Na in artificially mummified remains. Lastly, it is also possible to conduct spectroscopic analyses with magnetic resonance (Lynnerup 2009), though use of this aspect of the technology has to date been infrequent (e.g., Karlik et al. 2007; Stødkilde-Jørgensen et al. 2008). Though CT images offer better resolution and are still the preferred modality for imaging mummified remains, magnetic resonance images "should be regarded as an adjunct modality to be used for non-invasive diagnostic imaging in unique cases" (Öhrström et al. 2013: 296).

Terahertz Imaging

On the electromagnetic spectrum, X-rays are radiation with wavelengths ranging from 0.01 to 10 nanometers, which corresponds to frequencies between 30 petahertz [1 petahertz = 10^{15} Hz] and 30 exahertz [1 exaertz = 10^{18} Hz]). Terahertz (1 THz = 10^{12} Hz) radiation falls between microwave and infrared radiation, with wavelengths between 1 mm and 0.1 mm. THz radiation has been used in clinical settings in cancer detection in superficial tissues (Yu et al. 2012) and in art conservation to examine 'hidden' (wrapped or otherwise inaccessible) papyri (Labaune et al. 2010), the presence of drawings and paint layers beneath mural paintings (Jackson et al. 2008), or surface damage (Fukunaga and Hosako 2010). THz imaging is particularly attractive because it is considered a completely nondestructive modality: it is nonionizing, and it does not heat up unbound protons.

Öhrström et al. (2010) explored the feasibility of using THz imaging on ancient mummified remains (a mummified fish and an isolated mummified hand from Egypt) and a modern bone. They found that although bone and cartilage were well differentiated from soft tissue and linens, image quality is influenced by object thickness. THz imaging of an approximately 5 mm thick mummified fish were better than the approximately 3 cm thick mummified hand (Figures 5.5 and 5.6). Although THz imaging has no unique features that make it particularly suited for paleopathological research, it could be used to detect *in situ* material artifacts (e.g., amulets, jewelry) as well as the chemical identification of embalming substances (Öhrström et al. 2010).

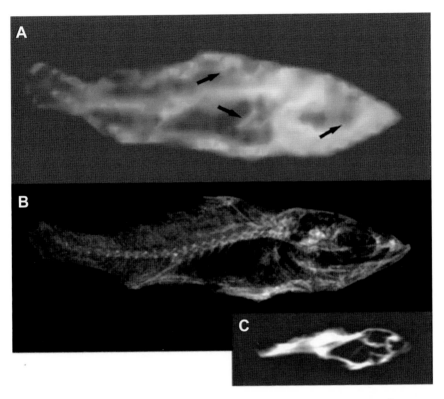

FIGURE 5.5 (A) Terahertz image and (B) X-ray image of a mummified fish (Öhrström et al. 2010).

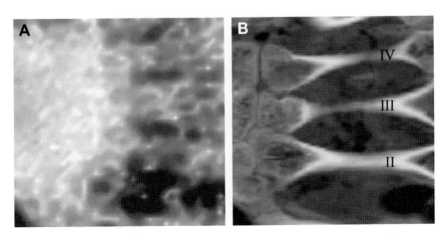

FIGURE 5.6 (A) Terahertz image and (B) X-ray image of a mummified hand (Öhrström et al. 2010).

Paleogenetics

Two studies in the mid-1980s launched the field of paleogenetics: Higuchi and colleagues' (1984) amplification of DNA from muscle and connective tissue from the preserved skin of a quagga and Pääbo's (1985a, b) amplification of DNA from an Egyptian mummy. Since then, paleogenetics has provided significant new insight into human evolution (e.g., Green et al. 2010; Meyer et al. 2012), population structure and migration (e.g., Hey 2005), and disease evolution (e.g., Bos et al. 2014; Harkins and Stone 2014). Paleogenetics have been incorporated into several areas of mummy studies including the investigation of long-distance migration and population history based on human DNA (e.g., Francalacci 1995) and bacterial DNA (e.g., Castillo-Rojas et al. 2008; Guhl et al. 2000; Swanston et al. 2011), kinship and within-site analyses (e.g., Gamba et al. 2011; Gilbert et al. 2007; Hawass et al. 2010, 2012), and mortuary ritual (Hanna et al. 2012). Where paleogenetics has had the biggest impact on mummy studies, however, is in the area of health and disease.

Health and Disease

Paleomicrobiology is the study of disease pathogens (i.e., bacteria, viruses, parasites) in skeletal and mummified remains. The ability to isolate, amplify, and sequence host or pathogenic DNA from soft tissue has allowed researchers to circumvent the limitations of both skeletal material and soft tissue in paleopathological investigations. The following discussion will focus on three inter-related areas of investigation: the identification and amplification of pathogenic DNA, the evolutionary history of these pathogens, and the analysis of human DNA to examine genetic disorders and predispositions. Some of this research has also been used to supplement paleopathological diagnoses based on morphological, biochemical, and/or immunological data. The application of these methods has also facilitated a broader range of health-related research questions, including examining host susceptibility and environmental risk factors, pathogen evolution, and phylogeny, which can be fundamental in understanding emerging infections (Anastasiou and Mitchell 2013).

Pathogenic DNA and Evolution

DNA from several pathogenic bacteria have been isolated and identified in mummified remains, including

- Salo and colleagues (1994) amplified *M. tuberculosis* DNA from a pre-Columbian South American mummy
- *Escherichia coli* from samples recovered from the gut of Lindow Man (Fricker et al. 1997) and in the mummified remains of an eighteen-month old infant that dates to the Third Intermediate Period of Egypt (1000–700 BC) (Zink et al. 2000);

- Members of the *Corynebacterium* genus from a dental abscess observed in a mummified head dating to the New Kingdom (ca. 1550–1080 AD) of Egypt (Zink et al. 2001);
- *Bordetella pertussis* in seventeenth- to nineteenth-century mummies from Yakutia, Eastern Siberia (Thèves et al. 2011).

Additionally, researchers have successfully amplified DNA of endo- and ectoparasites including

- *Plasmodium falciparum* (Hawass et al. 2010; Nerlich et al. 2008)
- *Leishmania donovani* (Zink et al. 2006) and *Leishmania tarentolae* (Novo et al. 2015)
- *Ascaris* sp. (Loreille et al. 2001; Leles et al. 2008)
- *Enterobius vermicularis* (Iñiguez et al. 2003)
- *Clonorchis sinensis* (Shin et al. 2013; Liu et al. 2007)

Because the focus of this section is on paleogenetic data that can be retrieved from soft tissue, I will not be providing in-depth summations of research based on skeletonized remains, though I will try to provide key references for the reader. Further, although the most extensive paleogenetic research on the paleoepidemiology and evolution of pathogens in mummy studies has been conducted on tuberculosis and Chagas disease, I will also summarize smaller, case-study-based research as these deal with modern pathogens that are significant causes of morbidity and mortality.

Wilmar Salo and colleagues (1994) produced one of the first studies that successfully extracted pathogenic DNA from mummified remains. During dissection of a spontaneously mummified forty- to forty-five-year old female from the Chiribaya culture of southern Peru (AD 1000–1300), it was noted that the upper-right lung was adhered to the chest wall and had a large calcified nodule. Tissue samples from the nodule led to the successful extraction and sequencing of *Mycobacterium tuberculosis* DNA.

M. tuberculosis DNA has also been successfully extracted from mummified remains from prehistoric Chile (Arriaza et al. 1995), sixteenth- to nineteenth-century Eastern Siberia (Dabernat et al. 2014; Figure 5.7), pre-Hispanic Brazil (Sotomayor et al. 2004), eighteenth-century Hungary (Donoghue et al. 2011; Fletcher et al. 2003a), and ancient Egypt (Donoghue et al. 2010; Zink and Nerlich 2003; Zink et al. 2004, 2007).[2] Although some studies were based on a small number of individuals, recent works have focused on larger collections. For example, Zink and Nerlich (2003) collected bone and soft tissue samples from eighty-five Egyptian mummies dating between 2050 and 500 BC. Of these, the researchers were able to amplify DNA from forty-eight individuals, and of these, twenty-five (52%) were positive for *M. tuberculosis* complex DNA. Additionally, Donoghue et al. (2011) report that 157 out of 232 (67.7 %) individuals from the Dominican Church in Vác, Hungary, tested positive for *M. tuberculosis* complex DNA.

FIGURE 5.7   Frozen mummies from Yakut. Skeletal lesions attributed to tuberculosis were observed in these individuals (Dabernat et al. 2014).

Although the focus of this research was on paleopathological diagnosis, the results also speak to the evolution and natural history of *Mycobacterium tuberculosis*. In 2002, Brosch and colleagues demonstrated that contrary to prevailing thought, *M. tuberculosis* did not originate from *M. bovis* but rather belongs to a separate branch. These results are echoed in the work on Egyptian mummies (Zink and Nerlich 2003), eighteenth-century Hungarian mummies (Fletcher et al. 2003b), and seventeenth and eighteenth-century frozen mummies from Yakutia in Eastern Siberia (Dabernat et al. 2014).

In contrast to the success that researchers have had in isolating *M. tuberculosis*, it has been much more difficult to isolate DNA from treponemal bacteria (e.g., *Treponema pallidum*) even in individuals with pathognomonic skeletal indicators (e.g., Barnes and Thomas 2006; Bouwman and Brown 2005). Bouwman and Brown (2005) have suggested that this is due to variation in pathogen load throughout the course of the disease. Pathogen load is highest during the secondary phase of venereal syphilis and in congenital syphilis, thus providing the highest probability of successfully isolating DNA (Bouwman and Brown 2005). Conversely, in tertiary phase venereal syphilis, with its diagnostic caries sicca, pathogen load is lowest. Based on this, recent attempts utilizing skeletal material have been more successful isolating *T. pallidum* DNA in individuals with congenital syphilis (Montiel et al. 2012).

I could locate only one study that attempted to isolate *T. pallidum* DNA from mummified remains. As discussed in the previous chapter, Gino Fornaciari and colleagues (1989) concluded based on immunological, histological, and ultrastructural analyses of her mummified remains that Maria of Aragon had tertiary stage venereal syphilis. Several years later, Marota and colleagues (1996) successfully amplified short fragments of the 16S ribosomal rRNA gene of *Treponema pallidum*. Sequencing of one of the fragments (95 bp) demonstrated close similarity (85%) with reference samples (Marota et al. 1996; Rollo and Marota 1999). Sequencing of cloned amplicons, however, resulted in no *T. pallidum* sequence. Instead, the authors found sequences from a variety of oral bacteria (e.g., *Propionibacterium*, *Peptostreptococcus*, *Clostridium*, and *Capnocytophaga*) and *Mycobacterium*.

Studies that have successfully amplified viral DNA from mummified remains are not common. Aside from the work by Li et al. (1999) and Sonoda et al. (2000) discussed later, the majority are isolated case studies or based on small samples. Nonetheless, the viruses that have been identified are significant human pathogens throughout history, and, therefore, the results of this research have implications for our understanding of viral evolution.

Smallpox is an acute viral infection caused by *Variola major* or *Variola minor* in humans. The latter causes a milder form of the disease with about a 1% mortality rate, whereas infection by *Variola major* kills 15% to 45% of those infected (Behbehani 1983). The antiquity of the disease is unclear, for although historical evidence suggests it was present in China in the twelfth century BC and India by the fifteenth century BC (Li et al. 2007), soft tissue evidence is lacking. Skin lesions thought to represent smallpox were observed by Ruffer and Ferguson (1911) in Ramses V (1200–1100 BC) but have not been confirmed histologically (Aufderheide 2003). More recent examples of smallpox have been identified in mummified remains from sixteenth-century AD Italy (Fornaciari G. and Marchetti 1986), though it was not possible to recover any viral DNA (Marennikova et al. 1989). Researchers were, however, able to amplify three segments of the *Variola* genome from Siberian mummies dating to the seventeenth to nineteenth century (Biagini et al. 2012). Based on phylogenetic analysis, the strain isolated from these mummies is distinct from modern clades and "could be a direct progenitor of modern viral strains or a member of an ancient lineage that did not cause outbreaks in the 20th century" (Biagini et al. 2012: 2059).

Hepatitis is an infection of the liver caused by one of five different viruses; A, B, C, D, and E. Each virus has different modes of transmission, symptoms, and outcomes. For instance, hepatitis A (HAV) is contracted through ingesting food or water contaminated with infected fecal matter, and although an infected individual may display some symptoms (e.g., fatigue, loss of appetite, fever), many people recover without treatment or lasting liver damage (WHO Fact Sheet N°328, accessed April 7, 2015). On the other hand, HBV is a chronic infection transmitted through contact with infected bodily fluids (e.g., blood, semen) that can lead to death from cirrhosis and liver cancer (WHO Fact sheet N°204, accessed April 7, 2015). There is significant genotypic diversity within each of these viruses; HBV has a short (3214 bp) double-stranded DNA genome with a worldwide distribution of ten different genotypes (A through J) with several subgenotypes (Araujo et al. 2011); HEV is a positive-sense, single-stranded RNA genome (7.5 kb) with four different genotypes and, though currently spreading to developed nations, has its highest prevalence in South and East Asia (WHO Fact sheet N°280, accessed April 7, 2015; Panda et al. 2007). There are two examples in the mummy paleopathological literature where researchers have extracted and amplified hepatitis viral DNA.

Using the same samples scraped from the bandage found on the mummified remains of Maria of Aragon, Marota et al. (1998) amplified a 24 bp complementary DNA sequence for one segment of the HEV RNA genome. Because HEV is composed solely of RNA and has no DNA stage, the authors (1998: 57) admit that this "cannot be explained easily." One idea is that Maria of Aragon was infected by HEV *and* a retrovirus, the latter being responsible for the production of the complementary DNA sequence. Alternatively, the authors suggest that the sequence represents a "normal component of the human genome present since very ancient times" (Marota et al. 1998: 58).

In 2003, Shin and colleagues (2003a, b) reported on their gross and radiological examination of the mummified remains of a young male child (4.5–6.6 years of age at death) dating to the Chosun Dynasty (1392–1910 AD) in Korea (Figure 5.8). Endoscopic examination of the internal organs by Kim et al. (2006) identified nodules on the surface of the liver, though the authors avoided characterizing this as a pathology. In 2012, Kahila Bar-Gal et al. (2012) confirmed the presence of HBV genotype C2 DNA in liver samples taken from the child. Modern clinical data indicates the HBV genotype C is a more aggressive and virulent strain with an

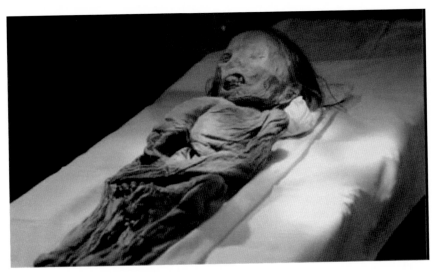

FIGURE 5.8 The mummified remains of a four- to six-year-old child from the Chosun Dynasty (1392–1910 AD) in Korea. Adapted from Kim et al. 2006.

elevated risk for early onset of liver inflammation, fibrosis, cirrhosis, and liver cancer (Araujo et al. 2011; Kao et al. 2002). Based on comparison with the modern HBV genome the authors conclude that the ancient HBV sequence diverged at least 3000 years ago. Given the estimated age of the individual, the most likely mode of virus transmission was from the mother during birth, which increases the likelihood (>90%) that this child would have developed a chronic form of the infection (Araujo et al. 2011).

The human lymphotropic virus-1 (HTLV-1) is one of a group of four human retroviruses that causes adult T-cell leukemia/lymphoma (ATLL) and HTLV-1-associated myelopathology/tropical spastic paraparesis (HAM/TSP). Although most individuals infected by the virus will remain asymptomatic, 1–5% will develop ATLL, a fatal infection of the T-cells. This low incidence suggests additional factors influence its development (Nicot 2005). The virus has a broad geographic distribution, and in an effort to determine the origin of HTLV-1 in Japan and South America, Li et al. (1999) and Sonoda et al. (2000) analyzed 104 bone marrow samples taken from 1500-year-old mummies from northern Chile.[3] The researchers were able to identify two regions (LTR and pX) of HTLV-1, and when compared to modern Chilean and Japanese HTLBv-1, concluded that the virus had an Asian origin and was introduced during initial New World colonization. These publications were followed by a short series of responses that questioned the antiquity of the strain identified by Li and colleagues (Gessain et al. 2000; Vandamme et al. 2000). A more recent phylogenetic analysis of the sequences led Coulthart et al. (2006: 95) to conclude that "the ancient versus modern status of the putatively mummy-derived HTLV-1 LTR sequences of Li et al. (1999) and Sonoda et al. (2000) remains open."

Worldwide, human papillomavirus (HPV) is a significant source of morbidity and mortality. There are five major genera of HPV with 174 different types with manifestations ranging from benign epithelial lesions to cancer (Bzhalava et al. 2013). Twelve HPV types are responsible for 99.7% of all cervical cancers, with HPV 16 and HPV 18 alone accounting for 70% of cases worldwide (Ault 2006).

Despite its modern-day prevalence and a long coevolutionary history with our species (Chan et al. 1992; Ong et al. 1993), only one example of HPV infection presented in the mummy literature. In part, this may be due to the fact that HPV targets epithelial cells (Longworth and Laimins 2004), and these cells commonly decompose rapidly. During the course of their examination of the mummified remains of Maria of Aragon (Figure 1.11), Gino Fornaciari and colleagues (2003: 1160) observed "a large pedunculated branching skin neoformation" in the "right paravulvar region," which they suggest was an anogenital wart. They were able to amplify DNA that targeted a 141 bp sequence from several different types of HPVs. Hybridization and subsequent sequencing of the amplified DNA indicated the presence of HPV 18 as well as JC9813, an HPV type that was discovered in 1998.

The literature in mummy studies devoted to documenting parasitic infection is quite extensive. This research has predominantly been predicated upon morphological or immunological evidence (e.g., Bianucci Mattutino et al. 2008; Deelder et al. 1990; Reinhard 1990). As mentioned earlier, paleogenetic evidence of *Plasmodium falciparum*, *Leishmania donovani* and *Leishmania tarentolae*, *Clonorchis sinensis*, and *Pulex* sp., have been described. Although the epidemiology of schistosomiasis in Egypt has been extensively examined (e.g., Kloos and David 2002) only more recently has the question has been approached using DNA (Matheson et al. 2014). To date the most extensive paleogenetic research on parasitic infection has focused on Chagas disease.

Chagas disease is caused by the protozoan parasite *Trypanosoma cruzi*, which is passed onto a human host by triatomine bugs as it bites and defecates on the skin of its victim. Although it is more common in Latin American countries, it is spreading and currently affects between six and seven million people worldwide (WHO Fact sheet N°340, accessed April 7, 2015). In the acute phase of the disease the parasite proliferates within cells, eventually causing them to burst. The chronic phase of Chagas disease may be predominantly asymptomatic though interspersed with periods of fever. Myocardial tissue is progressively damaged due to chronic inflammation and fibrosis whereas nerve damage in the peripheral autonomic nervous system can lead to enlargement of the heart, esophagus, and colon (Köberle 1963). Approximately 10% of those infected die from myocarditis or meningoencephalitis (Aufderheide et al. 2004b).

The earliest efforts to diagnosis Chagas disease in mummified material were based on immunochemistry and gross morphological changes (Fornaciari G. et al. 1992; Rothhammer et al. 1985). Rothhammer and colleagues (1985) autopsied thirty-five mummies from four different sites in northern Chile dating between 470 BC and 600 AD. Twenty-two mummies were sufficiently well preserved for analysis, with nine exhibiting some form of megalopathy. Gino Fornaciari and colleagues (1992) identified 'nests' of *T. cruzi* amastigotes in cardiac and esophageal tissues in a fifteenth- to sixteenth-century highland mummy from Peru.

Guhl and colleagues (1997, 1999) were able to successfully amplify a segment of *T. cruzi* DNA from soft tissue sample collected from twenty-seven northern Chilean/southern Peruvian mummies dating between 2000 BC and 1800 AD. Several subsequent studies have expanded upon these results including; Ferreira et al. (2000), Madden et al. (2001), and Aufderheide et al. (2004b). In the latter study, the authors tested tissue samples from 283 mummies ranging in time from 7050 BC to 1850 AD. Based on their results, the authors estimated a 40.6% prevalence rate of Chagas, with no significant differences between the different cultural periods sampled. *T. cruzi* is endemic and has a natural, 'wild' cycle consisting of various mammalian reservoir species and insect vectors. When humans colonized the area, they introduced themselves into this cycle. Once established, an equilibrium was established "between the biology of the trypanosome and its vector, the environment, and human behavior/biology" (Aufderheide et al. 2004b: 2036), leading to the stability evidence in prevalence rate through time.

Researchers are also beginning to examine the presence of *T. cruzi* and Chagas disease in prehistoric Brazil. Lima and colleagues (2008) took rib samples from a 4500- to 7000-year-old mummy from the site known as Abrigo do Malhador in the Peruaçu Valley. Fernandes and colleagues (2008) took both bone and soft tissue samples from a 560-year-old mummy (± 40 years), also from the Peruaçu Valley, that exhibited evidence of megacolon. Both groups of researchers were able to isolate segments of *T. cruzi* DNA. Given the age of the mummies, both authors conclude that Chagas disease was present in Brazil before the arrival of Europeans.

Genetic Disorders and Predispositions

The impact of molecular analyses within the modern clinical context on diagnosis and treatment of diseases is profound. It is now possible to perform genetic screening that may indicate a susceptibility to specific pathological conditions or the presence of genetic disorders. Generation of this type of genetic information has been obtained from archaeological remains, but at present has been limited to single individuals and cannot provide population-level data. Still, this represents a significant new direction in paleopathological research. Soft tissue evidence of genetic conditions or disorders is rare, and I will present the work of Hershkovitz and colleagues (2014) on a case study from the Joseon Dynasty (1392–1910 AD) of Korea. Evidence of genetic predisposition has been discussed for atherosclerosis, colorectal cancer, and rheumatoid arthritis.

Over the last decade, there have been a number of publications on spontaneous or spontaneously enhanced mummies dating to the Joseon Dynasty of Korea. This research has predominantly focused on issues related to health and disease, employing both gross morphological, radiographic, and paleoparasitological methodologies. Recently, Hershkovitz et al. (2014) described a case of cherubism observed in an eighteen- to twenty-five-year-old female. Cherubism, an autosomal dominant disease resulting from the mutation of the SH3BP2 gene on chromosome 4p16.3 (Li and Yu 2006; Ueki et al. 2001), is a benign childhood disease, first manifesting between four months and four years that regresses postpuberty. The typical manifestation is hypertrophy of the maxilla and mandible with bone being replaced by fibrous tissue cysts. This hypertrophy encroaches on the orbits and when coupled with depression of the maxillae the eyes appear to gaze upward (Figure 5.9).

Given the morphological, radiological, and histological evidence that pointed to cherubism, the authors wanted to confirm their diagnosis by attempting to amplify mutations in the SH3BP2 gene and the PTPN11 gene (chromosome 12q24). Ultimately, however, the authors concluded that "it was technically non-feasible to extract viable DNA from our subject" (Hershkovitz et al. 2014: e102441).

Atherosclerosis is a chronic immunoinflammatory disease of medium and large arteries and is the most common cause of coronary artery disease, carotid artery disease, and peripheral arterial disease, being responsible for 78% of cardiovascular related deaths in 2008 (13.5 out of 17.2 million; Mendis et al. 2011). Leaky endothelial linings allow the passage of atherogenic lipoproteins, initiating an inflammatory response, which in turn is followed by a fibroproliferative response by the intimal smooth muscle (Falk 2006). There are environmental and behavioral risk factors

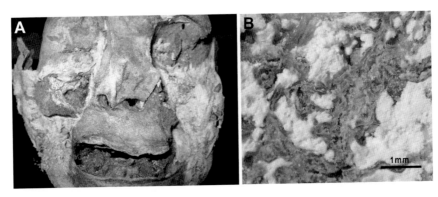

FIGURE 5.9   Anterior view of the mummy discussed by Hershkovitz et al. (2014). In Panel (A) the authors note expansion of the lower portion of the face. Photo (B) is a low-magnification view of a section through the maxillary sinus. The brownish substance is trabecular bone; the white substance is partially calcified fibrous tissue.

associated with atherosclerosis as well as several single-nucleotide polymorphisms (SNP) that increases one's risk.

Until very recently, paleopathological identification of atherosclerosis has been only sporadically reported (e.g, Ruffer 1911; Nerlich et al. 1997b; Zimmerman et al. 1971). Since 2003, however, seventeen articles have been published on atherosclerosis (e.g., Allam et al. 2011; Kim et al. 2015; Piombino-Mascali et al. 2014). Further, a special session that focused atherosclerosis in both skeletal and mummified remains was held at the Eighty-Fourth Annual Meetings of the American Association of Physical Anthropologists. The most extensive study to date was conducted by the Horus Group in which whole body CT scans were performed on 137 mummies from Egypt, Peru, and North America. The authors concluded that forty-seven (34%) had probable or definite atherosclerosis (Thompson et al. 2013).

In their interpretation of CT scans made from the Tyrolean Iceman, Murphy et al. (2003) identified several calcifications that indicated atherosclerosis. These findings, along with the subsequent work by other authors, run counter to the general understanding of the etiology of atherosclerosis as being associated with modern risk factors (e.g., diet, stress, etc.). For example, Murphy and colleagues (2003: 627) conclude that "In combination, these calcifications may present a surprising amount of evidence for arteriosclerotic cardiovascular disease, particularly if we share the perspective that this condition is a modern affliction facilitated by lifestyle, diet, and tobacco use." Then, in the course of sequencing the Iceman's genome, researchers were able to determine that he was homozygous for allele rs10757274, located in chromosomal region 9p21, which would have doubled his risk of cardiac heart disease (Zink et al. 2014). They also identified several other SNPs that would have predisposed him to cardiovascular diseases (Table 5.1).

In 1994, Gino Fornaciari and colleagues identified a mucinous adenocarcinoma in the colon of King Ferrante I of Aragon. Today, colorectal cancers (CRC) are the

TABLE 5.1 Single-nucleotide polymorphisms associated with cardiovascular disease risk identified in Ötzi the Tyrolean Iceman (modified from Zink et al. 2014).

Chromosome# (dbSNP#)	Gene	SNP Association
1 (rs1801133)	MTHFR	Cardiovascular disease
1 (rs1764391)	GJA4	Atherosclerosis
4 (rs1870377)	KDR	Coronary heart disease
9 (rs10757274)	CDKNBAS	Ischemic stroke, sudden cardiac death
9 (rs2383206)	CDKNBAS	Coronary heart disease
13 (rs5351)	EDNRB	Atherosclerosis
19 (rs1613662)	GP6	Myocardial infarction, age

third most commonly diagnosed cancer and are the second leading cause of cancer-related death (50,830 deaths in 2013, 50,310 deaths in 2014) in the United States (American Cancer Society 2013, 2014). Though risk of colorectal cancer is age-progressive, there are a number of behavioral and diet-related risk factors including high red meat consumption, low fruit and vegetable consumption, long-term smoking, lack of physical activity, and alcohol consumption. Several genetic factors can predispose one for CRC including mutation at the microsatellite loci BAT 25 and BAT26 and point mutations at codon 12 of the oncogene K-Ras (involved in tissue signaling) and at V599E on the BRAF gene (involved in protein production that influences cell growth) (Oliveira et al. 2007).

Several articles report results of molecular analyses on the remains of King Ferrante I (Falchetti et al. 2006; Marchetti et al. 1996; Ottini et al. 2011). Using tissue from the tumor, all report that although there were no changes in the BAT25 microsatellite or the BRAF V599E but that the codon 12 mutation on the K-Ras gene was present. In the most recent study, given the dietary and behavioral risk factors known to be associated with CRC, Ottini et al. (2011) reconstructed the diet of King Ferrante based on $\delta^{13}C$ and $\delta^{15}N$ stable isotopic analyses. They concluded that his diet consisted of a high proportion of meat ($\delta^{15}N$ equal to 11.9‰) with very little marine foods ($\delta^{13}C$ equal to −18.1‰).

Rheumatoid arthritis (RA) is an autoimmune disease resulting in chronic inflammation and fibrosis of joint capsules. Current clinical data from the United States indicates a prevalence rate of 0.72%, which translates to an estimated 1.5 million adults suffering from rheumatoid arthritis (Myasoedova et al. 2010). The main environmental risk factor is smoking (Scott et al. 2010), and there is a large genetic component (50%) to RA susceptibility. More than thirty regions are thought to be associated with the condition (Scott et al. 2010), but the most significant are the HLA—DRB1 and the single-nucleotide polymorphism N22 (PTPN22) genes (Barton and Worthington 2009).

In 2002, Cirianni and colleagues examined a late-sixteenth-century mummy dubbed the "Braids Lady": a fifty- to fifty-five-year-old woman buried in the San Francisco Church in Arezzo, Italy. Based on gross and radiographic examination, the authors documented several lesions that indicated a severe form of arthritis including erosions of the joint surfaces, deviation of the toes, and "z" deformation of the second ray of the left hand. The authors ultimately concluded that the Braids Lady suffered from rheumatoid arthritis.

As indicated earlier, alleles of the HLA-DRB1 gene (i.e., DRB1*0101, DRB1*0401, DRB1*0404, DRB1*0405, DRB1*1402, and DRB1*1001) are thought to be a major genetic contributor to RA susceptibility. Fontecchio et al. (2006a, b, 2012) extracted and amplified DNA from this individual to try to determine her HLA genotype, ultimately identifying the presence of the DRB1*0101 and DRB1*1101 alleles.

Notes

1. The authors do not offer any further clarification on the latter four samples.
2. This does not of course include the paleogenetic work on tuberculosis from skeletal material. Excellent summaries of this work are provided by Roberts and Buikstra (2003, 2014).
3. The text offers no further insight into the time or cultural period of the mummies other than that the samples were taken from mummies held at the Museo Archeologia San Miguel around the Azapa valley and the Museo Padre le Paige in the Atacama Desert.

6

MUMMY STUDIES AND BIOARCHAEOLOGY

The goal of this book has been to consider the state of mummy research relative to the field of bioarchaeology. Bioarchaeology developed as an interdisciplinary approach melding archaeological and skeletal data in a biocultural, population-level, problem-oriented research design. My goal was to consider if mummy studies was influenced by the same paradigmatic shifts that drove the development of bioarchaeology. Has it moved from a focus on cultural-historical explication to population-based, hypothesis-testing explanation? To what extent has mummy studies managed to successfully merge the biomedical and the anthropological paradigms that characterize the bioarchaeological investigation of paleopathology?

The modern manifestation of mummy studies was developing at the same time as bioarchaeology in both the UK and the United States. As Grahame Clark was introducing the term 'bioarchaeology,' Michael Zimmerman was publishing his experimental research on the histology of mummified tissues. When Vilhem Møller-Christensen was publishing his description of osteoarchaeology, Aidan and Eve Cockburn were bringing together scientists to examine the mummy PUM II and Rosalie David was revitalizing the Manchester Mummy Project. As Robert Blakely and Jane E. Buikstra articulated bioarchaeology as a problem-oriented biocultural approach to the study of human remains, the results of the autopsy of ROM I were published in the *Canadian Medical Association Journal*. The fields were developing alongside each other, but although there are many points of connection between bioarchaeology and mummy studies, and some researchers have a foot in both disciplines, the field of mummy studies has largely been isolated from the major paradigmatic shifts that archaeology and biological anthropology have experienced over the last forty-five years.

Summary of Publication Trends

The interdisciplinary nature of mummy studies is reflected in the fact that mummy research is published in a very broad array of journals, ranging from highly specialized biomedical (e.g., *The Prostate*, Ciranni et al. 2000) and natural science journals (e.g., *Journal of Synchrotron Radiation*, Bertrand et al. 2003) to the earth sciences (e.g., *Quaternary International*, Oller et al. 2012) and humanities (e.g., *Journal of Humanistic Ideology*, Hawass 2013). The number of journals categorized as 'nonanthropological' (n = 298) far exceeds those journals categorized as related to anthropology (n = 69). The number of articles published in nonanthropology venues (n = 622) exceeds those published in anthropology journals (n = 441). Although the journals that published the greatest number of mummy articles, the *American Journal of Physical Anthropology* and the *Journal of Archaeological Science*, are anthropological journals, they only published a total of 152 articles (14.3% of the total number of articles) over the last forty-five years.

There is a distinct trend in mummy studies of increasingly specialized, laboratory-based, biomedically orientated research that focuses on questions related to health and disease. There has also been a shift where mummy research is being published. Although the frequency of publication in most of the top journals discussed has remained relatively constant over the last twenty years, the *American Journal of Physical Anthropology* has actually seen a general decline. The two journals that have seen an increase in the frequency of mummy research in the same time span are the *Journal of Archaeological Science* and *PLoS ONE*. It is significant that the diversity of topics within *JAS* is greater than in most of the other venues; indeed *JAS* is one of the few journals in which health and disease-related articles are *not* the most frequent. This topical diversity also reflects a greater emphasis on the archaeology and anthropology sides of bioarchaeology. On the other hand, the articles published in *PLoS ONE* are more focused on the *bio* side of bioarchaeology and do not engage as deeply with archaeological data or social theory.

The field has increasingly moved away from autopsy as the main investigative method, and it is possible to observe non- or minimally invasive methods being used more frequently though time. The majority of paleopathology articles in the earlier decades covered by this analysis were based on gross visual observation of morphology (see Figure 3.14).[1] Beginning in the late 1980s and early 1990s, immunological, molecular, and biochemical techniques became integrated into the mummy toolkit. Although some of the methodological advances were being fueled by the growing recognition that researchers should avoid destructive or invasive analyses (e.g., Harwood-Nash 1979), it was also the recognition that the presence of soft tissue afforded new opportunities to investigate health based on immunological response (e.g., Deelder et al. 1990; Sawicki et al. 1976) or pathogenic DNA (e.g., Guhl et al. 1997; Nerlich et al. 1997a).

Despite the importance that a clear understanding of postmortem taphonomic processes has for all mummy-related research questions, research of this type has been limited (Aufderheide 2011). This is a major concern because assessing the impact of postmortem processes is foundational for interpretation; understanding how soft tissues are preserved and the impact of these processes on morphology and biochemistry is essential for all subsequent research agendas. Although it is possible to observe that the overall frequency of taphonomy-related articles has increased over the last forty-five years, these still represent only 13% of the 496 articles published in the top journals. The journals that published the greatest number of taphonomy-related articles were the *Journal of Archaeological Science* (n = 14), *American Journal of Physical Anthropology* (n = 12), and the *Yearbook of Mummy Studies* (n = 7). On the other hand, articles focused on taphonomy are less frequent (or absent) in the biomedical journals (e.g., *Canadian Medical Association Journal, Journal of Parasitology*, and *The Lancet*).

This is not to say that there has been some significant research published on taphonomy. The taphonomic history of the mummy known as Ötzi has been intensively investigated (e.g., Janko et al. 2010), the results of which have also been used in comparative analyses (e.g., Rollo et al. 2005, 2007). Other notable research includes the work of researchers at Cova des Pas (Prats-Muñoz et al. 2013; Oller et al. 2012) as well as the work of Parker Pearson and colleagues (Parker Pearson et al. 2005, 2007). Although less frequent, there are examples of experimental research that focus on taphonomy (e.g., Brier and Wade 1997; Garcia et al. 2014; Gill-Robinson 1996; Gill-Frerking 2010; Papageorgopoulou et al. 2015; Zimmerman 1972; Zimmerman et al. 1998).

Given the history of mummy studies, it is not surprising that the reconstruction of mortuary behavior is a significant area of research. The frequency of articles that reconstruct or consider mortuary behavior has remained relatively constant over the first three decades considered by this study, though there has been a small increase in the number of articles since 2004. Excellent examples of recent research in this area that combines advanced laboratory methodologies and mortuary theory includes Wade and colleagues (Wade et al. 2011; Wade and Nelson 2013a, b) and Ceruti (2015).

The Future of Mummy Studies

Two main figures of modern mummy studies recently discussed the future of the discipline, highlighting both potentials and pitfalls. Michael Zimmerman (2011: 164) noted that new developments in paleoimaging, paleoserology, and paleogenetics will expand "our knowledge of the life stories and fate of ancient individuals, their relationships to others, ancient migrations, the evolution of disease, and the role of ancient disease in human evolution and social history . . ." Arthur Aufderheide (2013) focused his comments on limitations the field must overcome, including issues pertaining to legislation restricting access to mummies, the lack of clear funding sources, and the organization and long-term survival of the discipline. Both authors are discussing big-picture issues, yet there are several other fundamental challenges facing mummy studies.

Standardization and Research Protocols

Data collection and methodological standards are common features of scientific disciplines, as they ensure reproducibility, cross-study comparability, and a common frame of reference for evaluating published results. In skeletal bioarchaeology, the *Standards for Data Collection from Human Skeletons* manual compiled by Jane Buikstra and Doug Ubelaker (1994) is one of the most widely employed. The manual establishes procedures for generating data on specific aspects of skeletal bioarchaeology (e.g., age and sex estimation, pathology, metrics and nonmetric features, etc.) while also providing a general research protocol that structures data collection.

A number of studies will be highlighted next that offer key components for the initial construction of a unified set of standards for mummy studies. Although action on the individual-researcher level is a step in the right direction, development of fieldwide standards must occur at a higher level. For instance, the *Standards for Data Collection from Human Skeletons* were developed in response to a very specific issue facing biological anthropology in the late 1980s and early 1990s; lack of standardized in data collection and legislation calling for the repatriation of Native American skeletal remains. In response to this, a workshop supported by the National Science Foundation was held at the Field Museum of Natural History in Chicago in 1989. Eleven different contributors were invited based upon their research expertise and were asked to present recommendations regarding data-collection standards.

The point of this small tangent is that while individual authors can advocate for particular standards, establishing a fieldwide data-collection protocol and method standardization will likely require a much more comprehensive and centralized effort. There are indications that such efforts are in the works. For instance, Ronald Beckett is chairing the Ad Hoc Committee on Recording Standards for Scientific Approaches to Mummy Studies for the Paleopathology Association. Moissidou and colleagues (2015: 4) advocated for a special session at the 2016 World Congress on Mummy Studies in Lima to establish "a scientific committee and, subsequently, of promoting the standardization of a bioethical protocol on mummified remains," though unfortunately this didn't materialize.

Research Protocols

Aufderheide (2003) provides readers with his mummy dissection protocol forms, which he attributes to Marvin Allison. Ikram (2015) provides similar protocol forms, though with entries related specifically to Egyptian mummies. These protocols structure the preliminary examination of a mummy and provide a specific order in which data should be collected. Both begin with an external examination, describing any wrappings or surface treatment, followed by recording presence/absence and treatment of features such as hair, eyes, and nose. Aufderheide's (2003) protocol includes a scoring system for recording soft tissue preservation (which I will return to later) and skeletal metric data. He also provides a detailed description of how to evaluate major features and regions of the body. Except for Aufderheide's soft tissue preservation index, these protocols, however, do not provide standardized methods for recording these data.

Recently, Moissidou and colleagues (2015: 4) identify "a lack of internationally established guidelines" and call "for an international mummy research protocol to be instituted." According to the authors, such a protocol should answer the following questions:

"Are we showing adequate respect to the corpse we are analyzing?"

"Which scientific hypothesis necessitates our study of mummified remains?"

"Do we propose to study mummies for scientific/cultural purposes or for business?"

The authors recommend that these guidelines be enforced by an international committee "composed of scholars of high repute" that would "reestablish a series of priorities in the study of mummified bodies" (Moissidou et al. 2015: 4). The authors do not seem to be proposing a research protocol (i.e., recommended sequence of observations/procedures for data acquisition) so much as a code of ethics. Though I do not disagree with their central point, a much simpler course of action would be to officially adopt research guidelines and codes of ethics of an existing association such as the Paleopathology Association or any number of other professional academic societies (e.g., American Association of Physical Anthropologists, British Association of Biological Anthropology and Osteoarchaeology, Canadian Association of Physical Anthropology), all of which have published guidelines that speak to the questions raised by Moissidou and colleagues. No doubt many mummy researchers already belong to one or more of these professional societies.

Soft Tissue Preservation

The manner in which soft tissue preservation is described in published reports is not standardized. Most of the descriptions of soft tissue preservation are qualitative assessments ranging from "excellently preserved" (Panzer et al. 2014: 4) to "not well preserved" (Gaudio et al. 2014: 36). Indeed, in the last example, the only evidence of soft tissue preservation provided by the authors is the "preservation of adipocere near the chest, and pseudo-mummification of residual muscle" (Gaudio et al. 2014: 36). In my own research, I have used qualitative statements such as "significant amounts of soft tissue" (Nystrom et al. 2010: 485) and "considerable amount of soft tissue" (Nystrom et al. 2005: 178). In response to this type of imprecise and variable language, there have been several recent attempts to standardize the assessment of soft tissue preservation.

Aufderheide (2003) developed the Soft Tissue Index (STI), a ratio of the percentage of preserved bone that is covered by soft tissue. The body is divided into five regions (head, chest, abdomen, arms, legs), and each is assigned a total of five points if the bones are present. The extent of soft tissue preservation is determined by whether the bone is completely covered by skin and/or muscle. The degree of preservation of eight major internal organs and two external organs are assessed on a ten-point scale.

The Soft Tissue Preservation System (STPS) published by Wittmers et al. (2011) is based upon Aufderheide's Soft Tissue Index. Wittmers and colleagues provide some elaboration on the scoring procedure for determining external soft tissue preservation. For instance, the five points assigned to the head are divided into the following point scale: one-half point for each eye, and one point each for hair, scalp, mandible, and face. The principal focus of this study, however, was to determine if the STPS was useful in predicting internal organ preservation because this could prevent unnecessary dissections. Based on data derived from a large sample of mummies from southern coast of Peru, the authors concluded that the STPS was indeed useful for predicting internal organ preservation.

Contrary to the STI and the STPS, Panzer and colleagues (2015) developed a method for assessing soft tissue preservation based on full-body computed tomography scans. The authors created a checklist of ninety-seven anatomical landmarks divided into two main categories: (1) soft tissues of the head and musculoskeletal system and (2) organs and organ systems. These are in turn subdivided into several categories. Although this appears to be quite a long list, the authors report that it took anywhere between fifteen and thirty minutes to go through the checklist and that there was a high degree of both intra- and interobserver reliability.

There are advantages and limitations associated with each method. The STI and STPS are based on gross observation and are rapid and easy methods for nonradiologists to employ. They are also well suited for in-field examinations and for larger collections. Although the scoring procedures are straightforward, one limitation however, is that the authors do not report intra- or interobserver error.

The method developed by Panzer and colleagues (2015) involves a much more extensive evaluation of soft tissue preservation and they were also able to demonstrate a high level of interobserver agreement. Having this level of detail could also stimulate research on taphonomy as the scoring system could facilitate comparative analyses. The principal drawbacks are that the method requires access to a CT machine and thus is not feasible for in-field assessment. Further, the logistics and costs of getting full-body CT scans of larger collection of mummies might limit its applicability. Alternatively, it may be possible to retroactively produce estimates of soft tissue preservation based on previously conducted CT studies. Although both methods have the same goal and promote standardization of soft tissue preservation, it is an open question as to the correlation between the methods.

Though Sydler and colleagues (2015) research was not explicitly articulated as a means of quantifying soft tissue preservation, the technique they propose to evaluate the degree of soft tissue shrinkage certainly is related. The authors calculated the ratio of cross-sectional area of soft tissue to bone at thirteen different locations in mummified remains relative to modern reference bodies (Figure 6.1). Seventeen different mummies were grouped into categories based on mummification process: ice mummies, Egyptian mummies, bog bodies, South American mummies, and

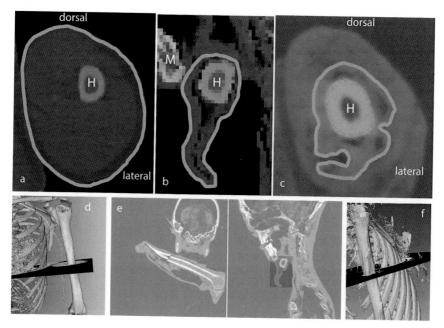

FIGURE 6.1 Axial slices through humeral midshaft in (a) modern body, (b) ice mummy, and (c) Egyptian mummy. In the top images, H represents the humerus. The light grey immediately surrounding this represents bone while the outlined area is soft tissue. (Sydler et al. 2015).

desiccated mummies. The authors documented differences in percentage of soft tissue shrinkage between categories, with the ice mummies exhibiting the lowest rate of shrinkage. The authors also noted within-group and within-body variability in tissue shrinkage stemming from a variety of both antemortem and postmortem factors.

Before any of these methods can become standard protocols, however, they would need to be independently validated by other researchers. Additionally, it would be good to examine the correlation between soft tissue preservation indices and tissue shrinkage estimates. These steps represent basic exploratory steps in research design and thus are analogous to recording skeletal inventory and element completeness, common features of osteology standards (e.g., Buikstra and Ubelaker 1994).

Paleoimaging

The development of different paleoimaging modalities has arguably had the biggest impact on mummy studies relative to any other technology or analytical method. From the discovery of X-rays to the development of computed tomography, advances in radiographic technology have been rapidly applied to the examination of mummified remains. Although the field is exploring the feasibility of other modalities, such as terahertz and magnetic resonance imaging, computed tomography has became central to many mummy investigations. Despite the fact that CT was first used on mummified remains nearly thirty years ago, recent critiques raise several serious concerns.

O'Brien and colleagues' (2009) analysis reveals a fundamental problem in the employment of paleoimaging in mummy studies. The authors identified thirty-one articles published before 2005 that featured computed tomography of human mummified remains. From these articles, O'Brien et al. (2009) generated data on how authors articulated their research hypotheses and statement of purpose, if there was a description of CT imaging protocols, type and quality of conclusions (e.g., general vs. specific answer to a research question), strength and level of evidence, and author disciplinary background.

Out of the thirty-one studies, O'Brien and colleagues report that only three articles (9.7%) were explicitly hypothesis-driven, with 84% stating either a general or specific focus for the use of CT scans. Of the latter, the majority (62%) provided only a general statement regarding expected outcomes. Only ten (32%) articles clearly articulated a set of research objectives. Conversely, CT scans were employed "to investigate human mummies for curiosity and without specific" research questions in 65% of the articles (O'Brien et al. 2009: 93).

The authors also indicate that only 68% of the authors reported CT imaging protocols (i.e., slice thickness, manufacturer, etc.). Several researchers, including Nelson and Wade (2015) and Beckett and Conlogue (2010) have noted that there is no standardized protocol for conducting a CT scan of a mummy, a fact that has several consequences. Because there are no standards, there is little consistency in exposure parameters between different studies, making it impossible to make the data "meaningful beyond the scope of more than the one individual scanned" (Cox 2015: 1109; see also Nelson and Wade 2015). Numerous authors have also pointed out that the software used to reconstruct the CT images are intended for living people and therefore cannot be uncritically applied to mummified remains (Beckett and Conlogue 2010; Conlogue 2015; Lynnerup 2007; Villa and Lynnerup 2012). Without a comparative database or the benefit of previous experience, the chances of incorrectly identifying pathologies increases. Lastly, although CT scans are commonly used to aid in paleopathological diagnosis (O'Brien et al. (2009) indicate that 58.1% of the articles in their sample reported on paleopathology), there is no "comprehensive guide to diagnosing paleopathology in radiology" and little attention is paid to the potentially confounding influence of taphonomy or the mummification process itself (Cox 2015: 1101).

Soft Tissue Differentiation and Artifact Identification

As the use of paleoimaging technology becomes increasingly common in mummy research it is imperative that researchers have the ability to reliably differentiate between tissues, between tissues and material artifacts, and between different types of material artifacts. This may influence any number of research questions, though to date the focus has been on tissue differentiation to improve pathological diagnosis: "Knowledge of the typical HU range for the different tissues in mummies may help to avoid misinterpretation of increased or reduced radiodensity as evidence of paleopathological conditions" (Villa and Lynnerup 2012: 127).

In the broadest study to date, Villa and Lynnerup (2012) present HU values derived from mummified remains recovered from bogs, cold-dry, and hot-dry environments. The researchers noted differences in within- and between-tissue HU values based on these environmental contexts. For instance, although the authors identified largely homogenous results between three frozen Inca mummies, values derived from bog bodies were more heterogenous across tissue type. Panzer and colleagues (2013a) documented an overall increase in HU density across four different classes of soft tissue and bone in an experimentally mummified lower limb. The primary limitation of this study is that it represents density changes associated with a single specific mummification procedure.

Computed tomography is the most commonly employed imaging technology in mummy studies, yet it is limited in its ability to differentiate between desiccated soft tissues. Rühli and colleagues (2007a) used magnetic resonance imaging to investigate tissue differentiation. Although there are several limitations to the application of MRI to imaging mummified remains, the authors used a device called the NMR-MOUSE or MObile Universal Surface Explorer, "an open and portable sensor that can detect NMR signals from a volume external to the magnet, giving access to a variety of applications which cannot be tackled in closed magnet geometries" (Rühli et al. 2007a: 259). Using this machine, the authors were able to differentiate between superficial layers of bandages and tissue in a mummified hand as well as between different tissues in both dry and frozen remains.

The same principles that facilitate tissue differentiation in CT also facilitates identification of any material artifacts contained within a mummy bundle. In the only study to date that has published a large set of results, Gostner et al. (2013) provide the Hounsfield Units of a wide range of material artifacts, including gemstones and minerals, metals, fired clay, wood, bitumen, amber, and calcified tissues.

Data Archiving and Reporting

Growth of the field and increased utilization of imaging technology has raised concerns about data storage, access, and reporting. Beyond just ensuring that imaging data is archived, Nelson and Wade (2015: 942) note that "limited access to these primary data and the means by which to analyze them has reduced mummy studies to a highly limiting case-study approach . . ." and has restricted the fields' "ability to perform meaningful analyses of patterns of paleopathology and mummification traditions." As discussed in Chapter 2, the IMPACT database was established to serve as a centralized archive for imaging data and to foster standardization. One of the most significant aspects, however, is that this database facilitates the development of larger-scale comparative studies and thus would counter the predominance of the case study in mummy research.

In their review articles, Zweifel et al. (2009) and Dagefőrde et al. (2014) focus on variability in how paleopathological data has been reported. The authors' common objective is the development an 'evidence-based' approach to paleopathology and to encourage diagnostic accuracy and reducing methodological variability. Several of Zweifel and colleagues' (2009) results deserve comment. First, they found that "roughly a third of all individually described mummies were of indeterminate (or unreported) sex" (Zweifel et al. 2009: 415) and that sex estimation methods were often not reported. They found a similar lack of clarity on age estimations and methods. Clearly this problem limits interpretation and cross-study comparison. Though the authors did not address this, it would be interesting to delve deeper into these data to examine several issues. Is the degree of soft tissue preservation influencing sex and age estimation? What is the correlation between the disciplinary background of the authors and the frequency of reporting age/sex estimation and the methods employed to derive them?

The authors note that out of 131 articles, only 16 reported a cause of death. In the remaining cases, cause of death was either not reported or remained equivocal. Zweifel and colleagues (2009: 416) conclude that this "diagnostic uncertainty is a general problem in any palaeopathological research and thus, clinical standards of diagnostic sensitivity and specificity have rarely been applied in ancient mummy studies." Dagefőrde and colleagues (2014: 15) conclude that the "overall quality of palaeopathological studies (in terms of minimum standards) was not one would expect but can be improved." Because these authors focused exclusively on articles discussing soft tissue paleopathology, and in general seem to find reporting of information inadequate, it would be interesting to conduct a similar examination of reporting in skeletal paleopathology.

Disciplinary Journal and Home

In their introduction to the first volume of the *Yearbook of Mummy Studies*, the editors note that the field lacks a dedicated journal and that this hampers development into a strong independent discipline (Gill-Frerking et al. 2011). This concern for the future of the discipline was also expressed by Aufderheide (2013: 134): "It is possible but unlikely that the field of mummy studies will ever be large enough to be an independent scientific discipline. Thus, to survive and flourish, the field will need to join a related discipline." I would agree with these authors in the sense that a dedicated mummy studies journal could foster a sense of community among mummy researchers, though I question the need for the field to "be seen as a strong discipline in its own right" (Gill-Frerking et al. 2011: 5) and consider biological anthropology as the disciplinary home of mummy studies. The fact is, however, that only a small proportion (20.5%) of mummy-related articles published between 1970 and 2015 appear in bioanthropology-related journals (e.g., *American Journal of Physical Anthropology, Journal of Archaeological Science, International Journal of Osteoarcheology*, and *International Journal of Paleopathology*). Therefore, while I commend the efforts and vision of the *Yearbook* editors, I believe we need to encourage cross-field integration rather than accentuating disciplinary distinctiveness.

Training

Bioarchaeologists, no matter what 'school' of bioarchaeology we adhere to, take similar graduate coursework that is ultimately grounded in anthropological and archaeological method and theory. Further, despite differences in approach and perspective, fundamentally most bioarchaeologists ground their research in the bio-cultural framework. So, despite some differences in research foci, methodological approach, and theoretical perspective, bioarchaeology is largely united.

Those engaged in mummy research, however, come from a wide range of backgrounds including pathologists, general medical practitioners, radiologists, anatomists, forensic scientists, cardiologists, parasitologists, and of course bioarchae-ologists. We do not take the same graduate-level courses, and we do not get the same level of training in all the aspects necessary for a research project that involves mummified remains.

Because there are few large collections of mummies, opportunities to acquire formalized training in 'mummy research' are limited. I would hazard a guess that most skeletal bioarchaeologists begin their careers examining skeletal material first and then become more involved in the analysis of mummified remains as opportu-nities present themselves, acquiring 'on-the-job' training in the biomedical aspects of mummy research (e.g., radiography, soft tissue paleopathology). Medical profes-sionals get called upon to participate in mummy research because of their special-ized knowledge, particularly in the fields of soft tissue pathology and imaging. This is reflected in the manner in which multidisciplinary teams are constructed and how the research is published.

Take for example the examination of ROM I in 1974 (Hart et al. 1977). During the autopsy of the mummy, directed by Theodore Reyman, Michael Zimmerman, and Peter Lewin, tissue specimens were collected from the remains and "distributed to qualified participants and observers as this had the advantage of ensuring greater coverage in the search for abnormalities" (Millet et al. 1998: 91). So, George Lynn and Jamie Benitez (1977), a professor of audiology and otoneurologist, respectively, examined the ears while U. de Boni, while U. de Boni (physiologist), M. Lenczner (a tropical disease expert) and J. W. Scott (physiologist) examined a cyst resulting from *Trichinella spiralis* infection (1977). Although the preservation of soft tissue structures encourages the involvement of specialists and the formation of multi-disciplinary teams, it also fosters atomization and the perception that a mummy is simply a collection of different tissue types.

Some training opportunities are available for those interested in mummy research. In 2014, the University of Innsbruck and the European Academy of Bozen/Bolzano (EURAC) Institute for Mummies and the Iceman held a two-week course called Mummies and Glacial Archaeology. Topics covered in the course included conservation, paleoecology and archaeobotany, glacial archaeology, climate, and ecology, forensic anthropology, paleopathology, historical anthropology, and finally molecular genetics. In 2016, researchers from the Sicily Mummy Project and the University of Nebraska-Lincoln hosted the Mummy Studies Field School in Santa Lucia del Mela, Sicily. The course included modules on human anatomy, osteology, taphonomy, paleopathology, paleoparasitology, paleobotany, death and burial, and crypt architecture.

These types of intensive courses represent a significant step forward, and from the perspective of bioarchaeology, it is easy to envision how this type of experience could be incorporated into graduate training. Bioarchaeology graduate students commonly gain practical experience in archaeological excavation and osteological analyses in field schools. Similarly, these training opportunities would provide biomedical professionals experience in skeletal biology methods (e.g., age, sex estimation) and a basic understanding of the biocultural approach.

Ethics

Standards and guidelines structure the development of ethical research designs, publication, community involvement, and so on in anthropology, archaeology, and biomedical fields. There is a substantial literature on closely allied topics including the ethics of DNA analyses (Kaestle and Horsburgh 2002; Pullman and Nicholas 2011), the rights of the dead (Bahn 1994; Scarre 2003, 2006; Tarlow 2006; Wilkinson 2002), as well as discussions aimed specifically at bioarchaeologists and biohistorians (Alfonso and Powell 2007; Buikstra 2016; DeWitte 2015; Lambert 2012; Larsen and Walker 2004; Paradise and Andrews 2007; Turner and Andrushko 2011; Walker 2000; Winston and Kittles 2005; Zimmerman 2014).

Yet ethics has not been a significant focus of discussion in mummy studies until recently (e.g., Day 2014; Elliott 2009; Holm 2001; Kaufmann and Rühli 2010; Lonfat et al. 2015). As noted in several places in this book, there has been a significant shift in how researchers approach studying mummified remains. The first decades of the modern scientific investigation of mummies very much proceeded from a clinical, medical perspective (Lynnerup 2007) where the autopsy and the collection of tissue samples were standard practices. It is increasingly recognized, however, that the mummy itself is a culturally important artifact and that these types of destructive analyses should be avoided. Mirroring developments in skeletal bioarchaeology, recent discussions of research ethics in mummy studies have touched on topics related to the display of mummified remains (Day 2014), tissue collection and DNA analyses (Elliott 2009; Holm 2001), and the concept of informed consent (Kaufmann and Rühli 2010).

A significant ethical question that confronts researchers working with prehistoric remains is establishing who speaks for the dead—who can give consent to study the remains? Holm (2001) raises two main issues regarding genetic research on tissue samples in which there is no possibility of informed consent: Are relatives or descendants legitimate proxy decision makers, and do the dead have interests in how their tissues may be used? Holm argues that in the absence of any information regarding what the deceased may have actually wanted, decisions made by any relative or descendant is really just what the living want and therefore does not really constitute proxy consent. Further, if the remains are sufficiently old, the identification of any living relatives may not be possible. In such instances, it may be possible to identify a cultural affiliation, though as Holm notes several potential issues may arise, including competing claims or that remains may be so old that a reasonable estimation of affiliation is simply not possible.

In his discussion, Holm uses Ötzi as a case study. In this instance, there is no possibility of identifying cultural affiliation, and we cannot really ask ourselves what he may have wanted because we have only a limited understanding of his culture. Any decision therefore comes down to ownership of the body, which thought officially settled (the body is 'owned' by the Süd-Tirol government) is still problematic as this disregards the possibility that Ötzi could have what Holm refers to as residual rights in his body.

Residual rights include "(1) an interest in a dignified treatment after death and (2) an interest in maintaining one's good name" (Holm 2001: 446). Both of these 'rights' are fundamentally, however, culturally contingent. In the absence of any knowledge or understanding of what constitutes 'dignified' or 'good name' in a specific culture, the decision ultimately rests in the hands of those people or institutions that control the body (e.g., scientists, museum officials, etc.). Holm (2001) notes that maintaining the 'good name' of a past person is predicated upon knowing the name in the first place and then anticipating how research results could impact that name. There are many examples of mummified remains of historical individuals (some with more widely recognizable names, some not) in which this could be an issue:

- Rosalia Lombardo in the Capuchin Catacombs of Palermo (Panzer et al. 2013b);
- Ferrante I (Fornaciari G. et al. 1999), Ferdinand II (Fornaciari G. et al. 2009), and Mary of Aragon (Fornaciari G. et al. 2003);
- Cangrande della Scala, Lord of Verona (Apostoli et al. 2009; Fornaciari G. et al. 2015);
- Cardinal Giulo della Rovere, Archbishop of Ravenna (Masetti et al. 2008);
- Queen Giovanna IV and the Marquis of Pescara Franceso Ferdinando d'Avalos (Fornaciari G. 1985);
- Blessed Christina from Spoleto (Fornaciari A. et al. 2008);
- Salimbene Capacci, rector of the Hospital of Santa Maria dells Scala, and his wife Margherita Sozzini (Giuffra et al. 2011);
- Charles Francis Hall (Paddock et al. 1970);
- Swedish engineer and North Pole explorer Salomon Andrée (Aufderheide 2003);
- John Paul Jones (Eckert, 1982);
- Saint Zita from the Basilica of Saint Frediano in Lucca, Italy (Fornaciari G. et al. 1989);

- Antónia Tauber (Kustár et al. 2011);
- Antal Simon (Kustár 2004);
- the embalmed heart of King Richard I (Charlier et al. 2013).

Examples of mummy research that could be considered to impugn someone's 'good name' are prevalent. For instance, we know that Ferdinand II of Aragon, King of Naples suffered from an infestation of head and pubic lice (Fornaciari G. et al. 2011). One of the research objectives articulated by Kustár and colleagues (2011: 84) was to determine if Antónia Tauber, a eighteenth-century nun from Hungary, was indeed "really ugly and frightening in life."

A recent example in which research results were considered to negatively impact an individual's 'good name' involves Tutankhamen. In the last months of 2014, the BBC aired a documentary in which the following DNA and CT results were presented: Tutankhamen was the product of an incestuous relationship between brother and sister, and he had a club foot, possibly suffered from gynecomastia, which would have produced enlarged breasts and rounded, fuller hips, and temporal lobe epilepsy. The show produced a full frontal 3-D reconstruction, one that differs dramatically from previous representations. The 'results' of this documentary and the subsequent backlash played out in the mainstream media. As one of the most visible and outspoken Egyptian archaeologists, Zahi Hawass, former Secretary General of the Egyptian Supreme Council of Antiquities, responded to these results in a series of articles published by *Al-Ahram Weekly*. Hawass criticizes the film's producers, presenters, and the purported findings. The most interesting aspect of Hawass's retorts is the way in which he articulated how the documentary had humiliated and slandered the boy king himself.

Kaufmann and Rühli (2010) and Lonfat and colleagues (2015) echo Holm's concern regarding informed consent and privacy but also introduce two other ethical issues that influence mummy research. First, they stress the concept of the integrity of the body and link this explicitly with the integrity and continuity of the individual self.

> The right of integrity is understood as the elemental right of each human being to be protected from any kind of harm. Research on mummies has to consider the aspects of individualism and the right of integrity. Bodily integrity is therefore an important issue in maintaining the integrity of a person and as such is important for the practice of research
> *(Kaufmann and Rühli 2010: 611–612).*

> Intact wholeness strongly mirrors a religious aspect of bodily wholeness. This means that the body is intrinsically important for personal identity.
> *(Kaufmann and Rühli 2010: 613)*

This focus on structural integrity of the body, and in turn its connection to the integrity of the individual, reflects a modern biomedical perspective of body in which we own our bodies and that our individuality is linked with our bodies (Tarlow 2006). This is, however, grounded in our Western understanding of the body and self, and both archaeological (e.g., Chapman 2000; Jones 2005), and bio-archaeological (e.g., Duncan and Schwarz 2014; Geller 2012) research has explored the fragmentary, relational, *dividual* body and that continued social existence or significance is not predicated upon an intact body.

Kaufmann and Rühli (2010) also consider the type of mummification and how this may impact ethical considerations. In particular, the authors suggest that due to the intentionality behind the production of an anthropogenic mummy, invasive and/or destructive analyses would violate the principle of informed consent, whereas in cases of spontaneous mummification, "this may be regarded differently" (Kaufmann and Rühli 2010: 614):

> In ethical judgment, one should also differentiate between whether a child or adult mummy is involved. This is especially true in cases of artificial mummification, where an adult individual intentionally underwent preservation and thus indirectly took into consideration the possibility of his physical availability to later generations. In the case of accidental mummification, such as for ice mummies, this may be regarded differently. For such mummies including artificially embalmed minors done [sic] may assume that the deceased was not aware of the possibility of preservation and of the scientific availability of his body remains to future generations.
>
> *(Kaufmann and Rühli 2010: 614)*

This introduces the possibility that our treatment of remains will, at least in part, rest on our ability to reconstruct the intentionality behind different components of mortuary behavior. Although these authors do not explicitly state that it is more appropriate to perform destructive analyses on spontaneous mummies, the implication is there and raises some interesting epistemological and ethical concerns. First, by differentiating the treatment of remains based on age, the authors are suggesting that an adult has control over the mortuary behavior that accompanies their death. In actuality, funerary behavior may reflect the influence of any number of sociopolitical and economic forces beyond the control of the individual. For a modern example, consider the story of how Lenin's body was treated, against his stated wishes, upon his death (Quigley 1998). Secondly, the argument hinges upon our ability to reconstruct the intention behind mummification. As discussed in Chapter 2, it is easier to observe some forms of anthropogenic mummification (e.g., evisceration, excerebration) than others (e.g., smoking, wrapping). The modern Western definition of intentionality may not accurately reflect the concept in any number of prehistoric non-Western contexts. If the body mummifies spontaneously, and therefore unintentionally, this does not directly obviate the need to consider any principle of informed consent. The implication of the distinction highlighted by Kaufmann and Rühli (2010) is that there is some inherent value in anthropogenic mummies, such that destructive analyses violate an ethical standard.

Researchers at the Institute of Evolutionary Medicine (IEM) at the University of Zurich have developed an internal code of ethics, explicitly outlining standards for research involving mummified human remains.[2] This code outlines ethical standards for the following topics: researcher qualifications, invasiveness of investigation, appropriateness of research design/question, sample processing and storage, data generation, interpretation, diversification, and publication. Although this code of ethics would serve as a good starting point in the development of discipline-wide guidelines, the interdisciplinary nature of mummy studies necessitates expanding the discussion of ethical considerations outside of the biomedical specialties.

Recent discussion within bioarchaeology have focused more explicitly on the ethics of conducting research on human remains (e.g. DeWitte 2015; Lambert 2012; Turner and Andrushko 2011; Walker 2000). In his discussion of the ethical issues facing bioarchaeologists Walker (2000) identifies three core ethical principles that should structure research with human remains: (1) remains should be treated with dignity and respect because they were once living individuals, (2) descendant groups should have the authority to determine the fate of any remains, and (3) given their importance for investigating our history, skeletal collections should be preserved. Several things can make realization of these guidelines difficult, including the lack of clear ancestor-descendant relationships and cross-cultural and diachronic variability in the treatment of the dead. Further, when dealing with prehistoric remains, or with skeletal or mummified remains for which there is no proxy decision maker, it may become more difficult or impossible to obtain informed consent. If we acknowledge that agency can exist after death, the possibility that we can harm the dead still exists (Scarre 2006).

Further, as researchers we have to acknowledge that we occupy a position of power with respect to remains that we are studying. Zuckerman and colleagues (2014), drawing on the concept of embodiment, advocate for a relational ethical principle that would guide the analyses of human remains that represent those that were oppressed during life; those that were discriminated against, socially marginalized, and disenfranchised. The authors argue that "researchers would explicitly engage in an ethics of social responsibility, wherein they would explicitly recognize that skeletons are not inert archives of information but are, symbolically, participants in the research process whose values and interests must be recognized" (Zuckerman et al. 2014: 517). As the authors are explicitly discussing research focused on the remains of socially marginalized groups, it is also important that researchers be aware of the inherent structural inequalities that may exist between themselves, the skeletons or mummies they study, and the descendant communities.

Mummy Studies as Anthropology

I return to the quote by Arthur Aufderheide that opened this book as it speaks to the future of mummy studies:

> Due to their spectacular nature, mummies have often been decontextualized, because interest in the preserved body has overridden the importance

of archaeological contexts. Integrative, hypothesis-driven, multidisciplinary approaches . . . are essential to a more holistic understanding of these remains.

(2013: 134)

Several measures attest to the fact that mummy studies is increasing in popularity and visibility. Just in the last ten years alone, 496 articles have been published on mummies, a significant number when compared to the number (n = 567) published in the preceding thirty-five years. A number of books that are written for a more general audience (e.g., James Dickson's *Ancient Ice Mummies* and Albert Zink's *The World of Mummies: From Ötzi to Lenin*) as well as academic volumes (e.g., Pauline Asingh and Niels Lynnerup's *Grauballe Man: An Iron Age Body Revisited*) have been published in the last several years. A dedicated journal was launched in 2011, and international training programs are now being offered. These same measures, however, also indicate that the field is entering a critical juncture in its development.

Although bioarchaeology and mummy studies share a common ancestry and are certainly related, they have taken different directions. As the merging of methods and theory derived from skeletal biology and archaeology, bioarchaeology ultimately linked more closely with anthropology, whereas mummy studies, with its emphasis on soft tissue paleopathology, allied more closely with the biomedical professions. In the 1970s when mummy studies began to coalesce, studies were very descriptive and principally focused on individual-level paleopathology. Although topical and methodological diversity increased in the 1980s and 1990s, descriptive case studies remained common (e.g., Bloomfield 1985; Vahey and Brown 1984; Zimmerman and Aufderheide 1984). During these decades, both skeletal and soft tissue paleopathology were more allied with the biomedical sciences than with the biocultural perspective of anthropology and were hampered by a lack of "problem orientation and a reliance on the newest technology to drive the research" (Armelagos 1994: 240). In the previous chapter I synthesized research in three broad methodological categories (i.e., biochemical studies, paleogenetics, and paleoimaging) to consider the following question: Has the incorporation of these technologies and methodologies into mummy studies spurred development of new and novel research questions or is the technology driving research?

Relative to skeletal bioarchaeology, the application of biogeochemical methods within mummy studies is nascent, with only a small number of articles published in the top journals involving stable isotopic analyses (n = 32). Yet it is here we can see some of the clearest evidence for the development of new approaches and questions in mummy studies. For instance, Bethany Turner and colleagues adopt a life-course perspective on diet in their research on nine naturally mummified bodies from southern Mongolia. Viewing diet as the "intersection between political economy, ecology, and physiological well-being" Turner and colleagues (2012: 3125) utilize a suite of stable isotopes ($\delta^{13}C$, $\delta^{15}N$, $\delta^{18}O$, $^{87}Sr/^{86}Sr$, and $^{20n}Pb/^{204}Pb$) to explore macro-scale cultural processes and document dietary stability in the face of marked political and economic turmoil. In another study, Turner and colleagues (2013) provide insight on the impact of imperialism based on the reconstruction of diet and mobility from isotopes.

Similarly, Wilson and colleagues (2007, 2013) were able to reconstruct approximately two-and-a-half years' worth of isotopic data from scalp hair and cut hair recovered in association with the Llullaillaco Maiden from Argentina. The results indicated that the Maiden's diet became significantly richer in animal protein and C_4 plants approximately one year before her death, consumption of the latter steadily increasing during the final four-and-a-half months. Additionally, mass spectrometry analysis of the Maiden's hair indicates a significant and prolonged increase in coca and alcohol consumption beginning approximately twelve months before her death (Wilson et al. 2013). These results, coupled with ethnohistorical accounts, provide a detailed reconstruction of this individual's transition to a new social status as *capacocha*.

The analysis of ancient DNA in mummy studies has focused primarily on issues related to health and disease and can be separated into three broad categories: paleoepidemiological studies, reconstruction of evolutionary history of pathogens/conditions, and confirmation of diagnosis. In regard to the latter category, molecular analyses have been employed to confirm diagnoses based on gross soft tissue observations. Although documenting these conditions contributes at some level to our understanding of disease evolution, these efforts do not contribute to our understanding of incidence or distribution. In the best cases, however, these case studies serves as a springboard for additional analyses. For instance, the molecular analyses that confirmed the presence of colorectal cancer in King Ferrante I of Aragon, ultimately lead to the work of Ottini and colleagues (2011) and their examination of the impact of environmental and dietary risk factors based on stable isotopic analyses.

To date, the most extensive paleoepidemiological research that has employed molecular analyses have examined tuberculosis (Chan et al. 2013; Dabernat et al. 2014; Zink et al. 2007) and Chagas disease (Aufderheide et al. 2004b; Fernandes et al. 2008; Ferreira et al. 2000; Guhl et al. 1997, 1999; Madden et al. 2001). Though in some instances the molecular data is used to confirm previous soft tissue diagnoses (e.g., Fernandes et al. 2008; Salo et al. 1994), the availability of larger samples of mummies facilitates an epidemiological approach. Further, establishing the genetic relationship between these pathogens and modern strains represent significant new areas of investigation (e.g., Fletcher et al. 2003b; Dabernat et al. 2014; Zink et al. 2007). Molecular analyses have also been key in reconstructing the evolutionary history of various parasites (e.g., Iñiguez et al. 2003; Loreille et al. 2001; Oh et al. 2010; Shin et al. 2013) and in some instances are linked to paleoepidemiological studies of parasitic infection.

One of the most significant technological advances for mummy studies over the last forty-five years has been the development of paleoimaging, principally X-rays and computed tomography. With the field generally moving away from conducting 'traditional' autopsies, computed tomography, first used in mummy studies in 1977, is widely considered to one of the best noninvasive, nondestructive methods of examination. X-ray units are widely available, adaptable to field situations (e.g., Conlogue 1999), and even nonspecialists like myself can make use of them (e.g.,

Nystrom et al. 2004). Computed tomography has become the 'gold-standard' (Öhrström et al. 2010) for paleopathological diagnosis and for the general examination of mummies. As discussed earlier, however, critical reviews of the literature indicate that this research is not hypothesis-driven and lacks explicit problem orientation.

It seems clear that CT scans are commonly used as an exploratory tool, and the identification of any pathology or the description of mortuary behavior is often *post hoc* without being grounded in a discrete problem-orientated research design. The frequency of these studies in mummy studies in many ways reflects the concerns raised by Armelagos and Van Gerven in their critique of the state of skeletal biology and paleopathology and the impact of new technology on descriptive analyses: "Give an osteologist a CAT scan, and every specimen is scanable" (Armelagos and Van Gerven 2003: 60).

Although mummy studies have diversified in scope, the detection and documentation of pathology remains the dominant focus. The most visible texts on mummy studies, such as Arthur Aufderheide's *Scientific Study of Mummies*, Aidan and Eve Cockburn's *Mummies, Disease, and Ancient Culture*, and Rosalie David's *Egyptian Mummies and Modern Science*, all emphasize the manner in which mummified remains can contribute to our understanding of disease experiences in the past. This disciplinary emphasis is also reflected in a number of recent publications. The majority of Lynnerup's (2007) review of the current state of mummy studies is devoted to highlighting methodological advances and the discussion of soft tissue paleopathology. Although his chapter was published in a volume specifically on paleopathology, Zimmerman (2014: 120–121) states that "The examination of mummies has two goals: fitting the diagnosis of diseases in individual mummies into a picture of the health status of a given ancient population; and providing information on the evolution of disease." In their introduction to a recent special issue of *The Anatomical Record* on mummies, Monge and Rühli (2015: 936) stated that "The *raison d'être* for the scientific study of mummies is to gain an understanding of the evolution of health and disease in previous or extinct populations of humans."

There seems little doubt that the reconstruction of health and disease will continue to be a dominant research topic and feature of the discipline. This, however, must be balanced by a more explicit problem orientation and contextualization of data. The contextualization of paleopathological data in reference to concepts such as disease, health care, disability, and pain (Fay 2006; Marsteller et al. 2011; Roberts 2011; Tilley and Cameron 2014; Tilley and Oxenham 2011; Tilley 2015; Toyne 2015) would be productive approach for mummy studies. Indeed, given the current state and disciplinary composition of the field, these areas seem particularly well-suited.

I hope critically considering the current state of mummy studies will stimulate greater integration and cross-fertilization with bioarchaeology. Addressing the issues facing mummy studies is critical in the near term and should not be postponed. In particular, it is important for the field to reaffirm its connections to anthropology and bioarchaeology through the adoption of a more holistic approach. Anthropology marks itself as being distinct from other social sciences in part based on its holistic approach to the study of human culture, which means that researchers do not consider aspects of society (e.g., economics, religion, sexuality, language) in isolation from one another. Perhaps the single biggest difference between the modern manifestations of bioarchaeology and mummy studies is the degree to which the fields engage with the biocultural approach and the integration of social theory. A biocultural perspective requires the consideration of the mummified body as actively structuring society, moving beyond being a passive reflection of social, political, and economic factors in the environment. In this sense too, acknowledgment of the structuring influence of the biomedical perspective on sex and gender opens up alternative explanations and possibilities. Approaching paleopathological data from a bioarchaeological and biocultural perspective provides insight into the human and societal response to disease and illness. There are areas where mummy studies can more fully engage with social theory that would complement current research foci. In my opinion, mummy studies is inherently a part of anthropology and as such should strive to integrate methodological advances within a biocultural framework to expand the interpretative significance of data.

Notes

1. Although I did not collect data on how many studies conducted autopsies and therefore cannot track any temporal trends, autopsies, though much less common, still occur (e.g., Dedouit et al. 2010; Giuffra et al. 2011; Lim et al. 2008). Indeed, while he acknowledges the value of nonanatomical methods (e.g., immunological, biochemical) of investigating disease in human remains, Aufderheide (2003: 323) comments that "The study of morphological changes in the tissues of mummified human remains is still the cornerstone upon which the science of mummy studies is based" and outlines a detailed protocol for a mummy dissection.
2. A. pdf version of the code of ethics is available at the following website: www.iem.uzh. ch/institute/iemcodeofethics/Code_of_Ethics_IEM_2014.pdf.

APPENDIX I

In most instances, the following journal abbreviations were taken from the Web of Science website. Three journals, *Yearbook of Mummy Studies*, *Journal of Paleopathology*, and *Papers on Anthropology*, are not currently listed on that website. These are the abbreviations that appear in the figures used in Chapter 3. Other abbreviations used in the text (*AJPA*, *JAS*, and *IJOA*) are more 'colloquial' names for some journals.

American Journal of Physical Anthropology	*Am J Phys Anthropol*
Journal of Archaeological Science	*J Archaeol Sci*
Yearbook of Mummy Studies	*Yearb Mum S*
Anatomical Record	*Anat Rec*
Chungará—Revista de Antropologia Chilena	*Chungará*
The Lancet	*Lancet*
International Journal of Osteoarchaeology	*Int J Osteoarchaeol*
PLoS ONE	*PLoS ONE*
Journal of Human Evolution	*J Hum Evol*
Journal of Parasitology	*J Parasitol*
Forensic Science International	*Forensic Sci Int*
American Journal of Roentgenology	*Am J Roentgenol*
Medicina nei Secoli	*Med Secoli*
Anthropologischer Anzeiger	*Anthropol Anz*
Bulletin of the New York Academy of Medicine	*B New York Acad Med*
Canadian Medical Association Journal	*Can Med Assoc J*
Journal of Paleopathology	*J Paleopath*
Science	*Science*
Papers on Anthropology	*Papers Anth*
Antiquity	*Antiquity*
Journal of Egyptian Archaeology	*J Egypt Archaeol*
Memórias do Instituto Oswaldo Cruz	*Mem I Oswaldo Cruz*

BIBLIOGRAPHY

[AAPA].2003. *Code of Ethics of the American Association of Physical Anthropologists.*http://physanth. org/about/position-statements/; Accessed January 23, 2015.

Aboelsoud N. 2010. Herbal Medicine in Ancient Egypt. *Journal of Medicinal Plants Research* 4:82–86.

Adams JE, and Alsop CW. 2008. Imaging in Egyptian Mummies. In: David R, editor. *Egyptian Mummies and Modern Science.* Cambridge: Cambridge University Press. pp. 21–42.

Ahrenholt-Bindslev D, Josephsen K, and Jurik AG. 2007. Grauballe Man's Teeth and Jaws. In: Asingh P and Lynnerup N, editors. *Grauballe Man: An Iron Age Bog Body Revisited. Aarhus.* Aarhus, Denmark: Aarhus University Press. pp. 140–153.

Alfonso MP, and Powell JF. 2007. Ethics of Flesh and Bone, or Ethics in the Practice of Paleopathology, Osteology, and Bioarchaeology. In: Cassman V, Odegaard N, and Powell JF, editors. *Human Remains: Guide for Museums and Academic Institutions.* Lanham, MD: AltaMira Press. pp. 5–19.

Allam AH, Mandour Ali MA, Wann LS, Thompson RC, Sutherland ML, Sutherland JD, Frohlich B, Michalik DE, Zink A, Lombardi GP, Watson L, Cox SL, Finch CE, Miyamoto MI, Sallam SL, Narula J, and Thomas GS. 2014. Atherosclerosis in Ancient and Modern Egyptians: The Horus Study. *Global Heart* 9(2):197–202.

Allam AH, Nureldin A, Adelmaksoub G, Badr I, Amer HA, Soliman MA-T, Thomas GS, Thompson RC, Miyamoto MI, and Thomas IG. 2010. Something Old, Something New—Computed Tomography Studies of the Cardiovascular System in Ancient Egyptian Mummies. *The American Heart Hospital Journal* 20:10–13.

Allam AH, Thompson RC, Wann LS, Miyamoto MI, Nur el-Din A el-H, el-Maksoud GA, Al-Tohamy Soliman M, Badr I, el-Rahman Amer HA, Sutherland ML, Sutherland JD, and Thomas GS. 2011. Atherosclerosis in Ancient Egyptian Mummies: The Horus Study. *JACC: Cardiovascular Imaging* 4(4):315–327.

Allam AH, Thompson RC, Wann LS, Miyamoto MI, and Thomas GS. 2009. Computed Tomographic Assessment of Atherosclerosis in Ancient Egyptian Mummies. *Journal of the American Medical Association* 302:2091–2094.

Allison MJ, Focacci G, Arriaza B, Standen V, Rivera M, and Lowenstein JM. 1984. Chinchorro, momias de preparación complicada: Métodos de momificación. *Chungara* 13:155–173.

Allison MJ, Gerszten E, Munizaga J, and Santoro C. 1980. Metastatic Tumor of Bone in a Tiahuanaco Female. *Bulletin of the New York Academy of Medicine* 56(6):581.

Allison MJ, Hossaini AA, Castro N, Munizaga J, and Pezzia A. 1976. ABO Blood Groups in Peruvian Mummies. I: An Evaluation of Techniques. *American Journal of Physical Anthropology* 44(1):55–61.

Allison MJ, Hossaini AA, Munizaga J, and Fung R. 1978. ABO Blood Groups in Chilean and Peruvian Mummies. II: Results of Agglutination-Inhibition Technique. *American Journal of Physical Anthropology* 49(1):139–142.

Allison MJ, Lindberg L, Santoro C, and Focacci G. 1981. Tatuajes y pintura corporal de los indígenas precolombinos de Peru y Chile. *Chungara* 7:218–236.

Allison MJ, Mendoza D, and Pezzia A. 1973. Documentation of a Case of Tuberculosis in Pre-Columbian America. *The American Review of Respiratory Disease* 107(6):985–991.

Allison MJ, Mendoza D, and Pezzia A. 1974a. A Radiographic Approach to Childhood Illness in Precolumbian Inhabitants of Southern Peru. *American Journal of Physical Anthropology* 40(3):409–415.

Allison MJ, Pezzia A, Gerszten E, and Mendoza D. 1974b. A Case of Carrion's Disease Associated with Human Sacrifice from the Huari Culture of Southern Peru. *American Journal of Physical Anthropology* 41(2):295–300.

Allison MJ, Pezzia A, Hasegawa I, and Gerszten E. 1974c. A Case of Hookworm Infestation in a Precolumbian American. *American Journal of Physical Anthropology* 41(1):103–106.

Alt KW, Burger J, Simons A, Schön W, Grupe G, Hummel S, Grosskopf B, Vach W, Buitrago Téllex C, Fischer C-H, Möller-Wiering S, Shrestha SS, Pichler SL, von den Driesch A. 2003. Climbing into the Past—First Himalayan Mummies Discovered in Nepal. *Journal of Archaeological Science* 30(11):1529–1535.

Alvrus A, Wright D, and Merbs CF. 2001. Examination of Tattoos on Mummified Tissue Using Infra-Red Reflectography. *Journal of Archaeological Science* 28(4):395–400.

Ambrose SH, Buikstra JE, and Krueger HW. 2003. Status and Gender Differences in Diet at Mound 72, Cahokia, Revealed by Isotopic Analysis of Bone. *Journal of Anthropological Archaeology* 22:217–226.

Amenta A, Piombino-Mascali D, and Panzer S. 2013. Vatican Mummy Project: L'indagine paleoradiologica della mummia di Ni-Maat-Ra. *Bollettino dei Monumenti Musei E Gallerire Pontificie* 31:6–22.

American Cancer Society. 2013. *Cancer Facts & Figures.* Atlanta: American Cancer Society

American Cancer Society. 2014. *Cancer Facts & Figures.* Atlanta: American Cancer Society.

Amory S, Keyser C, Crubézy E, and Ludes B. 2007. STR Typing of Ancient DNA Extracted from Hair Shafts of Siberian Mummies. *Forensic Science International* 16:218–229.

Amy R, Bhatnagar R, Damkjar E, and Beattie O. 1986. The Last Franklin Expedition: Report of a Postmortem Examination of a Crew Member. *Canadian Medical Association Journal* 135:115–117.

Anastasiou E, and Mitchell PD. 2013. Palaeopathology and Genes: Investigating the Genetics of Infectious Diseases in Excavated Human Skeletal Remains and Mummies from Past Populations. *Gene* 528:33–40.

Andrushko VA, Torres Pino EC, and Bellifemine V. 2006. The Burials at Sacsahuaman and Chokepukio: A Bioarchaeological Case Study of Imperialism from the Capital of the Inca Empire. *Nawpa Pacha* 28:63–92.

Apostoli P, De Palma G, Catalani S, Bortolotti F, and Tagliaro F. 2009. Multielemental Analysis of Tissues from Cangrande della Scala, Prince of Verona, in the 14th Century. *Journal of Analytical Toxicology* 33(6):322–327.

Appelboom T, and Struyven J. 1999. Medical Imaging of the Peruvian Mummy Rascar Capac. *The Lancet* 354(9196):2153–2155.

Arana-Chavez VE, and Massa LF. 2004. Odontoblasts: The Cells Forming and Maintaining Dentine. *The International Journal of Biochemistry & Cell Biology* 36(8):1367–1373.

Araujo NM, Waizbort R, and Kay A. 2011. Hepatitis B Virus Infection from an Evolutionary Point of View: How Viral, Host, and Environmental Factors Shape Genotypes and Sub-genotypes. *Infection, Genetics and Evolution* 11(6):1199–1207.

Ardren T. 2008. Studies of Gender in the Prehispanic Americas. *Journal of Archaeological Research* 16(1):1–35.

Argarwal SC, and Glencross BA, editors. 2011a. *Social Bioarchaeology.* West Sussex: Wiley-Blackwell.

Argarwal SC, and Glencross BA. 2011b. Building a Social Bioarchaeology. In: Argarwal SC and Glencross BA, editors. *Social Bioarchaeology.* West Sussex: Wiley-Blackwell. pp. 1–11.

Argent G. 2013. Inked: Human-Horse Apprenticeship, Tattoos, and Time in the Pazyryk World. *Soceity and Animals* 21(2):178–193.

Argüello MRH. 2006. New Paleoparasitological Techniques. *Journal of Archaeological Science* 33(3):372–377.

Armelagos GJ. 1994. Review of Human Paleopathology: Current Syntheses and Future Options. *Journal of Field Archaeology* 21(2):239–243.

Armelagos GJ. 2003. Bioarchaeology as Anthropology. *Archeological Papers of the American Anthropological Association* 13(1):27–40.

Armelagos GJ, and Van Gerven DP. 2003. A Century of Skeletal Biology and Paleopathology: Constrasts, Contradictions, and Conflicts. *American Anthropologist* 105(1):53–64.

Arnold B. 2014. Life After Life: Bioarchaeology and Post-Mortem Agency. *Cambridge Archaeological Journal* 24(3):523–529.

Arriaza BT. 1994. Tipología de las momias Chinchorro y evolución de las prácticas de momificación. *Chungara* 26(1):11–24.

Arriaza BT. 1995a. *Beyond Death: The Chinchorro Mummies of Ancient Chile.* Washington, DC: Smithsonian Institution Press.

Arriaza BT. 1995b. Chinchorro Bioarchaeology: Chronology and Mummy Seriation. *Latin American Antiquity* 6:35–55.

Arriaza BT. 2005. Arseniasis as an Environmental Hypothetical Explanation for the Origin of the Oldest Artificial Mummification Practice in the World. *Chungara* 37:255–260.

Arriaza BT, Allison M, and Standen V. 1984. Líneas de Harrris en una población Arcaica tardía del extremo norte de Chile: Morro-1. *Chungara* 13:187–193.

Arriaza BT, Allison M, Standen V, Focaccia G, and Chacama R J. 1986. Peinados precolombinos en momias de Arica. *Chungara* 16–17:353–375.

Arriaza BT, Amarasiriwardena D, Cornejo L, Standen V, Byrne S, Bartkus L, and Bandak B. 2010. Exploring Chronic Arsenic Poisoning in Pre-Columbian Chilean Mummies. *Journal of Archaeological Science* 37(6):1274–1278.

Arriaza BT, Cartmell LL, Moragas C, Nerlich AG, Salo W, Madden M, and Aufderheide AC. 2008. The Bioarchaeological Value of Human Mummies Without Provenience. *Chungará (Arica)* 40(1):55–65.

Arriaza BT, Doubrava M, Standen VG, and Haas H. 2005. Differential Mortuary Treatment Among the Andean Chinchorro Fishers: Social Inequalities or in Situ Regional Cultural Evolution. *Current Anthropology* 46:662–671.

Arriaza BT, Orellana NC, Barbosa HS, Menna-Barreto RFS, Araujos A, and Standen V. 2012. Severe Head Lice Infestation in an Andean Mummy in Arica, Chile. *Journal of Parasitology* 98(2):433–436.

Arriaza BT, Salo W, Aufderheide AC, and Holcomb TA. 1995. Pre-Columbian Tuberculosis in Northern Chile: Molecular and Skeletal Evidence. *American Journal of Physical Anthropology* 98:37–45.

Arriaza BT, Standen V, Nuñez H, and Reinhard K. 2013. Study of Archaeological Nits/Eggs of *Pediculus Humanus Capitis* by Scanning Electron Microscopy. *Micron* 45:145–149.

Arriaza BT, Standen V, Reinhard K, Araújo A, Heukelbach J, and Dittmar K. 2013. On Head Lice and Social Interaction in Archaic Andean Coastal Populations. *International Journal of Paleopathology* 3(4):257–268.

Ashworth JT, Allison MJ, Gerszten E, and Pezzia A. 1976. The Pubic Scars of Gestation and Parturition in a Group of Pre-Columbian and Colonial Peruvian Mummies. *American Journal of Physical Anthropology* 45(1):85–89.

Asingh P, and Lynnerup N, editors. 2007. *Grauballe Man: An Iron Age Bog Body Revisited.* Aarhus, Denmark: Aarhus University Press.

Aspöck H, Auer H, and Picher O. 1996. Trichuris trichiura Eggs in the Neolithic Glacier Mummy from the Alps. *Parasitology Today* 12(7):255–256.

Aufderheide AC. 1981. Soft Tissue Paleopathology—An Emerging Subspecialty. *Human Pathology* 12(10):865–867.

Aufderheide AC. 2000. Progress in Soft Tissue Paleopathology. *Journal of the American Medical Association* 284(20):2571–2573.

Aufderheide AC. 2003. *The Scientific Study of Mummies.* Cambridge: Cambridge University Press.

Aufderheide AC. editor. 2009. *Overmodeled Skulls.* Duluth, MN: Heide Press, LLC.

Aufderheide AC. 2011. Soft Tissue Taphonomy: A Paleopathology Perspective. *International Journal of Paleopathology* 1:75–80.

Aufderheide AC. 2013. A Brief History of Soft Tissue Paleopathology. In: Lozada Cerna MC and O'Donnabhain B, editors. *The Dead Tell Tales: Essays in Honor of Jane E Buikstra.* Los Angeles: Cotsen Institute of Archaeology Press. pp. 130–135.

Aufderheide AC, and Aufderheide ML. 1991. Taphonomy of Spontaneous ("Natural") Mummification with Applications to Mummies of Venzone, Italy. In: Ortner DJ and Aufderheide AC, editors. *Human Paleopathology: Current Syntheses and Future Options.* Washington, DC: Smithsonian Institution Press. pp. 79–86.

Aufderheide AC, Cartmell LW, Zlonis M, and Sheldrick P. 2004a. Mummification Practices at Kellis Site in Egypt's Dakhleh Oasis. *Journal of the Society for the Study of Egyptian Antiquities* 31:63–77.

Aufderheide AC, Kelley MA, Rivera M, Gray L, Tieszen LL, Iversen E, Krouse HR, and Carevic A. 1994. Contributions of Chemical Dietary Reconstruction to the Assessment of Adaptation by Ancient Highland Immigrants (Alto Ramirez) to Coastal Conditions at Pisagua, North Chile. *Journal of Archaeological Science* 21:515–524.

Aufderheide AC, Munoz I, and Arriaza BT. 1993. Seven Chinchorro Mummies and the Prehistory of Northern Chile. *American Journal of Physical Anthropology* 91:189–201.

Aufderheide AC, and Rodríguez-Martin C. 1998. *The Cambridge Encyclopedia of Human Paleopathology.* Cambridge: Cambridge University Press.

Aufderheide AC, Salo W, Madden M, Streitz J, Buikstra JE, Guhl F, Arriaza BT, Renier C, Wittmers LE, Fornaciari G, and Allison M. 2004b. A 9,000-Year Record of Chagas' Disease. *Proceedings of the National Academy of Sciences of the United States of America* 101:2034–2039.

Aufderheide AC, Salo W, Madden M, Streitz JM, de la Cruz KD, Buikstra JE, Arriaza BT, and Wittmers LE. 2005. Aspects of Ingestion Transmission of Chagas Disease Identified in Mummies and Their Coprolites. *Chungara Revista de Antropología Chilena* 37(1):85–90.

Aufderheide AC, Zlonis M, Cartmell LL, Zimmerman MR, Sheldrick P, Cook M, and Molto JE. 1999. Human Mummification Practices at Ismant El-Kharab. *The Journal of Egyptian Archaeology* 85:197–210.

Ault KA. 2006. Epidemiology and Natural History of Human Papillomavirus Infections in the Female Genital Tract. *Infectious Diseases in Obstetrics and Gynecology* 2006, Article ID 40470, 5 pages.

Baadsgaard A. 2011. Mortuary Dress as Material Culture: A Case Study from the Royal Cemetery of Ur. In: Baadsgaard A, Boutin AT, and Buikstra JE, editors. *Breathing New Life into the Evidence of Death.* Santa Fe: School for Advanced Research. pp. 179–200.

Baadsgaard A, Boutin AT, and Buikstra JE, editors. 2011. *Breathing New Life into the Evidence of Death.* Santa Fe: School for Advanced Research.

Báez H, Castro MM, Benavente MA, Kintze P, Cirimelee V, Camargo C, and Thomas C. 2000. Drugs in Prehistory: Chemical Analysis of Ancient Human Hair. *Forensic Science International* 108:173–179.

Bahn P. 1994. Do Not Disturb? Archaeology and the Rights of the Dead. *Journal of Applied Philosophy* 1:213–225.

Baker BJ, and Judd MA. 2012. Development of Paleopathology in the Nile Valley. In: Buikstra JE and Roberts CA, editors. *The Global History of Paleopathology: Pioneers and Prospects.* Oxford: Oxford University Press. pp. 209–234.

Balabanova S, Parsche S, and Pirsig W. 1992. First Identification of Drugs in Egyptian Mummies. *Naturwissenschaften* 79(8):358.

Balabanova S, Teschler-Nicola M, and Strouhal E. 1994. Evidence of Nicotine in Scalp Hair of Naturally Mummified Bodies from the Christian Sayala (Egyptian-Nubian). *Anthropologischer Anzeiger* 52(2):167–173.

Bárcena R. 1989. Pigmentos en el Ritual Funerario de la Momia del Cerro Aconcagua. *Xama* 2:61–116.

Barnes I, and Thomas MG. 2006. Evaluating Bacterial Pathogen DNA Preservation in Museum Osteological Collections. *Proceedings of the Royal Society Biological Sciences* 273:645–653.

Barraco RA. 1977. Autopsy of an Egyptian Mummy. 8: Analysis of Protein Extract. *Canadian Medical Association Journal* 117:474.

Barraco RA, Reyman TA, and Cockburn A. 1977. Paleobiochemical Analysis of an Egyptian Mummy. *Journal of Human Evolution* 6:533–546.

Barrett J, and Richards M. 2004. Identity, Gender, Religion and Economy: New Isotope and Radiocarbon Evidence for Marine Resource Intensification in Early Historic Orkney, Scotland, UK. *European Journal of Archaeology* 7:249–271.

Barton A, and Worthington J. 2009. Genetic Susceptibility to Rheumatoid Arthritis: An Emerging Picture. *Arthritis Care & Research* 61(10):1441–1446.

Bastien JW. 1995. The Mountain/Body Metaphor Expressed in a Kaatan Funeral. In: Dillehay TD, editor. *Tombs for the Living: Andean Mortuary Practices.* Washington, DC: Dumbarton Oaks Research Library and Collection. pp. 355–378.

Bauer BS, and Rodríguez AC. 2007. The Hospital of San Andrés (Lima, Peru) and the Search for the Royal Mummies of The Incas. *Fieldiana Anthropology* 39:1–31.

Beck LA. 2006. Kidder, Hooton, Pecos, and the Birth of Bioarchaeology. In: Buikstra JE and Beck LA, editors. *Bioarchaeology: The Contextual Analysis of Human Remains.* Burlington, MA: Elsevier. pp. 83–94.

Beckett RG. 2015. Application and Limitations of Endoscopy in Anthropological and Archaeological Research. *The Anatomical Record* 298(6):1125–1134.

Beckett RG, and Conlogue GJ. 2010. *Paleoimaging: Field Applications for Cultural Remains and Artifacts.* Boca Raton: CRC Press.

Beckett RG, Lohmann U, and Bernstein J. 2011a. A Field Report on the Mummification Practices of the Anga of Koke Village. *Yearbook of Mummy Studies* 1:11–17.

Beckett RG, Lohmann U, and Bernstein J. 2011b. A Unique Field Mummy Conservation Project in Papua New Guinea. *Yearbook of Mummy Studies* 1:19–26.

Behbehani AM. 1983. The Smallpox Story: Life and Death of an Old Disease. *Microbiological Reviews* 47(4):455–509.

Belén Dazio M, Santos DM, Abramzon F, Lesyk S, and Pucciarelli HM. 2014. A Late-Period Mummy from an Egyptian Non-Elite Cemetery, Curated in Buenos Aires: 3D-Volumetric Study. *Yearbook of Mummy Studies* 2:71–76.

Bellard FG, and Cortés JLA. 1991. A Muscular Parasite in a Mummified Girl. *International Journal of Osteoarchaeology* 1(3–4):215–218.

Bereuter TL, Mikenda W, and Reiter C. 1997. Iceman's Mummification-Implications from Infrared Spectroscopical and Histological Studies. *Chemistry: A European Journal* 3(7):1032–1038.

Bernschneider-Reif S, Alt KW, Meier S, Rühli F, and Rosendahl W. 2010. Egyptian Mummies—The Merck Archives in Darmstadt. In: Wieczorek A and Rosendahl W, editors. *Mummies of the World*. New York: Prestel. pp. 319–321.

Bertrand L, Doucet J, Dumas P, Simionovici A, Tsoucaris G, and Walter P. 2003. Microbeam Synchrotron Imaging of Hairs from Ancient Egyptian Mummies. *Journal of Synchrotron Radiation* 10(5):387–392.

Bertrand L, Vichi A, Doucet J, Walter P, and Blanchard P. 2014. The Fate of Archaeological Keratin Fibres in a Temperate Burial Context: Microtaphonomy Study of Hairs from Marie de Bretagne (15th c., Orléans, France). *Journal of Archaeological Science* 42:487–499.

Besom T. 2010. Inka Sand the Mummy of Salinas Grandes. *Latin American Antiquity* 21(4):399–422.

Besom T. 2013. *Inka Human Sacrifice and Mountain Worship: Strategies for Empire Unification*. Albuquerque: University of New Mexico Press.

Biagini P, Thèves C, Balaresque P, Géraut A, Keyser C, Nikolaeva D, Gérard P, Duchesne S, Orlando L, Willerslev E et al. 2012. Variola Virus in a 300-Year-Old Siberian Mummy. *The New England Journal of Medicine* 367(21):2057–2059.

Bianchi RS. 1988. Tattoo in Ancient Egypt. In: Rubin A, editor. *Marks of Civilization: Artistic Transformations of the Human Body*. Los Angeles: Museum of Cultural History, University of California. pp. 21–28.

Bianucci R, Jeziorska M, Lallo R, Mattutino G, Massimelli M, Phillips G, and Appenzeller O. 2008. A Pre-Hispanic Head. *PLoS One* 3(4):e2053.

Bianucci R, Mattutino G, Lallo R, Charlier P, Jouin-Spriet Hln, Peluso A, Higham T, Torre C, and Rabino Massa E. 2008. Immunological Evidence of *Plasmodium Falciparum* Infection in an Egyptian Child Mummy from the Early Dynastic Period. *Journal of Archaeological Science* 35(7):1880–1885.

Binford LR. 1962. Archaeology as Anthropology. *American Antiquity* 28(2):217–225.

Binford LR. 1971. Mortuary Practices: Their Study and Their Potential. *Memoirs of the Society for American Archaeology* 25:6–29.

Bird J. 1979. The "Copper Man": A Prehistoric Miner and His Tools from Northern Chile. In: Benson E, editor. *Pre-Columbian Metallurgy of South America*. Washington, DC: Dumbarton Oaks Research Library and Collections. pp. 106–131.

Blakely RL. 1977. Introduction: Changing Strategies for the Biological Anthropologist. In: Blakely RL, editor. *Biocultural Adaptation in Prehistoric America*. Athens, GA: University of Georgia Press. pp. 1–9.

Bloch M, and Parry J, editors. 1982. *Death and the Regeneration of Life*. Cambridge: Cambridge University Press.

Blom DE. 2005. Embodying Borders: Human Body Modification and Diversity in Tiwan-aku Society. *Journal of Anthropological Archaeology* 24:1–24.

Bloomfield JA. 1985. Radiology of Egyptian Mummy. *Australasian Radiology* 29:64–66.

Boano R, Fulcheri E, Martina MC, Ferraris A, Grilletto R, Cremo R, Cesarani F, Giovanni G, and Massa ER. 2009. Neural Tube Defect in a 4000-Year-Old Egyptian Infant Mummy: A Case of Meningocele from the Museum of Anthropology and Ethnography of Turin (Italy). *European Journal of Paediatric Neurology* 13:481–487.

Boel LW, and Dalstra M. 2007. Microscopical Analyses of Bone Specimens: Structural Changes Related to Chronological Age and Possible Diseases. In: Asingh P and Lynnerup N, editors. *Grauballe Man: An Iron Age Bog Body Revisited.* Aarhus, Denmark: Aarhus University Press. pp. 130–139.

Bos KI, Harkins KM, Herbig A, Coscolla M, Weber N, Comas I, Forrest SA, Bryant JM, Harris SR, and Schuenemann VJ. 2014. Pre-Columbian Mycobacterial Genomes Reveal Seals as a Source of New World Human Tuberculosis. *Nature* 514(7523):494–497.

Bou C, Pomar P, Pessey JJ, and Rabino-Massa E. 1998. Three-Dimensional Facial Reconstruction of Computerized Tomography Images by Computer-Aided Design: Example of an Anthropologic Study. *Revue de Laryngologie Otologie Rhinologie* 119:333–335.

Bourke JB. 1986. The Medical Investigation of Lindow Man. In: Stead M, Bourke JB, and Brothwell D, editors. *Lindow Man: The Body in the Bog.* London: British Museum. pp. 46–51.

Boutin AT. 2012. Crafting a Bioarchaeology of Personhood: Osteobiographical Narratives from Alalakh. In: Baadsgaard A, Boutin AT, and Buikstra JE, editors. *Breathing New Life into the Evidence of Death.* Santa Fe: School for Advanced Research Press. pp. 109–133.

Bouwman AS, and Brown TA. 2005. The Limits of Biomolecular Palaeopathology: Ancient DNA Cannot Be Used to Study Venereal Syphilis. *Journal of Archaeological Science* 32(5):703–713.

Bower NW, McCants SA, Custodio JM, Ketterer ME, Getty SR, and Hoffman JM. 2007. Human Lead Exposure in a Late 19th Century Mental Asylum Population. *Science of the Total Environment* 372:463–473.

Boyd LG, and Boyd WC. 1939. Blood Group Reactions of Preserved Bone and Muscle. *American Journal of Physical Anthropology* 25(3):421–434.

Boyer RS, Rodin EA, Grey TC, and Connolly RC. 2003. The Skull and Cervical Spine Radiographs of Tutankhamen: A Critical Appraisal. *American Journal of Neuroradiology* 24:1142–1147.

Böni T, Rühli FJ, and Chhem RK. 2004. History of Paleoradiology: Early Published Literature, 1896–1921. *Canadian Association of Radiologists Journal* 55(4):203–210.

Brenner E. 2014. Human Body Preservation—Old and New Techniques. *Journal of Anatomy* 224(3):316–344.

Brier B, and Wade R. 1997. The Use of Natron in Human Mummification: A Modern Experiment. *Z Ägypt Sprache Altertumskunde* 124:89–100.

Brosch R, Gordon SV, Marmiesse M, Brodin P, Buchrieser C, Eiglmeier K, Garnier T, Gutierez C, Hewinson G, and Kremer K. 2002. A New Evolutionary Scenario for the *Mycobacterium Tuberculosis* Complex. *Proceedings of the National Academy of Sciences* 99(6):3684–3689.

Brothwell DR, and Sandison AT. 1967. *Diseases in Antiquity.* Springfield: Thomas.

Brown JA, editor. 1971a. *Approaches to the Social Dimensions of Mortuary Practices.* Washington, DC: Memoirs of the Society for American Archaeology, 25.

Brown JA. 1971b. The Dimensions of Status in the Burials at Spiro. In: Brown JA, editor. *Approaches to the Social Dimensions of Mortuary Practices.* Washington, DC: Memoirs of the Society for American Archaeology, 25. pp. 92–112.

Buckland PC, and Panagiotakopulu E. 2001. Rameses II and the Tobacco Beetle. *Antiquity* 75:549–556.

Buckley SA, Stott AW, and Evershed RP. 1999. Studies of Organic Residues from Ancient Egyptian Mummies Using High Temperature-Gas Chromatography-Mass Spectrometry and Sequential Thermal Desorption-Gas Chromatography-Mass Spectrometry and Pyrolysis-Gas Chromatography-Mass Spectrometry. *Analyst* 124(4):443–452.

Buikstra JE. 1977. Biocultural Dimensions of Archaeological Study: A Regional Perspective. In: Blakely RL, editor. *Biocultural Adaptation in Prehistoric America*. Athens, GA: University of Georgia Press. pp. 67–84.

Buikstra JE. 1995. Tombs for the Living . . . or . . . for the Dead: The Osmore Ancestors. In: Dillehay TD, editor. *Tombs for the Living: Andean Mortuary Practices*. Washington, DC: Dumbarton Oaks Research Library and Collection. pp. 229–280.

Buikstra JE. 2006a. A Historical Introduction. In: Buikstra JE and Beck LA, editors. *Bioarchaeology: The Contextual Analysis of Human Remains*. Burlington, MA: Elsevier. pp. 7–25.

Buikstra JE. 2006b. On to the 21st Century. In: Buikstra JE and Beck LA, editors. *Bioarchaeology: The Contextual Analysis of Human Remains*. Burlington, MA: Elsevier. pp. 347–357.

Buikstra JE. 2016. Ethical Issues in Biohistory: NO Easy Answers! In: Stojanowski CM and Duncan WN, editors. *Studies in Forensic Biohistory: Anthropological Perspectives*. Cambridge: Cambridge University Press. pp. 288–314.

Buikstra JE, Baadsgaard A, and Boutin AT. 2011. Introduction. In: Baadsgaard A, Boutin AT, and Buikstra JE, editors. *Breathing New Life into the Evidence of Death*. Santa Fe: School for Advanced Research Press. pp. 3–26.

Buikstra JE, and Beck LA, editors. 2006. *Bioarchaeology: The Contextual Analysis of Human Remains*. Burlington, MA: Elsevier.

Buikstra JE, and Cook DC. 1980. Palaeopathology: An American Account. *Annual Review of Anthropology* 9:433–470.

Buikstra JE, and Nystrom KC. 2003. Embodied Traditions: The Chachapoya and Inca Ancestors. In: Jeske RJ and Charles DK, editors. *Theory, Method, and Practice in Modern Archaeology*. Westport, CT: Praeger Publishers. pp. 29–48.

Buikstra JE, and Nystrom KC. 2015. Ancestors and Social Memory: A South American Example of Dead Body Politics. In: Shimada I and Fitzsimmons J, editors. *Between the Dead and the Living: Cross-Disciplinary and Diachronic Visions*. Tucson: University of Arizona Press. pp. 245–266.

Buikstra JE, and Roberts CA, editors. 2012. *The Global History of Paleopathology: Pioneers and Prospects*. Oxford: Oxford University Press.

Buikstra JE, and Scott RE. 2009. Key Concepts in Identity Studies. In: Knudson KJ and Stojanowski CM, editors. *Bioarchaeology and Identity in the Americas*. Gainesville: University Press of Florida. pp. 24–55.

Buikstra JE, Tomczak PD, Lozada MC, and Rakita GFM. 2005. Chiribaya Political Economy: A Bioarchaeological Perspective. In: Rakita GFM, Buikstra JE, Beck LA, and Williams SR, editors. *Interacting with the Dead: Perspectives on Mortuary Archaeology for the New Millennium*. Gainesville: University Press of Florida. pp. 66–80.

Buikstra JE, and Ubelaker DH. 1994. *Standards for Data Collection from Human Skeletal Remains*. Fayetteville: Arkansas Archaeological Survey.

Buikstra JE, and Williams S. 1991. Tuberculosis in the Americas: Current Perspectives. In: Ortner DJ, and Aufderheide AC, editors. *Human Paleopathology, Current Syntheses and Future Options*. Washington, DC: Smithsonian Institution Press. pp. 161–172.

Buzon MR. 2012. The Bioarchaeological Approach to Paleopathology. In: Grauer AL, editor. *A Companion to Paleopathology*. West Sussex: Wiley-Blackwell. pp. 58–75.

Buzon MR, and Richman R. 2007. Traumatic Injuries and Imperialism: The Effects of Egyptian Colonial Strategies at Tombos in Upper Nubia. *American Journal of Physical Anthropology* 133:783–791.

Byrne S, Amarasiriwardena D, Bandak B, Bartkus L, Kane J, Jones J, Yanez J, Arriaza B, and Cornejo L. 2010. Were Chinchorros Exposed to Arsenic? Arsenic Determination in Chinchorro Mummies' Hair by Laser Ablation Inductively Coupled Plasma-Mass Spectrometry (LA-ICP-MS). *Microchemical Journal* 94(1):28–35.

Bzhalava D, Guan P, Franceschi S, Dillner J, and Clifford G. 2013. A Systematic Review of the Prevalence of Mucosal and Cutaneous Human Papillomavirus Types. *Virology* 445(1–2):224–231.

Cagigao ET, Peters A, Lund M, and Ayarza A. 2013. Body Modification at Paracas Necropolis, South Coast of Peru, ca. 2000 BP. In: Della Casa P and Witt C, editors. *Tattoos and Body Modification in Antiquity: Proceedings of the Sessions at the Annual Meetings of the European Association of Archaeologists in the Hague and Oslo, 2010/11*. Zurich Studies in Archaeology 9. Chronos-Verlag, Zurich. pp. 49–58.

Callister LC. 2003. Cultural Influences on Pain Perceptions and Behaviors. *Home Health Care Management & Practice* 15(3):207–211.

Campbell JM. 2008. Pharmacy in Ancient Egypt. In: David AR, editor. *Egytpian Mummies and Modern Science*. Cambridge: Cambridge University Press. pp. 216–233.

Candela PB. 1939a. Blood-Group Determinations Upon the Bones of Thirty Aleutian Mummies. *American Journal of Physical Anthropology* 24(3):361–383.

Candela PB. 1939b. Blood-Group Tests on Stains, Mummified Tissues, and Cancellous Bone. *American Journal of Physical Anthropology* 25(2):187–214.

Candela PB. 1943. Blood Group Tests on Tissues of Paracas Mummies. *American Journal of Physical Anthropology* 1(1):65–67.

Cano RJ, Tiefenbrunner F, Ubaldi M, Cueto CD, Luciani S, Cox T, Orkand P, Künzel KH, and Rollo F. 2000. Sequence Analysis of Bacterial DNA in the Colon and Stomach of the Tyrolean Iceman. *American Journal of Physical Anthropology* 112:297–309.

Capasso L. 1993. A Preliminary Report on the Tattoos of the Val Senales Mummy (Tyrol, Neolithic). *Journal of Paleopathology* 5:173–182.

Capasso L. 1994. Ungueal Morphology and Pathology of the Human Mummy Found in the Val Senales (Eastern Alps, Tyrol, Bronze-Age). *Munibe Ciencias Naturales* 46:123–132.

Capasso L. 1998. 5300 Years Ago, the Ice Man Used Natural Laxatives and Antibiotics. *The Lancet* 352(9143):1864.

Capasso L, Caramiello S, and D'Anastasio R. 1999. The Anomaly of Santa Rosa. *The Lancet* 353(9151):504.

Capasso L, Sciubba M, Hua Q, Levchenko VA, Viciano J, D'Anastasio R, and Bertuch F. 2016. Embryotomy in the 19th Century of Central Italy. *International Journal of Osteoarchaeology* 26(2):345–347.

Carancini GL, and Mattioli T. 2011. 'The Iceman is a burial': New Remarks. *Antiquity* 85. www.antiquity.ac.uk/projgall/carancini327/.

Carlton R, and Adler A. 2012. *Principles of Radiographic Imaging: An Art and a Science*. Clifton Park, NY: Delmar/Cengage Learning.

Carminati P, Begerock A-M, and Gill-Frerking H. 2014. Surface Treatment of Mummies: Mummification, Conservation, or Beautification. *Yearbook of Mummy Studies* 2:159–166.

Carod-Artal FJ, and Vázquez-Cabrera CB. 2006. Myelomeningocele in a Peruvian Mummy from the Moche Period. *Neurology* 66(11):1775–1776.

Carter DO, Yellowlees D, and Tibbett M. 2007. Cadaver Decomposition in Terrestrial Ecosystems. *Naturwissenschaften* 94:12–24.

Cartmell LW, Aufderheide AC, Capara D, Klein J, and Koren G. 2005. What Were They Drinking? A Preliminary Study of Alcohol Metabolites in Andean Mummy Hair. *Journal of Biological Research* 80:114–116.

Cartmell L, Aufderheide AC, Lorentz E, Wittmers J, and Weems C. 2001. The Predictive Value of Cocaine Hair/Visceral Tissue Ratios in Andean Mummies—A Pilot Study. *Proceedings of the Fourth World Congress on Mummy Studies* Nuuk, Greenland 79–81.

Cartmell LW, Aufderheide AC, Springfield AC, Buikstra J, Arriaza B, and Weems C. 1994. Analisis Radio-Inmunológico de cocaina en cabello de momias del sur de peru y norte de chile. *Chungara* 26:125–136.

Cartmell LW, Aufderheide AC, Springfield A, Weems C, and Arriaza B. 1991a. The Frequency and Antiquity of Prehistoric Coca-Leaf-Chewing Practices in Northern Chile: Radio-immunoassay of a Cocaine Metabolite in Human-Mummy Hair. *Latin American Antiquity* 2:260–268.

Cartmell LW, Aufderheide AC, and Weems C. 1991b. Cocaine Metabolites in Pre-Columbian Mummy Hair. *Journal of the Oklahoma State Medical Association* 84:11–12.

Castilla Ramirez GA. 2014. Funeral Traditions, Premature Burials and Mummification. *Yearbook of Mummy Studies* 2:133–142.

Castillo-Rojas G, Cerbon MA, and Lopez-Vidal Y. 2008. Presence of *Helicobacter pylori* in a Mexican Pre-Columbian Mummy. *BMC Microbiology* 8:119.

Ceruti MC. 2004. Human Bodies as Objects of Dedication at Inca Mountain Shrines (North-Western Argentina). *World Archaeology* 36(1):103–122.

Ceruti MC. 2015. Frozen Mummies from Andean Mountaintop Shrines: Bioarchaeology and Ethnohistory of Inca Human Sacrifice. *BioMed Research International* 2015:12.

Cervini-Silva J, Palacios E, de Lourdes Muñoz M, del Angel P, Mejía-Pérez Campos E, Chávez-Balderas X, and Herrera A. 2013. A High-Resolution Electron Microscopic and Energy-Dispersive Spectroscopic Study on the Molecular Mechanism Underpinning the Natural Preservation of 2300 Y.O. Naturally-Mummified Human Remains and the Occurrence of Small-Sized [Zn][Al]Carbon Spheres. *Journal of Archaeological Science* 40(4):1966–1974.

Cesarani F, Martina MC, Grilletto R, Boano R, Donadoni Roveri AM, Capussotto V, Giuliano A, Celia M, and Gandini G. 2004. Facial Reconstruction of a Wrapped Egyptian Mummy Using MDCT. *American Journal of Roentgenology* 183:755–758.

Chan JZ-M, Sergeant MJ, Lee OY-C, Minnikin DE, Besra GS, Pap I, Spigelman M, Donoghue HD, and Pallen MJ. 2013. Metagenomic Analysis of Tuberculosis in a Mummy. *New England Journal of Medicine* 369(3):289–290.

Chan S, Ho L, Ong C-K, Chow V, Drescher B, Dürst M, Ter Meulen J, Villa L, Luande J, and Mgaya H. 1992. Molecular Variants of Human Papillomavirus Type 16 from Four Continents Suggest Ancient Pandemic Spread of the Virus and Its Coevolution with Humankind. *Journal of Virology* 66(4):2057–2066.

Chang BS, Uhm CS, Park CH, Kim HK, Jung HS, Ham JH, Lee GY, Kim DH, Lee KJ, Bang IS et al. 2008. Ultramicroscopic Investigation of the Preservation Status of Hair Collected from a Full-Term, Intrauterine Baby Mummy of the Joseon Dynasty, Korea. *International Journal of Osteoarchaeology* 18(6):624–631.

Chang BS, Uhm CS, Park CH, Kim HK, Lee GY, Cho HH, Kim MJ, Chung YH, Song KW, Lim DS et al. 2006. Preserved Skin Structure of a Recently Found Fifteenth-Century Mummy in Daejeon, Korea. *Journal of Anatomy* 209:671–680.

Chapman J. 2000. *Fragmentation in Archaeology: People, Places and Broken Objects in the Prehistory of South Eastern Europe*. London: Routledge.

Chapman R, Kinnes I, and Randsborg K, editors. 1981. *The Archaeology of Death*. Cambridge: Cambridge University Press.

Charles DK, and Buikstra JE. 1983. Archaic Mortuary Sites in Central Mississippi Drainage: Distribution, Structure, and Behavioral Implications. In: Phillips JL and Brown JA, editors. *Archaic Hunters and Gatherers in the American Midwest*. New York: Academic Press. pp. 117–145.

Charlier P, and Huynh I. 2010. Assessment of Atherosclerosis in Egyptian Mummies. *JAMA* 303(12):1149–1150.

Charlier P, Poupon J, Jeannel G-F, Favier D, Popescu S-M, Weil R, Moulherat C, Huynh-Charlier I, Dorion-Peyronnet C, and Lazar A-M. 2013. The Embalmed Heart of Richard the Lionheart (1199 AD): A Biological and Anthropological Analysis. *Scientific Reports* 3.

Charrie-Duhaut A, Connan J, Rouquette N, Adam P, Barbotin C, de Rozie'res M-F, Tchapla A, and Albrecht P. 2007. The Canopic Jars of Rameses II: Real Use Revealed by Molecular Study of Organic Residues. *Journal of Archaeological Science* 34(6):957–967.

Cheng TO. 2012. Coronary Arteriosclerotic Disease Existed in China over 2,200 Years Ago. *Methodist DeBakey Cardiovascular Journal* 8(2):47–48.

Cheremisin D. 2007. The Meaning of Representations in the Animal Style and Their Relevance for the Reconstruction of Pazyryk Ideology. *Archaeology, Ethnology and Anthropology of Eurasia* 31(1):87–102.

Chhem RK, and Brothwell DR. 2010. *Paleoradiology: Imaging Mummies and Fossils*. Berlin, Germany. Springer-Verlag.

Chhem RK, Schmit P, and Fauré C. 2004. Did Ramesses II Really Have Ankylosing Spondylitis? A Reappraisal. *Canadian Association of Radiologists Journal* 55(4):211–217.

Ciranni R, Garbini F, Neri E, Melai L, Giusti L, and Fornaciari G. 2002. The "Braids Lady" of Arezzo: A Case of Rheumatoid Arthritis in a 16th Century Mummy. *Clinical and Experimental Rheumatology* 20:745–752.

Ciranni R, Giusti L, and Fornaciari G. 2000. Prostatic Hyperplasia in the Mummy of an Italian Renaissance Prince. *The Prostate* 45(4):320–322.

Clark JGD. 1972. *Starr Carr: A Case Study in Bioarchaeology, Modular Publications, 10*. London: Addison-Wesley.

Clarke EM, Thompson RC, Allam AH, Wann LS, Lombardi GP, Sutherland ML, Sutherland JD, Cox SL, Soliman MA-T, Abd el-Maksoud G, Badr I, Miyamoto MI, Frohlich B, Nur el-din AH, Stewart AFR, Narula J, Zink AR, Finch CE, Michalik DE, and Thomas GS. 2014. Is Atherosclerosis Fundamental to Human Aging? Lessons from Ancient Mummies. *Journal of Cardiology* 63(5):329–334.

Cockburn A, Barraco RA, Reyman TA, and Peck WH. 1975. Autopsy of an Egyptian Mummy. *Science* 187(4182):1155–1160.

Cohen MN, and Armelagos GJ, editors. 1984. *Paleopathology at the Origins of Agriculture*. Orlando, FL: Academic Press.

Conlogue G. 1999. Low Kilovoltage, Nonscreen Mummy Radiography. *Radiologic Technology* 71(2):125–132.

Conlogue G. 2015. Considered Limitations and Possible Applications of Computed Tomography in Mummy Research. *The Anatomical Record* 298(6):1088–1098.

Connolly RC, Harrison RG, and Ahmed S. 1976. Serological Evidence for the Parentage of Tut'ankhamun and Smenkhkare. *The Journal of Egyptian Archaeology* 62:184–186.

Contis G, and David A. 1996. The Epidemiology of Bilharzia in Ancient Egypt: 5000 Years of Schistosomiasis. *Parasitology Today* 12(7):253–255.

Corr LT, Richards MP, Jim S, Ambrose SH, Mackie A, Beattie O, and Evershed RP. 2008. Probing Dietary Change of the Kwäday Dän Ts'ìnchí Individual, an Ancient Glacier Body from British Columbia: I. Complementary Use of Marine Lipid Biomarker and Carbon Isotope Signatures as Novel Indicators of a Marine Diet. *Journal of Archaeological Science* 35(8):2102–2110.

Corthals A, Koller A, Martin DW, Rieger R, Chen EI, Bernaski M, Recagno G, and Dávalos LM. 2012. Detecting the Immune System Response of a 500 Year-Old Inca Mummy. *PLoS One* 7(7):e41244. doi:41210.41371/journal.pone.0041244.

Counsell DJ. 2008. Intoxicants in Ancient Egypt? Opium, Nymphaea, Coca and Tobacco. In: David AR, editor. *Egytpian Mummies and Modern Science*. Cambridge: Cambridge University Press. pp. 195–215.

Coulthart MB, Posada D, Crandall KA, and Dekaban GA. 2006. On the Phylogenetic Placement of Human T Cell Leukemia Virus Type 1 Sequences Associated with an Andean Mummy. *Infection, Genetics and Evolution* 6(2):91–96.

Cox SL. 2015. A Critical Look at Mummy CT Scanning. *The Anatomical Record* 298(6):1099–1110.

Crandall JJ, and Martin DL. 2014. The Bioarchaeology of Postmortem Agency: Integrating Archaeological Theory with Human Skeletal Remains. *Cambridge Archaeological Journal* 24(3):429–435.

Crubézy E, Amor S, Keyser C, Bouakaze C, Bodner M, Gilbert M, Röck A, Parson W, Alexeev A, and Ludes B. 2010. Human Evolution in Siberia: From Frozen Bodies to Ancient DNA. *BMC Evolutionary Biology* 10:25.

Cuong NL. 1982–84. About the Dead Bodies of Two Buddhist Monks Preserved in the Form of Statues at the Dau Pagoda. *OSSA International Journal of Skeletal Research* 9(11):105–109.

Dabernat H, Thèves C, Bouakaze C, Nikolaeva D, Keyser C, Mokrousov I, Géraut A, Duchesne S, Gérard P, Alexeev AN et al. 2014. Tuberculosis Epidemiology and Selection in an Autochthonous Siberian Population from the 16th—19th Century. *PLOS One* 9(2):e89877.

Dageförde KL, Vennemann M, and Rühli FJ. 2014. Evidence Based Palaeopathology: Meta-Analysis of Pubmed®-Listed Scientific Studies on Pre-Columbian, South American Mummies. *HOMO—Journal of Comparative Human Biology* 65:214–231.

D'Altroy TN, Lorandi AM, Williams VI, Hastorf CA, DeMarrais E, Calderari M, and Hagstrum MB. 2000. Inka Rule in the Northern Calchaquí Valley, Argentina. *Journal of Field Archaeology* 27:1–26.

Dastugue J. 1980. Possibilities, Limits and Prospects in Paleopathology of the Human Skeleton. *Journal of Human Evolution* 9(1):3–8.

Davey J, Birchland Stewart ME, and Drummer OH. 2013. The Value of CT Imaging of Horus in Determining the Method of Mummification and the Sex of the Mummy. *Journal of Medical Imaging and Radiation Oncology* 57:657–662.

Davey J, Craig JGP, and Drummer OH. 2014. Dislodged Teeth in Four Intact Child Mummies from Graeco/Roman Egypt (332 BCE- c. 395 CE)—Child Abuse, Accident or Careless Embalmers? *Papers on Anthropology* 23:18–28.

David AR, editor. 1979. *The Manchester Museum Mummy Project: Multidisciplinary Research on Ancient Egyptian Mummifed Remains*. Manchester: Manchester Museum.

David AR, editor. 1986. *Science in Egyptology*. Manchester: Manchester University Press.

David AR. 2008a. Preface. In: David AR, editor. *Egyptian Mummies and Modern Science*. Cambridge: Cambridge University Press. pp. xix–xxi.

David AR. 2008b. The Background of the Manchester Mummy Project. In: David AR, editor. *Egyptian Mummies and Modern Science*. Cambridge: Cambridge University Press. pp. 3–9.

David AR. 2008c. Egyptian Mummies: An Overview. In: David AR, editor. *Egyptian Mummies and Modern Science*. Cambridge: Cambridge University Press. pp. 10–18.

David AR. 2008d. The Ancient Egyptian Medical System. In: David AR, editor. *Egyptian Mummies and Modern Science*. Cambridge: Cambridge University Press. pp. 181–194.

Day J. 2014. 'Thinking Makes It So': Reflections on the Ethics of Displaying Egyptian Mummies. *Papers on Anthropology* 23:29–44.

Dazio MB, Santos DM, Abramzon F, Lesyk S, and Pucciarelli HM. 2014. A Late-Period Mummy from an Egyptian Non-Elite Cemetery, Curated in Buenos Aires: 3D-Volumetric Study. *Yearbook of Mummy Studies* 2:71–76.

de Boni U, Lenczner MM, and Scott JW. 1977. Autopsy of an Egyptian Mummy. 6. Trichinella spiralic cyst. *Canadian Medical Association Journal* 117:472.

de la Cova C. 2012. Patterns of Trauma and Violence in 19th-Century-Born African American and Euro-American Females. *International Journal of Paleopathology* 2(2):61–68.

Decker SJ, Davy-Jow SL, Ford JM, and Hilbelink DR. 2011. Virtual Determination of Sex: Metric and Nonmetric Traits of the Adult Pelvis from 3D Computed Tomography Models. *Journal of Forensic Sciences* 56(5):1107–1114.

Dedouit F, Geraut A, Baranov V, Ludes B, Rouge D, Telmon N, and Crubezy E. 2010. Virtual and Macroscopical Studies of Mummies-Differences or Complementarity? *Report of a Natural Frozen Siberian Mummy Forensic Science International* 200:e7–e13.

Deelder AM, Miller RL, de Jonge N, and Kerijger FW. 1990. Detection of Schistisome Antigen in Mummies. *The Lancet* 335(8691):724.

Degano I, and Colombini MP. 2009. Multi-Analytical Techniques for the Study of Pre-Columbian Mummies and Related Funerary Materials. *Journal of Archaeological Science* 36(8):1783–1790.

DeLeonardis L, and Lau GF. 2004. Life, Death, and the Ancestors. In: Silverman H, editor. *Andean Archaeology*. Malden, MA: Wiley-Blackwell.

DeWitte SN. 2015. Bioarchaeology and the Ethics of Research Using Human Skeletal Remains. *History Compass* 13(1):10–19.

Di Lullo GA, Sweeney SM, Körkkö J, Ala-Kokko L, and Antonio JDS. 2002. Mapping the Ligand-binding Sites and Disease-associated Mutations on the Most Abundant Protein in the Human, Type I Collagen. *The Journal of Biological Chemistry* 277:4223–4231.

Dickson JH. 2011. *Ancient Ice Mummies*. Gloucestershire: The History Press.

Dickson JH, Hofbauer W, Porley R, Schmidl A, Kofler W, and Oeggl K. 2009. Six Mosses from the Tyrolean Iceman's Alimentary Tract and Their Significance for His Ethnobotany and the Events of His Last Days. *Vegetation History and Archaeobotany* 18:13–22.

Dickson JH, Richards MP, Hebda RJ, Mudie PJ, Beattie O, Ramsay S, Turner NJ, Leighton BJ, Webster JM, Hobischak NR, Anderson GS, Troffe PM, and Wigen RJ. 2004. Kwäday Dän Ts'ìnchí, the First Ancient Body of a Man from a North American Glacier: Reconstructing His Last Days by Intestinal and Biomolecular Analyses. *The Holocene* 14(4):481–486.

Dillehay TD. 1995. Introduction. In: Dillehay TD, editor. *Tombs for the Living: Andean Mortuary Practices*. Washington, DC: Dumbarton Oaks Research Library and Collection. pp. 1–26.

Dillehay TD, Rossen J, Ugent D, Karathanasis A, Vásquez V, and Netherly Patricia J. 2010. Early Holocene Coca Chewing in Northern Peru. *Antiquity* 84(326):939–953.

Donoghue HD, Lee OY-C, Minnikin DE, Besra GS, Taylor JH, and Spigelman M. 2010. Tuberculosis in Dr Granville's Mummy: A Molecular Re-Examination of the Earliest Known Egyptian Mummy to be Scientifically Examined and Given a Medical Diagnosis. *Proceedings of the Royal Society B* 277:51–56.

Donoghue HD, Pap I, Szikossy I, and Spigelman M. 2011. Detection and Characterization of *Mycobacterium Tuberculosis* DNA in 18th Century Hungarians with Pulmonary and Extra-Pulmonary Tuberculosis. *Yearbook of Mummy Studies* 1:51–56.

Dorfer L, Moser M, Bahr F, Spindler K, Egarter-Vigl E, Giullén S, Dohr G, and Kenner T. 1999. A Medical Report from the Stone Age? *The Lancet* 354(9183):1023–1025.

Dorfer L, Moser M, Spindler K, Bahr F, Egarter-Vigl E, and Dohr G. 1998. 5200-Year-Old Acupuncture in Central Europe? *Science* 282(5387):242–243.

Douglas M. 1966. *Purity and Danger: An Analysis of Concepts of Pollution and Taboo.* London: Penguin Press.

Drusini AG, Carrara N, Orefici G, and Bonati MR. 2001. Palaeodemography of the Nasca Valley: Reconstruction of the Human Ecology in the Southern Peruvian Coast. *Homo— Journal of Comparative Human Biology* 52(2):157–172.

Duncan WN, and Schwarz KR. 2014. Partible, Permeable, and Relational Bodies in a Maya Mass Grave. In: Osterholtz AJ, editor. *Commingled and Disarticulated Human Remains: Working Toward Improved Theory, Method, and Data.* New York: Springer. pp. 149–170.

Dupras TL, Wheeler SM, Williams L, and Sheldrick P. 2015. Birth in Ancient Egypt: Timing, Trauma, and Triumph? In: Ikram S, Kaiser J, and Walker R, editors. *Egyptian Bioarchaeology: Humans, Animals, and the Environment.* Leiden: Sidestone Press. pp. 53–65.

Dupras TL, Williams LJ, De Meyer M, Peeters C, Depraetere D, Vanthuyne B, and Willems H. 2010. Evidence of Amputation as Medical Treatment in Ancient Egypt. *International Journal of Osteoarchaeology* 20(4):405–423.

Ebert V, and Patterson TC. 2006. Gender in South American Archaeology. In: Nelson SM, editor. *Handbook of Gender in Archaeology.* London: AltaMira Press. pp. 853–874.

Echeverría J, and Niemeyer HM. 2013. Nicotine in the Hair of Mummies from San Pedro de Atacama (Northern Chile). *Journal of Archaeological Science* 40(10):3561–3568.

Eckert W. 1982. Identification of the remains of John Paul Jones: A look at early methods. *American Journal of Forensic Medicine and Pathology* 3:143–152.

Edwards HGM, Gniadecka M, Petersen S, Hart Hansen JP, Nielsen OF, Christensen DH, and Wulf HC. 2002. NIR-FT Raman Spectroscopy as a Diagnostic Probe for Mummified Skin and Nails. *Vibrational Spectroscopy* 28:3–15.

Ege M, Nerlich A, and Zink A. 2005. Epidemiological Analysis of Tomb Complexes from the Necroopolois of Thebes-West. *Journal of Biological Research* 80:75–77.

Egeland GM, Ponce R, Bloom NS, Knecht R, Loring S, and Middaugh JP. 2009. Hair Methylmercury Level of Mummies of the Aleutian Isalnds, Alaska. *Environmental Research* 109:281–286.

El-Harake WA, Furman MA, Cook B, Nair KS, Kukowski J, and Brodsky IG. 1998. Measurement of Dermal Collagen Synthesis Rate in Vivo in Humans. *American Journal of Physiology-Endocrinology and Metabolism* 274(4):E586–E591.

El Najjar M, Benitez JT, Fry G, Lynn GE, Ortner DJ, Reyman TA, and Small PA. 1980. Autopsies of Two Native American Mummies. *American Journal of Physical Anthropology* 53:197–202.

Elias J, Lupton C, and Klales A. 2014. Assessment of Arm Arrangements of Egyptian Mummies in Life of Recent CT Studies. *Yearbook of Mummy Studies* 2:49–62.

Elliott LM. 2009. Property Rights of Ancient DNA: The Impact of Cultural Importance on the Ownership of Genetic Information. *International Journal of Cultural Property* 16:103–129.

Epstein S. 2004. Bodily Differences and Collective Identities: The Politics of Gender and Race in Biomedical Research in the United States. *Body & Society* 10(2–3):183–203.

Falchetti M, Lupi R, and Ottini L. 2006. Molecular Analysis of a Colorectal Carcinoma from a Mummy of the XVth Century. *Medicina nei Secoli* 18(3):943–951.

Falk E. 2006. Pathogenesis of Atherosclerosis. *Journal of the American College of Cardiology* 47(8s1):C7–C12.

Fay I. 2006. Text, Space and the Evidence of Human Remains in English Late Medieval and Tudor Disease Culture: Some Problems and Possibilities. In: Gowland R and Knüsel CJ, editors. *Social Archaeology of Funerary Remains.* Oxford: Alden Press. pp. 190–208.

Fernandes A, Iñiguez AM, Lima VS, Souza SM, Ferreira LF, Vicente ACP, and Jansen AM. 2008. Pre-Columbian Chagas Disease in Brazil: Trypanosoma cruzi I in the Archaeological Remains of a Human in Peruaçu Valley, Minas Gerais, Brazil. *Memórias do Instituto Oswaldo Cruz* 103(5):514–516.

Fernández J, Panarello HO, and Schobinger J. 1999. The Inka Mummy from Mount Aconcagua: Decoding the Geographic Origin of the "Messenger to the Deities" by Means of Stable Carbon, Nitrogen, and Sulfur Isotope Analysis. *Geoarchaeology* 14:27–46.

Fernicola VC, and Samadelli M. 2011. Humidity- and Temperature-Related Preservation Challenges for the Iceman. *Yearbook of Mummy Studies* 1:159–164.

Ferreira LF, Britto C, Cardoso MA, Fernandes O, Reinhard K, and Araújo A. 2000. Paleoparasitology of Chagas Disease Revealed by Infected Tissues from Chilean Mummies. *Acta Tropica* 75(1):79–84.

Fiedler S, Buegger F, Klaubert B, Zipp K, Dohrmann R, Witteyer M, Zarei M, and Graw M. 2009. Adipocere Withstands 1600 Years of Fluctuating Groundwater Levels in Soil. *Journal of Archaeological Science* 36(7):1328–1333.

Fiedler S, and Graw M. 2003. Decomposition of Buried Corpses, with Special Reference to the Formation of Adipocere. *Naturwissenschaften* 90(7):291–300.

Field AM. 1986. Smallpox in an Italian Mummy. *The Lancet* 328(8510):816.

Figueiredo Á, Owens LS, and Oswald R. 2002. Egyptian Mummies at the Museu Nacional de Arqueologia, Lisbon: A Proposed Programme of Study. *Papers from the Institute of Archaeology* 12:101–105.

Figueroa L, Razmilic B, Allison M, and González UM. 1988. Evidencia de arsenicismo crónico en momias del Valle de Camarones. *Región de Tarapacá, Chile. Chungara* 21:33–42.

Finucane BC. 2007. Mummies, Maize, and Manure: Multi-Tissue Stable Isotopes Analysis of Late Prehistoric Human Remains from the Ayacucho Valley, Peru. *Journal of Archaeological Science* 34(12):2115–2124.

Fletcher HA, Donoghue HD, Holton J, Pap I, and Spigelman M. 2003a. Widespread Occurrence of Mycobacterium Tuberculosis DNA from 18th–19th Century Hungarians. *American Journal of Physical Anthropology* 120:144–152.

Fletcher HA, Donoghue HD, Taylor GM, van der Zanden AG, and Spigelman M. 2003b. Molecular Analysis of Mycobacterium Tuberculosis DNA from a Family of 18th Century Hungarians. *Microbiology* 149(1):143–151.

Fontecchio G, Fioroni M, Azzarone R, Battistoni C, Cervelli C, Ventura L, Mercurio C, Fornaciari G, and Papola F. 2006a. Genetic Predisposition to Rheumatoid Arthritis in a Tuscan (Italy) Ancient Human Remain. *International Journal of Immunopathology and Pharmacology* 20(1):103–109.

Fontecchio G, Ventura L, Azzarone R, Fioroni M, Fornaciari G, and Papola F. 2006b. HLA-DRB Genotyping of an Italian Mummy from the 16th Century with Signs of Rheumatoid Arthritis. *Annals of the Rheumatic Diseases* 65(12):1676–1677.

Fontecchio G, Ventura L, and Poma AM. 2012. Further Genomic Testing and Histological Examinations Confirm the Diagnosis of Rheumatoid Arthritis in an Italian Mummy from the 16th Century. *Annals of the Rheumatic Diseases* 71(4):630.

Forbes SL, Stuart BH, and Dent BB. 2005a. The Effect of Soil Type on Adipocere Formation. *Forensic Science International* 154:35–43.

Forbes SL, Stuart BH, and Dent BB. 2005b. The Effect of the Burial Environment on Adipocere Formation. *Forensic Science International* 154:24–34.

Fornaciari G. 1985. The Mummies of the Abbey of Saint Domenico Maggiore in Naples: A Preliminary Report. *Archivio per l'Antropologia e la Etnologia* 115:215–226.

Fornaciari G. 1999. Renassiance Mummmies in Italy. *Medicina nei Secoli* 11:85–105.

Fornaciari G. 2006. Le mummie aragonesi in San Domenico Maggiore di Napoli. *Medicina nei Secoli* 18:843–864.

Fornaciari G, Castagna M, Tognetti A, Tornaboni D, and Bruno J. 1989. Syphilis in a Renaissance Italian Mummy. *The Lancet* 334(8663):614.

Fornaciari G, Castagna M, Viacava P, Tognetti A, and Bevilacqua G. 1992. Chagas' Disease in Peruvian Inca Mummy. *The Lancet* 399(8785):128–129.

Fornaciari G, Giuffra V, Bortolotti F, Gottardo R, Marvelli S, Marchesini M, Marinozzi S, Fornaciari A, Brocco G, and Tagliaro F. 2015. A Medieval Case of Digitalis Poisoning: The Sudden Death of Cangrande della Scala, lord of verona (1291–1329). *Journal of Archaeological Science* 54:162–167.

Fornaciari G, Giuffra V, Marinozzi S, Picchi MS, and Masetti M. 2009. "Royal" Pediculosis in Renaissance Italy: Lice in the Mummy of the King of Naples Ferdinand II of Aragon (1467–1496). *Memórias do Instituto Oswaldo Cruz* 104(4):671–672.

Fornaciari A, Giuffra V, Marvelli S, and Fornaciari G. 2008. The Blessed Christina from Spoleto: A Case of 15th Century Artificial Mummy from Umbria (Cental Italy). In: Atoche P, Rodríguez C, and Ramírez Á, editors. *VI World Congress on Mummy Studies*, Lanzarote. Santa Cruz de Tenerife, Academia Canaria de la Historia. pp. 521–527.

Fornaciari G, and Marchetti A. 1986. Intact Smallpox Virus Particles in an Italian Mummy of Sixteenth Century. *The Lancet* 328(8507):625.

Fornaciari G, Marchetti A, Pellegrini S, and Ciranni R. 1999. K-ras Mutation in the Tumour of King Ferrante I of Aragon (1431–1494) and Environmental Mutagens at the Aragonese Court of Naples. *International Journal of Osteoarchaeology* 9(5):302–306.

Fornaciari G, Marinozzi S, Gazzaniga V, Giuffra V, Picchi MS, Giusiani M, and Masetti M. 2011. The Use of Mercury Against Pediculosis in the Renaissance: The Case of Ferdinand II of Aragon, King of Naples, 1467–96. *Medical History* 55(1):109–115.

Fornaciari G, Zavaglia K, Giusti L, Vultaggio C, and Ciranni R. 2003. Human Papillomavirus in a 16th Century Mummy. *The Lancet* 362(9390):1160.

Francalacci P. 1995. DNA Analysis of Ancient Desiccated Corpses from Xinjiang. *Journal of Indo-European Studies* 23(3–4):385–398.

Frederiksen J. 2007. Conservation and Analysis of Grauballe Man 2001–2002. In: Asingh P and Lynnerup N, editors. *Grauballe Man: An Iron Age Bog Body Revisited*. Aarhus, Denmark: Aarhus University Press. pp. 58–77.

Fricker E, Spigelman M, and Fricker C. 1997. The Detection of Escherichia Coli DNA in the Ancient Remains of Lindow Man Using the Polymerase Chain Reaction. *Letters in Applied Microbiology* 24(5):351–354.

Friedman SN, Nelson AJ, Granton PV, Holdsworth DW, Chhem RK, and Cunningham IA. 2011. Dual-Energy Computed Tomography Automated Bone Identification in Ancient Egyptian Mummies. *Yearbook of Mummy Studies* 1:63–68.

Friedman SN, Nguyen N, Nelson AJ, Granton PV, MacDonald DB, Hibbert R, Holdsworth DW, and Cunningham IA. 2012. Computed Tomography (CT) Bone Segmentation of an Ancient Egyptian Mummy A Comparison of Automated and Semiautomated Threshold and Dual-Energy Techniques. *Journal of Computer Assisted Tomography* 36(5):616–622.

Friedrich KM, Nemec S, Czerny C, Fisher H, Plischke S, Gahleitner A, Viola TB, Imhof H, Seidler H, and Guillen S. 2010. The Story of 12 Chachapoyan Mummies Through Multidetector Computed Tomography. *European Journal of Radiology* 76:143–150.

Fukunaga K, and Hosako I. 2010. Innovative Non-Invasive Analysis Techniques for Cultural Heritage Using Terahertz Technology. *Comptes Rendus Physique* 11(7):519–526.

Gaeta R, Giuffra V, and Fornaciari G. 2013. Atherosclerosis in the Renaissance Elite: Ferdinand I King of Naples (1431–1494). *Virchows Arch* 462(5):593–595.

Gamba C, Fernández E, Tirado M, Pastor F, and Arroyo-Pardo E. 2011. Brief Communication: Ancient Nuclear DNA and Kinship Analysis: The Case of a Medieval Burial in San Esteban Church in Cuellar (Segovia, Central Spain). *American Journal of Physical Anthropology* 144(3):485–491.

Garcia AMB, Beckett RG, and Watson JT. 2014. Internal Environmental Characteristics of a Chiribaya Style Tomb Holding Swine Remains and Their Taphonomic Impact on Decomposition Delay, a Requisit for Mummification. *Papers on Anthropology* 23:45–62.

Gardner JC, Garvin G, Nelson AJ, Vascotto G, and Conlogue G. 2004. Paleoradiology in Mummy Studies: The Sulman Mummy Project. *Canadian Association of Radiologists Journal* 55:228–234.

Gaudio D, Galassi A, Nicolis F, Cappellozza N, and Cattaneo C. 2014. First World War Soldiers Preserved in the Ice: Two Case Reports. *Yearbook of Mummy Studies* 2:31–38.

Geller PL. 2005. Skeletal Analysis and Theoretical Complications. *World Archaeology* 37(4):597–609.

Geller PL. 2008. Conceiving Sex: Fomenting a Feminist Bioarchaeology. *Journal of Social Archaeology* 8:113–138.

Geller PL. 2009. Bodyscapes, Biology, and Heteronormativity. *American Anthropologist* 111(4):504–516.

Geller PL. 2012. Parting (with) the Dead: Body Partibility as Evidence of Commoner Ancestor Veneration. *Ancient Mesoamerica* 23:115–130.

Geller PL. 2017. *The Bioarchaeology of Socio-Sexual Lives: Queering Common Sense About Sex, Gender, and Sexuality*. New York: Springer.

Georges L, Seidenberg V, Hummel S, and Fehren-Schmitz L. 2012. Molecular Characterization of ABO Blood Group Frequencies in Pre-Columbian Peruvian Highlanders. *American Journal of Physical Anthropology* 149(2):242–249.

Gerloni A, Cavalli F, Costantinides F, Costantinides F, Bonetti S, and Paganelli C. 2009. Dental Status of Three Egyptian Mummies: Radiological Investigation by Multislice Computerized Tomography. *Oral Surgery, Oral Medicine, Oral Pathology, Oral Radiology, and Endodontology* 107(6):e58–e64.

Gerszten E, Allison MJ, Maguire BE, and Gerszten PC, editors. 2012. *Atlas of Paleopathology: Autopsies in South American Mummies*. CAP Press: College of American Pathologists.

Gessain A, Pecon-Slattery J, Meertens L, and Mahieux R. 2000. Origins of HTLV-1 in South America. *Nature Medicine* 6(3):232.

Gilbert MTP, Barnes I, Collins MJ, Smith C, Eklund J, Goudsmit J, Poinar H, and Cooper A. 2005. Long-Term Survival of Ancient DNA in Egypt: Response to Zink and Nerlich (2003). *American Journal of Physical Anthropology* 128(1):110–114.

Gilbert MTP, Djurhuus D, Melchior L, Lynnerup N, Worobey M, Wilson AS, Andreasen C, and Dissing J. 2007. mtDNA from Hair and Nail Clarifies the Genetic Relationship of the 15th Century Qilakitsoq Inuit Mummies. *American Journal of Physical Anthropology* 133(2):847–853.

Gilbey BE, and Lubran M. 1952. Blood Groups of South American Indian Mummies. *Man* 52:115–117.

Gilbey BE, and Lubran M. 1953. The ABO and Rh Blood Group Antigens in Pre-Dynastic Egyptian Mummies. *Man* 53:23.

Gildow D, and Bingenheimer M. 2002. Buddhist Mummification in Taiwan: Two Case Studies. *Asia Major* 15:87–127.

Gill-Frerking H. 2010. Bog Bodies—Preserved Bodies from Peat. In: Wieczorek A and Rosendahl W, editors. *Mummies of the World*. New York: Prestel. pp. 60–71.

Gill-Frerking H. 2014. The Impact of Historical Post-Excavation Modifications on the Re-Examination of Human Mummies. *Papers on Anthropology* 23:63–75.

Gill-Frerking H, Begerock A-M, and Rosendahl W. 2013. Interpreting the Tattoos on a 700-Year-Old Mummy from South America. In: Della Casa P and Witt C, editors. *Tattoos and Body Modification in Antiquity Proceedings of the Sessions at the Annual Meetings of the European Association of Archaeologists in the Hague and Oslo, 2010/11*. Zurich Studies in Archaeology 9. Chronos-Verlag, Zurich. pp. 59–65.

Gill-Frerking H, Rosendahl W, Zink A, and Piombino-Mascali D. 2011. Editorial: The Yearbook of Mummy Studies. *Yearbook of Mummy Studies* 1:5.

Gill-Robinson H. 1996. Piglets in Peat: Experimental Archaeology in the Study of Bog Body Preservation. In: Coles B, Coles J, and Schou Jørgensen M, editors. *Bod Bodies, Sacred Sites and Wetland Archaeology*. Exeter: University of Exeter. WARP Occasional Papers no. 12. pp. 99–102.

Giuffra V, Fornaciari A, Marvelli S, Marchesini M, Caramella D, and Fornaciari G. 2011. Embalming Methods and Plants in Renaissance Italy: Two Artificial Mummies from Siena (Central Italy). *Journal of Archaeological Science* 38(8):1949–1956.

Goldstein LG. 1980. *Mississippian Mortuary Practices: A Case Study of Two Cemeteries in the Lower Illinois*. River Valley: Northwestern University Archaeological Program.

Goldstein LG. 2006. Mortuary Analysis and Bioarchaeology. In: Buikstra JE and Beck LA, editors. *Bioarchaeology: The Contextual Analysis of Human Remains*. Burlington, MA: Elsevier. pp. 375–387.

Gose P. 1994. *Deathly Waters and Hungry Mountains: Agrarian Ritual and Class Formation in an Andean Town*. Toronto: University of Toronto Press.

Gostner P, Bonelli M, Pernter P, Graefen A, and Zink A. 2013. New Radiological Approach for Analysis and Identification of Foreign Objects in Ancient and Historic Mummies. *Journal of Archaeological Science* 40(2):1003–1011.

Götherström A, Fischer C, and Linden K. 1995. X-raying Ancient Bone: A Destructive Method in Connection with DNA Analysis. *Laborativ Arkeologi* 8:26–28.

Gowland R. 2006. Aging the Past: Examining Age Identity from Funerary Evidence. In: Gowland R and Knüsel C, editors. *Social Archaeology of Funerary Remains*. Oxford: Oxbow Books. pp. 143–154.

Gowland R, and Knüsel C, editors. 2006. *Social Archaeology of Funerary Remains*. Oxford: Oxbow Books.

Gowland R, and Thompson T. 2013. *Human Identity and Identification*. Cambridge: Cambridge University Press.

Grabherr S, Cooper C, Ulrich-Bochsler S, Uldin T, Ross S, Oesterhelweg L, Bolliger S, Christe A, Schnyder P, and Mangin P. 2009. Estimation of Sex and Age of "Virtual Skeletons"—A Feasibility Study. *European Radiology* 19(2):419–429.

Green RE, Krause J, Briggs AW, Maricic T, Stenzel U, Kircher M, Patterson N, Li H, Zhai W, Fritz M, Hansen N, Durand E, Malaspinas A, Jensen J, Maruqes-Bonet T, Alkan C, Prufer K, Meyer M, Burbano H, Good J, Schultz R, Aximu-Petri A, Butthof A, Hober B, Siegemund M, Weihmann A, Nusbaum C, Lander E, Russ C, Novod N, Affourtit J, Egholm M, Verna C, Rudan P, Brajkovic D, Kucan Z, Gusic I, Doronichev V, Golovanova L, Lalueza-Fox C, Rasilla M, Fortea J, Rosas A, Schmitz R, Johnson P, Eichler E, Falush D, Birney E, Mullikin J, Slatkin M, Nielsen R, Kelso J, Lachmann M, Reich D, and Paabo S. 2010. A Draft Sequence of the Neanderthal Genome. *Science* 328:710–722.

Gregersen M, Jurik AG, and Lynnerup N. 2007. Forensic Evidence, Injuries and Cause of Death. In: Asingh P and Lynnerup N, editors. *Grauballe Man: An Iron Age Bog Body Revisited*. Aarhus, Denmark: Aarhus University Press. pp. 235–258.

Grieshaber BM, Osborne DL, Doubleday AF, and Kaestle FA. 2008. A Pilot Study into the Effects of X-ray and Computed Tomography Exposure on the Amplification of DNA from Bone. *Journal of Archaeological Science* 35(3):681–687.

Guhl F, Jaramillo C, Vallejo GA, Cárdenas-Arroyo F, and Aufderheide AC. 2000. Chagas Disease and Human Migration. *Memórias do Instituto Oswaldo Cruz* 95(4):553–555.

Guhl F, Jaramillo C, Vallejo GA, Yockteng F, Cárdenas-Arroyo F, Fornaciari G, Arriaza BT, and Aufderheide AC. 1999. Isolation of Trypanosoma cruzi DNA in 4,000-Year-Old Mummified Human Tissue from Northern Chile. *American Journal of Physical Anthropology* 108:401–407.

Guhl F, Jaramillo C, Yockteng R, Vallejo GA, and Cárdenas-Arroyo F. 1997. Trypanosoma cruzi DNA in Human Mummies. *The Lancet* 349(9062):1370.

Guillén SE. 1998. Laguna de los Condores: Donde Viven los Muertos. *Bien Venida* 6:43–48.

Guillén SE. 2003. Keeping Ancestors Alive: The Mummies from Laguna de los Cóndores, Amazonas, Peru. In: Lynnerup N, Andreasen C, and Berglund J, editors. *Mummies in the New Millenium: Proceedings of the 4th World Congress on Mummy Studies.* Nuuk, Greenland: Greenland National Museum and Archives and Danish Polar Center. pp. 162–164.

Guillén SE. 2004. Artificial Mummies from the Andes. *Coll Anthropol Suppl* 2:141–157.

Guillén SE. 2005. Mummies, Cults, and Ancestors: The Chinchorro Mummies of the South Central Andes. In: Rakita GFM, Buikstra JE, Beck LA, and Williams SR, editors. *Interacting with the Dead: Perspectives on Mortuary Archaeology for the New Millennium.* Gainesville: University Press of Florida. pp. 142–149.

Guillén SE. 2012. De Chinchorro a Chiribaya: los ancestros de los mallquis Chachapoya-Inca. *Boletín de Arqueología PUCP* (7):287–303.

Haas NA, Zelle M, Rosendahl W, Zink A, Preuss R, Laser KT, Gostner P, Arens S, Domik G, and Burchert W. 2015. Hypoplastic Left Heart in the 6500-Year-Old Detmold Child. *The Lancet* 385(9985):2432.

Handt O, Richards M, Trommsdorff M, Kilger C, Simanainen J, Georgiev O, Bauer K, Stone A, Hedges R, Schaffner W, Utermann G, Sykes B, and Pääbo S. 1994. Molecular Genetic Analyses of the Tyrolean Ice Man. *Science* 264(5166):1775–1778.

Hanna J, Bouwman AS, Brown KA, Pearson MP, and Brown TA. 2012. Ancient DNA Typing Shows That a Bronze Age Mummy Is a Composite of Different Skeletons. *Journal of Archaeological Science* 39(8):2774–2779.

Hansen HE, and Gürtler H. 1983. HLA Types of Mummified Eskimo Bodies from the 15th Century. *American Journal of Physical Anthropology* 61(4):447–452.

Harild JA, Robinson DE, and Hudlebusch J. 2007. New Analyses of Grauballe Man's Gut Contents. In: Asingh P and Lynnerup N, editors. *Grauballe Man: An Iron Age Bog Body Revisited.* Aarhus, Denmark: Aarhus University Press. pp. 154–187.

Harkins KM, and Stone AC. 2014. Ancient Pathogen Genomics: Insights into Timing and Adaptation. *Journal of Human Evolution* 79:137–149.

Harris JE, Wente EF, Cox CF, El Nawaway I, Kowalski CJ, Storey AT, Russell WR, Ponitz PV, and Walker GF. 1978. Mummy of the "Elder Lady" in the Tomb of Amenhotep II: Egyptian Museum Catalog Number 61070. *Science* 200(4346):1149–1151.

Harris M. 2014. Radiographic Evaluation of a Late Dynastic/Ptolemaic Mummy Demonstrating a Renal Calculus. *Yearbook of Mummy Studies* 2:77–80.

Harrod RP, Thompson JL, and Martin DL. 2012. Hard Labor and Hostile Encounters: What Human Remains Reveal About Institutional Violence and Chinese Immigrants Living in Carlin, Nevada (1885–1923). *Historical Archaeology* 46(4):85–111.

Hart GD, Cockburn A, Millet NB, and Scott JW. 1977. Lessons Learned from the Autopsy of an Egyptian Mummy. *Canadian Medical Association Journal* 117:415–418.

Hart Hansen J, and Gullov H. 1989. The mummies from Qilakitsoq–Eskimos in the 15th century. *Meddelelser om Grønland. Man & Society* 12:199.

Hart Hansen J, and Nordqvist J. 1996. The mummy find from Qilakitsoq in northwest Greenland. *Human Mummies: Springer.* pp. 107–121.

Harwood-Nash DC. 1979. Computed Tomography of Ancient Egyptian Mummies. *Journal of Computer Assisted Tomography* 3:768–773.

Hastorf CA. 1990. The Effect of the Inca State on Sausa Agricultural Production and Crop Consumption. *American Antiquity* 55:262–290.

Havelková P, Villotte S, Velemínský P, Poláček L, and Dobisíková M. 2011. Enthesopathies and Activity Patterns in the Early Medieval Great Moravian Population: Evidence of Division of Labour. *International Journal of Osteoarchaeology* 21(4):487–504.

Hawass Z. 2013. The Death of Tutankhamun. *International Journal on Humanistic Ideology* (1):13–27.

Hawass Z, Gad YZ, Ismail S, Khairat R, Fathalla D, Hasan N, Ahmed A, Elleithy H, Ball M, Gaballah F, Wasef S, Fateen M, Amer H, Gostner P, Selim A, Zink A, and Pusch CM. 2010. Ancestry and Pathology in King Tutankhamun's Family. *Journal of the American Medical Association* 303(7):638–647.

Hawass Z, Ismail S, Selim A, Saleem SN, Fathalla D, Wasef S, Gad AZ, Saad R, Fares S, Amer H, Gostner P, Gad YZ, Pusch CM, and Zink AR. 2012. Revisiting the Harem Conspiracy and Death of Ramesses III: Anthropological, Forensic, Radiological, and Genetic Study. *British Medical Journal* 345:e8268.

Hershkovitz I, Spigelman M, Sarig R, Lim D-S, Lee IS, Oh CS, May H, Boaretto E, Kim Y-S, Lee SD et al. 2014. A Possible Case of Cherubism in a 17th-Century Korean Mummy. *PLoS One* 9(8):e102441.

Hertz R. 1960 [1907]. *Death and the Right Hand: A Contribution to the Study of the Collective Representation of Death.* Glencoe, IL: Free Press.

Hess MW, Klima G, Pfaller K, Künzel KH, and Gaber O. 1998. Histological Investigations on the Tyrolean Ice Man. *American Journal of Physical Anthropology* 106(4):521–532.

Hey J. 2005. On the Number of New World Founders: A Population Genetic Portrait of the Peopling of the Americas. *PLos Biology* 3:965–975.

Higuchi R, Bowman B, Freiberger M, Ryder OA, and Wilson AC. 1984. DNA Sequences from the Quagga, an Extinct Member of the Horse Family. *Nature* 312(5991):282–284.

Hill B, Macleod I, and Watscon L. 1993. Facial Reconstruction of a 3500-Year-Old Egyptian Mummy Using Axial Computed Tomography. *Journal of Audiovisual Media in Medicine* 16:11–13.

Hodder I. 1980. Social Structure and Cemeteries: A Critical Appraisal. In: Rahtz P, Dickinson T, and Watts L, editors. *Anglo-Saxon Cemeteries.* Oxford: British Archaeological Reports. pp. 161–169.

Hodge CJ. 2013. Non-Bodies of Knowledge: Anatomized Remains from the Holden Chapel Collection, Harvard University. *Journal of Social Archaeology* 13:122–149.

Holden TG, and Núñez L. 1993. An Analysis of the Gut Contents of Five Well-Preserved Human Bodies from Tarapacá, Northern Chile. *Journal of Archaeological Science* 20(6):595–611.

Hollimon SE. 2001. The Gendered Peopling of North America: Addressing the Antiquity of Systems of Multiple Genders. In: Price N, editor. *The Archaeology of Shamanism.* London: Routledge. pp. 123–134.

Hollimon SE. 2006. The Archaeology of Nonbinary Genders in Native North American Societies. In: Nelson SM, editor. *Handbook of Gender in Archaeology.* Lanham, MD: AltaMira Press. pp, 435–450.

Hollimon SE. 2011. Sex and Gender in Bioarchaeological Research: Theory, Method, and Interpretation. In: Argarwal SC and Glencross BA, editors. *Social Bioarchaeology.* West Sussex: Wiley-Blackwell. pp. 149–182.

Holm S. 2001. The Privacy of Tutankhamen—Utilising the Genetic Information in Stored Tissue Samples. *Theoretical Medicine and Bioethics* 22:437–449.

Hoogewerff J, Papesch W, Kralik M, Berner M, Vroon P, Miesbauer H, Gaber O, Kunzel K, and Kleinjans J. 2001. The Last Domicile of the Iceman from Hauslabjoch: A Geochemical Approach Using Sr, C and O Isotopes and Trace Element Signatures. *Journal of Archaeological Science* 28:983–989.

Hori I. 1962. Self-Mummified Buddhas in Japan: An Aspect of the Shugen-Dô ("Mountain Asceticism") Sect. *History of Religions* 1(2):222–242.

Horne PD, and Ireland RR. 1991. Moss and a guanche Mummy: An Unusual Utilization. *The Bryologist* 94(4):407–408.

Horne PD, and Lewin PK. 1977. Autopsy of an Egyptian Mummy. 7: Electron Microscopy of Mummified Tissue. *Canadian Medical Association Journal* 117:472–473.

Hounsfield G. 1976. Historical Notes on Computerized Axial Tomography. *Journal of the Canadian Association of Radiologists* 27(3):135–142.

Iacumin P, Bocherens H, Chaix L, and Marioth A. 1998. Stable Carbon and Nitrogen Isotopes as Dietary Indicators of Ancient Nubian Populations (Northern Sudan). *Journal of Archaeological Science* 25(4):293–301.

Iacumin P, Bocherens H, Mariotti A, and Longinelli A. 1996. An Isotopic Palaeoenvironmental Study of Human Skeletal Remains from the Nile Valley. *Palaeogeography, Palaeoclimatology, Palaeoecology* 126(1):15–30.

Ikram S. 2015. Studying Egyptian Mummies in the Field. In: Ikram S, Kaiser J, and Walker R, editors. *Egyptian Bioarchaeology: Humans, Animals, and the Environment*. Leiden: Sidestone Press. pp. 67–76.

Ikram S, and Dodson A. 1998. *The Mummy in Ancient Egypt*. London: Thames and Hudson.

Ikram S, Kaiser J, and Walker R, editors. 2015a. *Egyptian Bioarchaeology: Humans, Animals, and the Environment*. Leiden: Sidestone Press.

Ikram S, Kaiser J, and Walker R. 2015b. Preface. In: Ikram S, Kaiser J, and Walker R, editors. *Egyptian Bioarchaeology: Humans, Animals, and the Environment*. Leiden: Sidestone Press. pp. 17–18.

Iñiguez AM, Araújo A, Ferreira LF, and Vicente ACP. 2003. Analysis of Ancient DNA from Coprolites: A Perspective with Random Amplified Polymorphic DNA-Polymerase Chain Reaction Approach. *Memórias do Instituto Oswaldo Cruz* 98:63–65.

Iwe K. 2013. Tattoos from Mummies of the Pazyryk Culture. In: Della Casa P, and Witt C, editors. *Tattoos and Body Modification in Antiquity Proceedings of the Sessions at the Annual Meetings of the European Association of Archaeologists in the Hague and Oslo, 2010/11*. Zurich Studies in Archaeology 9. Chronos-Verlag, Zurich. pp. 89–95.

Jackson J, Mourou M, Whitaker J, Duling I, Williamson S, Menu M, and Mourou G. 2008. Terahertz Imaging for Non-Destructive Evaluation of Mural Paintings. *Optics Communications* 281(4):527–532.

Jankauskas R, and Piombino-Mascali D. 2012. The Lithuanian Mummy Project: Bioanthropological and Paleopathological Investigation of the Human Remains Found in the Holy Spirit Dominican Church, Vilnius. *Paleopath Newsletter* 159:12.

Janko M, Stark RW, and Zink A. 2012. Preservation of 5300 Year Old Red Blood Cells in the Iceman. *Journal of the Royal Society Interface* 9:2581–2590.

Janko M, Zink A, Gigler AM, Heckl WM, and Stark RW. 2010. Nanostructure and Mechanics of Mummified Type I Collagen from the 5300-Year-Old Tyrolean Iceman. *Proceedings of the Royal Society B* 277:2301–2309.

Jarcho S. 1966. The Development and Present Condition of Human Palaeopathology in the United States. In: Jarcho S, editor. *Human Palaeopathology*. New Haven: Yale University Press. pp. 3–30.

Jay M, Fuller BT, Richards MP, Knüsel CJ, and King SS. 2008. Iron Age Breastfeeding Practices in Britain: Isotopic Evidence from Wetwang Slack, East Yorkshire. *American Journal of Physical Anthropology* 136(327–337).

Jones A. 2005. Lives in Fragments? Personhood and the European Neolithic. *Journal of Social Archaeology* 5(2):193–224.

Jones J, Higham TFG, Oldfield R, O'Connor TP, and Buckley SA. 2014. Evidence for Prehistoric Origins of Egyptian Mummification in Late Neolithic Burials. *PLoS One* 9(8):e103608.

Joyce RA. 2000. Girling the Girl and Boying the Boy: The Production of Adulthood in Ancient Mesoamerica. *World Archaeology* 31:473–483.

Joyce RA, editor. 2008. *Ancient Bodies, Ancient Lives: Sex, Gender, and Archaeology*. New York: Thames and Hudson.

Kaestle FA, and Horsburgh K. 2002. Ancient DNA in Anthropology: Methods, Applications, and Ethics. *Yearbook of Physical Anthropology* 45:92–130.

Kahila Bar-Gal G, Kim MJ, Klein A, Shin DH, Oh CS, Kim JW, Kim TH, Kim SB, Grant PR, and Pappo O. 2012. Tracing Hepatitis B Virus to the 16th Century in a Korean Mummy. *Hepatology* 56(5):1671–1680.

Kanias T, and Acker JP. 2006. Mammalian Cell Desiccation: Facing the Challenges. *Cell Preservation Technology* 4(4):253–277.

Kao J-H, Chen P-J, Lai M-Y, and Chen D-S. 2002. Genotypes and Clinical Phenotypes of Hepatitis B Virus in Patients with Chronic Hepatitis B Virus Infection. *Journal of Clinical Microbiology* 40(4):1207–1209.

Karlik SJ, Bartha R, Kennedy K, and Chhem RK. 2007. MRI and Multinuclear MR Spectroscopy of a 3,200-Year-Old Egyptian Mummy Brain. *American Journal of Roentgenology* 189:105–111.

Kaufmann IM, and Rühli FJ. 2010. Without 'Informed Consent'? Ethics and Ancient Mummy Research. *Journal of Medical Ethics* 36:608–613.

Kean WF, and Kean M. 2014. The Mechanicla Back Pain and Leg Neuroseonsory Pain of the Similaun Iceman: Relationship to "Medicinal" Tattoos. *Yearbook of Mummy Studies* 2:7–14.

Kean WF, Tocchio S, Kean M, and Rainsford KD. 2013. The Musculoskeletal Abnormalities of the Similaun Iceman ("ÖTZI"): Clues to Chronic Pain and Possible Treatments. *Inflammopharmacol* 21:11–20.

Kelly EP. 2013. An Archaeological Interpretation of Irish Iron Age Bog Bodies. In: Ralph S, editor. *The Archaeology of Violence: Interdisciplinary Approaches*. Albany: State University of New York Press. pp. 232–240.

Khairat R, Ball M, Chang C-CH, Bianucci R, Nerlich AG, Trautmann M, Ismail S, Shanab GML, Karim AM, Gad YZ and others. 2013. First Insights into the Metagenome of Egyptian Mummies Using Next-Generation Sequencing. *Journal of Applied Genetics* 54:309–325.

Kim MJ, Kim Y-S, Oh CS, Go J-H, Lee IS, Park W-K, Cho S-M, Kim S-K, and Shin DH. 2015. Anatomical Confirmation of Computed Tomography-Based Diagnosis of the Atherosclerosis Discovered in 17th Century Korean Mummy. *PLoS One* 10(3):e0119474.

Kim MJ, Oh CS, Lee IS, Lee BH, Choi JH, Lim D-S, Yi YS, Han W-J, Kim Y-S, Bok GD et al. 2008. Human Mummified Brain from a Medieval Tomb with Lime-Soil Mixture Barrier of the Joseon Dynasty, Korea. *International Journal of Osteoarchaeology* 18:614–623.

Kim SB, Shin JE, Park SS, Bok GD, Chang YP, Kim J, Chung YH, Yi YS, Shin MH, Chang BS, Shin DH, and Myeung JK. 2006. Endoscopic Investigation of the Internal Organs of a 15th-Century Child Mummy from Yangju, Korea. *Journal of Anatomy* 209:681–688.

Kim Y-S, Lee IS, Jung G-U, Kim MJ, Oh CS, Yoo DS, Lee W-J, Lee E, Cha SC, and Shin DH. 2014. Radiological Diagnosis of Congenital Diaphragmatic Hernia in 17th Century Korean Mummy. *PLoS One* 9(7):e99779.

Kirkpatrick RC. 2000. The Evolution of Human Homosexual Behavior. *Current Anthropology* 41(3):385–413.

Klaus HD. 2012. The Bioarchaeology of Structural Violence. In: Martin DL and Harrod RP, editors. *The Bioarchaeology of Violence*. Gainesville: University Press of Florida. pp. 29–62.

Klaus HD, and Tam ME. 2008. Contact in the Andes: Bioarchaeology of Systemic Stress in Colonial Morrope, Peru. *American Journal of Physical Anthropology* 138:356–368.

Klocke J. 2010. Conservation of Mummies—Having Bones to Pick with the Dead. In: Wieczorek A and Rosendahl W, editors. *Mummies of the World*. Munich: Prestel. pp. 250–253.

Klocke J, and Petersen K. 2010. Infested, Cursed, Contaminated—Microbial and Chemical Contamination in Mummies. In: Wieczorek A and Rosendahl W, editors. *Mummies of the World*. Munich: Prestel. pp. 244–249.

Kloos H, and David R. 2002. The Paleoepidemiology of Schistosomiasis in Ancient Egypt. *Human Ecology Review* 9(1):14–25.

Knudson KJ, Pestle WJ, Torres-Rouff C, and Pimentel G. 2012. Assessing the Life History of an Andean Traveller Through Biogeochemistry: Stable and Radiogenic Isotope Analyses of Archaeological Human Remains from Northern Chile. *International Journal of Osteoarchaeology* 22(4):435–451.

Knudson KJ, and Stojanowski CM. 2008. New Directions in Bioarchaeology: Recent Contributions to the Study of Human Social Identity. *Journal of Archaeological Research* 16:397–432.

Knudson KJ, and Stojanowski CM. 2009. *Bioarchaeology and Identity in the Americas*. Gainesville: University Press of Florida.

Knudson KJ, Tung TA, Nystrom KC, Price TD, and Fullagar PD. 2005. The Origin of the Juch'uypampa Cave Mummies: Strontium Isotope Analysis of Archaeological Human Remains from Bolivia. *Journal of Archaeological Sciences* 32(6):903–913.

Knüsel CJ. 2010. Bioarchaelogy: A Synthetic Approach. *Bulletins et mémoires de la Société d'anthropologie de Paris* 22:62–73.

Knüsel CJ. 2011. Men Take Up Arms for War: Sex and Status Distinctions of Humeral Medial Epicondylar Avulsion Fractures in the Archaeological Record. In: Baadsgaard A, Boutin AT, and Buikstra JE, editors. *Breathing New Life into the Evidence of Death*. Santa Fe: School for Advanced Research. pp. 221–249.

Knüsel CJ, and Smith M. 2013. *The Routledge Handbook of the Bioarchaeology of Human Conflict*. London: Routledge.

Köberle F. 1963. Enteromegaly and Cardiomegaly in Chagas Disease. *Gut* 4(4):399–405.

Kowal W, Beattie OB, Baadsgaard H, and Krahn PM. 1991. Source Identification of Lead Found in Tissues of Sailors from the Franklin Arctic Expedition of 1845. *Journal of Archaeological Science* 18:193–203.

Kowal W, Krahn P, and Beattie O. 1989. Lead Levels in Human Tissues from the Franklin Forensic Project. *International Journal of Environmental Analytical Chemistry* 35(2):119–126.

Krieger N. 2003. Genders, Sexes, and Health: What Are the Connections—and Why Does It Matter? *International Journal of Epidemiology* 32(4):652–657.

Krogman W. 1935. Life Histories Recorded in Skeletons. *American Anthropologist* 37(1):92–103.

Kromann NP, Kapel H, Løytved ER, and Hart Hansen JP. 1989. The Tattooings of the Qilakitsoq Eskimo Mummies. In: Hart Hansen JP and Gulløv H, editors. *The Mummies from Qilakitsoq: Eskimos in the 15th Century*. Copenhagen: Meddelelser om Grønland, Man & Society 12. pp. 168–171.

Krutak L. 2013. The Power to Cure: A Brief History of Therapeutic Tattooing. In: Della Casa P and Witt C, editors. *Tattoos and Body Modification in Antiquity Proceedings of the Sessions at the Annual Meetings of the European Association of Archaeologists in the Hague and Oslo, 2010/11*. Zurich Studies in Archaeology 9. Chronos-Verlag, Zurich. pp. 27–34.

Kumm KJ, Reinhard KJ, Piombino-Mascali D, and Araujo A. 2010. Archaeoparasitological Investigation of a Mummy from Sicily (18th-19th Century AD). *Anthropologie* 48(2):177–184.

Kustár A. 2004. The Facial Restoration of Antal Simon, a Hungarian Priest-Teacher of the 19th c. Homo. *Journal of Comparative Human Biology* 55:77–90.

Kustár Á, Pap I, Végvári Z, Kristóf LA, Pálfi G, Karlinger K, Kovács B, and Szikossy I. 2011. Use of 3D Virtual Reconstruction for Pathological Investigation and Facial Reconstruction of an 18th Century Mummified Nun from Hungary. *Yearbook of Mummy Studies* 1:83–93.

Labaune J, Jackson J, Pages-Camagna S, Duling I, Menu M, and Mourou G. 2010. Papyrus Imaging with Terahertz Time Domain Spectroscopy. *Applied Physics A* 100(3):607–612.

Lalremruata A, Ball M, Bianucci R, Welte B, Nerlich AG, Kun JFJ, and Pusch CM. 2013. Molecular Identification of Falciparum Malaria and Human Tuberculosis Co-Infections in Mummies from the Fayum Depression (Lower Egypt). *PLoS One* 8(4):e60307.

Lambert PM. 2012. Ethics and Issues in the Use of Human Skeletal Remains in Paleopathology. In: Grauer A, editor. *A Companion to Paleopathology.* West Sussex: Wiley-Blackwell. pp. 15–33.

Larsen CS. 1981. Functional Implications of Postcranial Size Reduction on the Prehistoric Georgia Coast, USA. *Journal of Human Evolution* 10(6):489–502.

Larsen CS. 1987. Bioarchaeological Interpretations of Subsistence Economy and Behavior from Human Skeletal Remains. *Advances in Archaeological Method and Theory* 10:339–445.

Larsen CS. 2002. Bioarchaeology: The Lives and Lifestyles of Past People. *Journal of Archaeological Research* 10(2):119–166.

Larsen CS. 2006. The Changing Face of Bioarchaeology: An Interdisciplinary Science. In: Buikstra JE and Beck LA, editors. *Bioarchaeology: The Contextual Analysis of Human Remains.* Burlington, MA: Elsevier. pp. 359–374.

Larsen CS, and Walker PL. 2004. The Ethics of Bioarchaeology. In: Turner TR, editor. *Biological Anthropology and Ethics: From Repatriation to Genetic Identity.* Albany: State University of New York Press. pp. 111–119.

Lasch KE. 2000. Culture, Pain, and Culturally Sensitive Pain Care. *Pain Management Nursing* 1(3):16–22.

Laurent GJ. 1982. Rates of Collagen Synthesis in Lung, Skin and Muscle Obtained in Vivo by Simplified Method Using [3H] Proline. *Biochemical Journal* 206(3):535–544.

Lee H-J, Shin D-H, and Seo M. 2011. Discovery of Taeniid Eggs from a 17th Century Tomb in Korea. *Korean Journal of Parasitology* 49(3):327–329.

Lee IS, Kim MJ, Yoo DS, Lee YS, Park SS, Bok GD, Han SH, Chung YH, Chang BS, Yi YS, Oh CS, and Sin DH. 2007. Three-Dimensional Reconstruction of Medieval Child Mummy in *Yangju*, Korea, Using Multi-Detector Computed Tomography. *Annals of Anatomy* 189:558–568.

Lee IS, Lee E-J, Park JB, Baek SH, Oh CS, Lee SD, Kim Y-S, Bok GD, Hong JW, Lim D-S, Shin MH, Seo M, and Shin DH. 2009. Acute Traumatic Death of a 17th Century General Based on Examination of Mummified Remains Found in Korea. *Annals of Anatomy* 191:309–320.

Leeson TS. 1959. Electron Microscopy of Mummified Material. *Stain Technology* 34:317–320.

Leles D, Araújo A, Ferreira LF, Vicente ACP, and Iñiguez AM. 2008. Molecular Paleoparasitological Diagnosis of Ascaris sp. from Coprolites: New Scenery of Ascariasis in Pre-Colombian South America Times. *Memórias do Instituto Oswaldo Cruz* 103(1):106–108.

Lewin E, and Leap WL, editors. 2002. *Out in Theory: The Emergence of Lesbian and Gay Anthropology.* Chicago: University of Illinois Press.

Lewin PK. 1967. Palaeo-Electron Microscopy of Mummified Tissue. *Nature* 213:416–417.

Lewin PK, and Harwood-Nash DC. 1977. X-ray Computed Axial Tomography of an Ancient Egyptian Brain. *International Research Communications System Medical Science* 5:78.

Li C-Y, and Yu S-F. 2006. A Novel Mutation in the SH3BP2 gene Causes Cherubism: Case Report. *BMC Medical Genetics* 7(1):84.

Li H-C, Fujiyoshi T, Lou H, Yashiki S, Sonoda S, Cartier L, Nunez L, Munoz I, Horai S, and Tajima K. 1999. The Presence of Ancient Human T-Cell Lymphotropic Virus Type I Pro-virus DNA in an Andean Mummy. *Nature Medicine* 5(12):1428–1432.

Li Y, Carroll DS, Gardner SN, Walsh MC, Vitalis EA, and Damon IK. 2007. On the Origin of Smallpox: Correlating Variola Phylogenics with Historical Smallpox Records. *Proceedings of the National Academy of Sciences* 104(40):15787–15792.

Lichtenberg R. 2015. Study of Growth Arrest Lines Upon Human Remains from Kharga Oasis. In: Ikram S, Kaiser J, and Walker R, editors. *Egyptian Bioarchaeology: Humans, Animals, and the Environment.* Leiden: Sidestone Press. pp. 87–94.

Lim D-S, Lee IS, Choi K-J, Lee SD, Oh CS, Kim Y-S, Bok GD, Kim MJ, Yi YS, Lee E-J et al. 2008. The Potential for Non-Invasive Study of Mummies: Validation of the Use of Computerized Tomography by *Post Factum* Dissection and Histological Examination of a 17th Century Female Korean Mummy. *Journal of Anatomy* 213:482–495.

Lima VS, Iniguez AM, Otsuki K, Ferreira LF, Araújo A, Vicente ACP, and Jansen AM. 2008. Chagas Disease in Ancient Hunter-Gatherer Population, Brazil. Emerging Infectious Diseases 14(6):1001–1002.

Lippold LK. 1971. The Mixed Cell Agglutination Method for Typing Mummified Human Tissue. *American Journal of Physical Anthropology* 34(3):377–383.

Liu W-Q, Liu J, Zhang J-H, Long X-C, Lei J-H, and Li Y-L. 2007. Comparison of Ancient and Modern Clonorchis Sinensis Based on ITS1 and ITS2 Sequences. *Acta tropica* 101(2):91–94.

Llop E, and Rothhammer F. 1988. A Note on the Presence of Blood Groups A and B in Pre-Columbian South America. *American Journal of Physical Anthropology* 75(1):107–111.

Lonfat BMK, Kaufmann IM, and Rühli F. 2015. A Code of Ethics for Evidence-Based Research with Ancient Human Remains. *The Anatomical Record* 298(6):1175–1181.

Longworth MS, and Laimins LA. 2004. Pathogenesis of Human Papillomaviruses in Differentiating Epithelia. *Microbiology and Molecular Biology Reviews* 68(2):362–372.

Loreille O, Roumat E, Verneau O, Bouchet F, and Hänni C. 2001. Ancient DNA from Ascaris: Extraction Amplification and Sequences from Eggs Collected in Coprolites. *International Journal for Parasitology* 31(10):1101–1106.

Lösch S, Grupe G, and Peters J. 2006. Stable Isotopes and Dietary Adaptations in Humans and Animals at Pre-Pottery Neolithic Nevallı Çori, Southeast Anatolia. *American Journal of Physical Anthropology* 131(2):181–193.

Lovejoy CO, Mensforth RP, and Armelagos GJ. 1982. Five Decades of Skeletal Biology as Reflected in the American Journal of Physical Anthropology. In: Spencer F, editor. *A History of American Physical Anthropology, 1930–1980.* New York: Academic Press. pp. 329–336.

Lovering S. 2006. Cultural Attitudes and Beliefs About Pain. *Journal of Transcultural Nursing* 17(4):389–395.

Lozada Cerna MC, and Buikstra JE. 2005. Pescadores and Labradores Among the Señorío of Chiribaya in Southern Peru. In: Reycraft RM, editor. *Us and Them: Archaeology and Ethnicity in the Andes.* Los Angeles: Cotsen Institute of Archaeology, University of California. pp. 206–225.

Lozada Cerna MC, Buikstra JE, Rakita GFM, and Wheeler JC. 2009. Camelid Herders: The Forgotten Specialists in the Coastal Senorio of Chiribaya, Southern Peru. In: Marcus J and Williams PR, editors. *Andean Civilization: A Tribute to Michael E. Moseley.* Los Angeles: Cotsen Institute of Archaeology, University of California. pp. 351–364.

Lozada Cerna MC, Knudson KJ, Haydon RC, and Buikstra JE. 2012. Social Marginalization Among the Chiribaya: The *Curandero* of Yaral, Southern Peru. In: Stodder ALW and Palkovich AM, editors. *The Bioarchaeology of Individuals.* Gainsville: University Press of Florida. pp. 85–95.

Lucas A. 1932. The Use of Natron in Mummification. *The Journal of Egyptian Archaeology* 18:125–140.

Lunardini A, Costantini L, Biasini LC, Caramella D, and Fornaciari G. 2012. Evidence of Congenital Syphilis and Tuberculosis in a XIX Century Mummy (Perugia, Italy). *Journal of Biological Research* 85(1):241–242.

Lynn GE, and Benitez JT. 1974. Temporal Bone Preservation in a 2600-Year-Old Egyptian Mummy. *Science* 183(4121):200–202.

Lynn GE, and Benitez JT. 1977. Examination of Ears. *Canadian Medical Association Journal* 117:469.

Lynnerup N. 2007. Mummies. *American Journal of Physical Anthropology* 134(S45):162–190.

Lynnerup N. 2009. Methods in Mummy Research. *Anthropologischer Anzeiger* 67(4):357–384.

Lynnerup N. 2012. Mummies and Bog Bodies. In: Buikstra JE and Roberts CA, editors. *The Global History of Paleopathology: Pioneers and Prospects*. Oxford: Oxford University Press. pp. 632–651.

Lynnerup N. 2015. The Thule Inuit Mummies from Greenland. *The Anatomical Record* 298(6):1001–1006.

Lynnerup N, Aufderheide A, Rodríguez-Martín C, Cárdenas-Arroyo F, Arriaza B, Rabino-Massa E, Peña PA, and Cordy-Collins A. 2012. The World Congresses on Mummy Studies. In: Buikstra JE and Roberts CA, editors. *The Global History of Paleopathology: Pioneers and Prospects*. Oxford: Oxford University Press. pp. 694–699.

Madden G, and Arriaza B. 2014. The Effects of Arsenic Poisoning in the Early Inhabitants of the Azapa Valley, Chile. *Yearbook of Mummy Studies* 2:147–151.

Madden M, Salo WL, Streitz J, Aufderheide AC, Fornaciari G, Jaramillo C, Vallejo GA, Yockteng F, Arriaza BT, Cárdenas-Arroyo F, and Guhl F. 2001. Identification of trypanosoma cruzi DNA in Ancient Human Chilean Mummies. *BioTechniques* 30(1):102–109.

Maixner F, Overath T, Linke D, Janko M, Guerriero G, Berg BHJ, Stade B, Leidinger P, Backes C, Jaremek M, Kneissl B, Meder B, Franke A, Egarter-Vigl E, Meese E, Schwarz A, Tholey A, Zink A, and Keller A. 2013. Paleoproteomic Study of the Iceman's Brain Tissue. *Cellular and Molecular Life Sciences* 70(19):3709–3722.

Maixner F, Thomma A, Cipollini G, Widder S, Rattei T, and Zink A. 2014. Metagenomic Analysis Reveals Presence of *Treponema denticola* in a Tissue Biopsy of the Iceman. *PLoS One* 9(6):e99994.

Makristathis A, Schwarzmeier J, Mader RM, Varmuza K, Simonitsch I, Chavez JC, Platzer W, Unterdorfer H, Scheithauer R, and Derevianko A. 2002. Fatty Acid Composition and Preservation of the Tyrolean Iceman and Other Mummies. *Journal of Lipid Research* 43(12):2056–2061.

Malgora S, Pieri A, Bernardo L, Elias J, Milani C, and Ceriani G. 2014. The Ankhpakhered Mummy Project: CT-Scan Analysis. *Yearbook of Mummy Studies* 2:63–70.

Marchetti A, Pellegrini S, Bevilacqua G, and Fornaciari G. 1996. K-RAS Mutation in the Tumour of Ferrante I of Aragon, King of Naples. *The Lancet* 347(9010):1272.

Marennikova S, Shelukhina E, Zhukova O, Yanova N, and Loparev V. 1989. Smallpox Diagnosed 400 Years Later: Results of Skin Lesions Examination of 16th Century Italian Mummy. *Journal of Hygiene, Epidemiology, Microbiology, and Immunology* 34(2):227–231.

Marota I, Basile C, Ubaldi M, and Rollo F. 2002. DNA Decay Rate in Papyri and Human Remains from Egyptian Archaeological Sites. *American Journal of Physical Anthropology* 117(4):310–318.

Marota I, Fornaciari G, and Rollo F. 1996. La sifilide nel rinascimento: identificazione di sequenze ribosomali batteriche nel DNA isolato dalla mummia di Maria d'Aragona (XVI secolo). *Antropologia Contemporanea* 19:157–174.

Marota I, Fornaciar G, and Rollo U. 1998. Hepatitis E Virus (HEV) RNA Sequences in the DNA of Maria of Aragon (1503–1563): Paleopathological Evidence or Anthropological Marker? *Journal of Paleopathology* 10(2):53–58.

Marquet PA, Santoro CM, Latorre C, Standen VG, Abades S, Rivadeneira MM, Arriaza BT, and Hochberg ME. 2012. Emergence of Social Complexity Among Coastal Hunter-Gatherers in the Atacama Desert of Northern Chile. *Proceedings of the National Academy of Sciences of the United States of America* 109(37):14754–14760.

Marsteller SJ, Torres-Rouff C, and Knudson KJ. 2011. Pre-Columbian Andean Sickness Ideology and the Social Experience Leishmaniasis: A Contextualized Analysis of Bioarchaeological and Paleopathological Data from San Pedro de Atacama, Chile. *International Journal of Paleopathology* 1:24–34.

Martin DL, Harrod RP, and Pérez VR. 2013. *Bioarchaeology: An Integrated Approach to Working with Human Remains*. New York: Springer.

Martin RT. 1970. The Role of Coca in the History, Religion, and Medicine of South American Indians. *Economic Botany* 24(4):422–438.

Martinson E, Reinhard KJ, Buikstra JE, and Cruz KD. 2003. Pathoecology of Chiribaya parasitism. *Memórias do Instituto Oswaldo Cruz* 98:195–205.

Marx M, and D'Auria SH. 1986. CT Examination of Eleven Egyptian Mummies. *Radio-Graphics* 6(2):321–330.

Masali M, and Chiarelli B. 1972. Demographic Data on the Remains of Ancient Egyptians. *Journal of Human Evolution* 1(2):167–169.

Masetti M, Gabrielli S, Menconi M, and Fornaciari G. 2008. Insect Remains Associated with the Mummy of Cardinal Giulo della Rovere, Archbishop of Ravenna (1522–1578). In: Atoche P, Rodríguez C, and Ramírez Á, editors. *VI World Congress on Mummy Studies*, Lanzarote. Santa Cruz de Tenerife, Academia Canaria de la Historia. pp. 379–385.

Matheson CD, David R, Spigelman M, and Donoghue HD. 2014. Molecular Confirmation of Schistosoma and Family Relationship in Two Ancient Egyptian Mummies. *Yearbook of Mummy Studies* 2:39–47.

Maurer J, Möhring T, Jürgen R, and Nissenbaum A. 2002. Plant Lipids and Fossil Hydrocarbons in Embalming Material of Roman Period Mummies from the Dakhleh Oasis, Western Desert, Egypt. *Journal of Archaeological Science* 29(7):751–762.

Mayer BX, Reiter C, and Bereuter TL. 1997. Investigation of the Triacylglycerol Composition of Iceman's Mummified Tissue by High-Temperature Gas Chromatography. *Journal of Chromatography* 692:1–6.

McAnulty RJ, and Laurent GJ. 1987. Collagen Synthesis and Degradation in Vivo: Evidence for Rapid Rates of Collagen Turnover with Extensive Degradation of Newly Synthesized Collagen in Tissues of the Adult Rat. *Collagen and Related Research* 7(2):93–104.

McCreesh NC, Gize AP, and David AR. 2011. Ancient Egyptian Hair Gel: New Insight into Ancient Egyptian Mummification Procedures Through Chemical Analysis. *Journal of Archaeological Science* 38(12):3432–3434.

McKinley LM. 1977. Bodies Preserved from the Days of the Crusades in St Micham's Church, Dublin. *The Journal of Pathology* 122(1):27–28.

McKnight LM, and Loynes RD. 2014. From Egyptian Desert to Scottish Highlands—The Radiographic Study of a Twenty-Fifth Dynasty Coffin and Mummy Bundle from the Perth Museum and Art Gallery, Scotland. *Papers on Anthropology* 23:108–117.

McKnight LM, McCreesh NC, and Gize A. 2014. The Weird and the Wonderful—The Scientific Study of a Miniature Mummy. *Papers on Anthropology* 23:97–107.

McLean S. 2008. Bodies from the Bog: Metamorphosis, Non-Human Agency and the Making of 'Collective' Memory. *Trames* 12:299–308.

Meier DK, Mendonça de Souza S, Tessarolo B, Sene GAM, and de Silva LPR. 2011. Acauã: CT Scanning a Mummified Body from Gentio II Cave, Minas Gerais, Brazil. *Yearbook of Mummy Studies* 1:99–108.

Melcher AH, Holowka S, Pharoah M, and Lewin PK. 1997. Non-Invasive Computed Tomography and Three-Dimensional Reconstruction of Dentition of a 2,800-Year-Old Egyptian Mummy Exhibiting Extensive Dental Disease. *American Journal of Physical Anthropology* 103:329–340.

Mendis S, Puska P, and Norrving B, editors. 2011. *Global Atlas on Cardiovascular Disease Prevention and Control.* Geneva: World Health Organization.

Meyer M, Kircher M, Gansauge M-T, Li H, Racimo F, Mallick S, Schraiber JG, Jay F, Prüfer K, and de Filippo C. 2012. A High-Coverage Genome Sequence from an Archaic Denisovan Individual. *Science* 338(6104):222–226.

Millet NB, Hard GD, Reyman TA, Zimmerman MR, and Lewin PK. 1998. ROM I: Mummification for the Common People. In: Cockburn A, Cockburn E, and Reyman TA, editors. *Mummies, Disease, and Culture.* Cambridge: Cambridge University Press. pp. 91–105.

Minkes W. 2008. *Warp the Loom—Wrap the Dead Trapezoid Shaped Textiles from the Chiribaya Culture, South Peru, AD 900–1375.* Textile Society of American Symposium Proceedings. Paper 232.

Moissidou D, Day J, Shin DH, and Bianucci R. 2015. Invasive Versus Non Invasive Methods Applied to Mummy Research: Will This Controversy Ever Be Solved? *Biomed Research International* 2015, Article ID 192829, 7 pages.Møller-Christensen V. 1973. Osteo-Archaeology as a Medico-Historical Auxiliary Science. *Medical History* 17:411–418.

Monge JM, and Rühli F. 2015. The Anatomy of the Mummy: Mortui Viventes Docent—When Ancient Mummies Speak to Modern Doctors. *The Anatomical Record* 298(6):935–940.

Montiel R, Solórzano E, Díaz N, Álvarez-Sandoval BA, González-Ruiz M, Cañadas MP, Simões N, Isidro A, and Malgosa A. 2012. Neonate Human Remains: A Window of Opportunity to the Molecular Study of Ancient Syphilis. *PLoS One* 7(5):e36371.

Morales Gamarra R. 2002. Los Pinchudos, arquitectura funeraria en Río Abiseo, San Martín. Parte I. *Arkinka* 76:92–101.

Morales Gamarra R, Álvarez LV, Church WB, and Tello LC. 2002. Los Pinchudos: Un estudio preliminar de su población. *Sian* 8(12):1–41.

Munizaga J, Allison MJ, and Aspillaga E. 1978a. Diaphragmatic Hernia Associated with Strangulation of the Small Bowel in an Atacamena Mummy. *American Journal of Physical Anthropology* 48(1):17–19.

Munizaga J, Allison MJ, and Paredes C. 1978b. Cholelithiasis and Cholecystitis in Pre-Columbian Chileans. *American Journal of Physical Anthropology* 48(2):209–212.

Münnemann K, Böni T, Colacicco G, Blümich B, and Rühli F. 2007. Noninvasive 1H and 23Na Nuclear Magnetic Resonance Imaging of Ancient Egyptian Human Mummified Tissue. *Magnetic Resonance Imaging* 25:1341–1345.

Murphy MS, Gaither C, Goycochea E, Verano JW, and Cock G. 2010. Violence and Weapon-Related Trauma at Puruchuco-Huaquerones, Peru. *American Journal of Physical Anthropology* 142(4):636–649.

Murphy WA Jr, Nedden DZ, Gostner P, Knapp R, Recheis W, and Seidler H. 2003. The Iceman: Discovery and Imaging. *Radiology* 226(3):614–629.

Musshoff F, Brockmann C, Madea B, Rosendahl W, and Piombino-Mascali D. 2013. Ethyl Glucuronide Findings in Hair Samples from the Mummies of the Capuchin Catacombs of Palermo. *Forensic Science International* 232:213–217.

Myasoedova E, Crowson CS, Kremers HM, Therneau TM, and Gabriel SE. 2010. Is the Incidence of Rheumatoid Arthritis Rising? Results from Olmsted County, Minnesota, 1955–2007. *Arthritis & Rheumatism* 62(6):1576–1582.

Nelson AJ. 1998. Wandering Bones: Archaeology, Forensic Science and Moche Burial Practices. *International Journal of Osteoarchaeology* 8(3):192–212.

Nelson AJ, and Wade AD. 2011. *IMPACT Radiological Mummy Database*. www.impactdb.uwo.ca.

Nelson AJ, and Wade AD. 2015. Impact: Development of a Radiological Mummy Database. *The Anatomical Record* 298(6):941–948.

Nelson SM, editor. 2006. *Handbook of Gender in Archaeology*. Lanham, MD: AltaMira Press.

Nerlich AG, Bachmeier BE, Zink A, and Egarter Vigl E. 2005. Histological and Biochemical Evidence for an intravital Stab Wound on Ötzi's Right Hand. *Journal of Biological Research* 80:321–323.

Nerlich AG, Haas CJ, Zink A, Szeimies U, and Hagedorn HG. 1997a. Molecular Evidence for Tuberculosis in an Ancient Egyptian Mummy. *The Lancet* 350(9088):1404.

Nerlich AG, Parsche F, Kirsch T, Wiest I, and Von Der Mark K. 1993. Immunohistochemical Detection of Interstitial Collagens in Bone and Cartilage Tissue Remnants in an Infant Peruvian Mummy. *American Journal of Physical Anthropology* 91(3):279–285.

Nerlich AG, Peschel O, and Egarter-Vigl E. 2009. New Evidence for Ötzi's Final Trauma. *Intensive Care Medicine* 35:1138–1139.

Nerlich AG, Schraut B, Dittrich S, Jelinek T, and Zink AR. 2008. *Plasmodium Falciparum* in Ancient Egypt. *Emerging Infectious Diseases* 14(8):1317–1319.

Nerlich AG, Wiest I, Löhrs U, Parsche F, and Schramel P. 1995. Extensive Pulmonary Haemorrhage in an Egyptian Mummy. *Virchows Archiv* 427(4):423–429.

Nerlich AG, Wiest I, and Tubel J. 1997b. Coronary Arteriosclerosis in a Male Mummy from Ancient Egypt. *Journal of Paleopathology* 9(2):83–89.

Nerlich AG, Zink A, Szeimies U, and Hagedorn HG. 2000. Ancient Egyptian Prosthesis of the Big Toe. *The Lancet* 356(9248):2176–2179.

Nerlich AG, Zink A, Szeimies U, Rohrbach H, Bachmeier R, and Hagedorn H. 1999. Paleopathological Evidence for Surgical Treatment in Ancient Egypt. *Journal of Paleopathology* 11(2):135.

Nezamabadi M, Aali A, Stöllner T, Mashkour M, and Le Bailly M. 2013a. Paleoparasitological Analysis of Samples from the Chehrabad Salt Mine (Northwestern Iran). *International Journal of Paleopathology* 3(3):229–233.

Nezamabadi M, Mashkour M, Aali A, Stollner T, and Le Bailly M. 2013b. Identification of *Taenia* sp. in a Natural Human Mummy (Third Century BC) from the Chehrabad Salt Mine in Iran. *Journal of Parasitology* 99(3):570–572.

Nicot C. 2005. Current Views in HTLV-I-Associated Adult T-Cell Leukemia/Lymphoma. *American Journal of Hematology* 78(3):232–239.

Nissen R, Cardinale GJ, and Udenfriend S. 1978. Increased Turnover of Arterial Collagen in Hypertensive Rats. *Proceedings of the National Academy of Sciences* 75(1):451–453.

Notman DNH, Anderson L, Beattie OB, and Amy R. 1987. Arctic Paleoradiology: Portable Radiographic Examination of Two Frozen Sailors from the Franklin Expedition (1845–1848). *American Journal of Radiology* 149:347–350.

Notman DNH, Tashjian J, Aufderheide AC, Cass OW, Shane OC, Berquist TH, Gray JE, and Gedgaudas E. 1986. Modern Imaging and Endoscopic Biopsy Techniques in Egyptian Mummies. *American Journal of Roentgenology* 146:93–96.

Novo SPC, Leles D, Bianucci R, and Araujo A. 2015. Leishmania Tarentolae Molecular Signatures in a 300 Hundred-Years-Old Human Brazilian Mummy. *Parasites & Vectors* 8:72.

Nystrom KC. 2009. The reconstruction of identity: A case study from Chachapoya, Peru. In: Knudson KJ, and Stojanowski CM, editors. *Bioarchaeology and Identity in the Americas*. Gainesville: University Press of Florida. pp. 82–102.

Nystrom KC. 2014. The Bioarchaeology of Structural Violence and Dissection in 19th Century United States. *American Anthropologist* 116(4): 765–779.

Nystrom KC, Buikstra JE, and Braunstein EM. 2004. Field Paleoradiography of Skeletal Material from Early Classic Period of Copan, Honduras. *Canadian Association of Radiologists Journal* 55(4):246–253.

Nystrom KC, Buikstra JE, and Muscutt K. 2010. Chachapoya Mortuary Behavior: A Consideration of Method and Meaning. *Chungara* 42(2):477–495.

Nystrom KC, and Cartmell L. 2012. "Profoundly Inspired": The Contributions of Arthur C. Aufderheide to Soft-Tissue Paleopathology. In: Buikstra JE and Roberts CA, editors. *The Global History of Paleopathology: Pioneers and Prospects*. Oxford: Oxford University Press. pp. 14–21.

Nystrom KC, Goff A, and Goff ML. 2005. Mortuary Behavior Reconstruction Through Paleoentomology: A Case Study from Chachapoya, Peru. *International Journal of Osteoarchaeology* 15(3):175–185.

Nystrom KC, and Piombino-Mascali D. 2017. Mummy Studies and the Soft Tissue Evidence of Care. In: Tilley L and Schrenk AA, editors. *New Developments in the Bioarchaeology of Care: Further Case Studies and Expanded Theory*. New York: Springer. pp. 199–218.

Nystrom KC, and Tilley, L. 2018. Mummy Studies and the Bioarchaeology of Care. *International Journal of Paleopathology*. DOI: 10.1016/j.ijpp.2018.06.004.

O'Brien JJ, Battista JJ, Romagnoli C, and Chhem RK. 2009. CT Imaging of Human Mummies: A Critical Review of the Literature. *International Journal of Osteoarchaeology* 19:90–98.

O'Connor S, Ali E, Al-Sabah S, Anwar D, Bergström E, Brown KA, Buckberry J, Buckley S, Collins M, Denton J et al. 2011. Exceptional Preservation of a Prehistoric Human Brain from Heslington, Yorkshire, UK. *Journal of Archaeological Science* 38(7):1641–1654.

Oeggl K, Kofler W, and Schmid A. 2005. New Aspects to the Diet of the Neolithic Tyrolean Iceman "Ötzi." *Journal of Biological Research* 80:344–347.

Oeggl K, Kofler W, Schmidl A, Dickson JH, Egarter-Vigl E, and Gaber O. 2007. The Reconstruction of the Last Itinerary of "Ötzi," the Neolithic Iceman, by Pollen Analysis from Sequentially Sampled Gut Extracts. *Quaternary Science Reviews* 26:853–861.

Ogalde JP, Arriaza BT, and Soto EC. 2009. Identification of Psychoactive Alkaloids in Ancient Andean Human Hair by Gas Chromatography/Mass Spectrometry. *Journal of Archaeological Science* 36(2):467–472.

Oh CS, Lee SY, Lee IS, Kim Y-S, Koh KS, and Shin DH. 2011. Differential Findings in Post-Factum Dissections of Medieval Korean Mummies Exhibiting Similar Preservation Patterns on Computerized Tomography Images. *Annals of Anatomy-Anatomischer Anzeiger* 193(6):544–549.

Oh CS, Seo M, Lim NJ, Lee SJ, Lee E-J, Lee SD, and Shin DH. 2010. Paleoparasitological Report on Ascaris aDNA from an Ancient East Asian Sample. *Memórias do Instituto Oswaldo Cruz* 105(2):225–228.

Öhrström L, Bitzer A, Walther M, and Rühli FJ. 2010. Technical Note: Terahertz Imaging of Ancient Mummies and Bone. *American Journal of Physical Anthropology* 142(3):497–500.

Öhrström L, Fischer BM, Bitzer A, Wallauer J, Walther M, and Rühli F. 2015. Terahertz Imaging Modalities of Ancient Egyptian Mummified Objects and of a Naturally Mummified Rat. *The Anatomical Record* 298(6):1135–1143.

Öhrström L, Von Waldenburg H, Speier P, Bock M, and Rühli FM. 2013. MR Imaging Versus CT of Ancient Peruvian and Egyptian Mummified Tissues. *RadioGraphics* 33:291–296.

Olivieri C, Ermini L, Rizzi E, Corti G, Bonnal R, Luciani S, Marota I, De Bellis G, and Rollo F. 2010. Characterization of Nucleotide Misincorporation Patterns in the Iceman's Mitochondrial DNA. *PLoS One* 5(1):e8629.

Oliveira C, Velho S, Moutinho C, Ferreira A, Preto A, Domingo E, Capelinha AF, Duval A, Hamelin R, Machado JC et al. 2007. KRAS and BRAF Oncogenic Mutations in MSS Colorectal Carcinoma Progression. *Oncogene* 26:158–163.

Oller NA, Grácia XE, Nociarová D, and Morera AM. 2012. Taphonomical Study of the Anthropological Remains from Cova Des Pas (Minorca). *Quaternary International* 275:112–119.

Ong C, Chan S, Campo M, Fujinaga K, Mavromara-Nazos P, Labropoulou V, Pfister H, Tay S, Ter Meulen J, and Villa L. 1993. Evolution of Human Papillomavirus Type 18: An Ancient Phylogenetic Root in Africa and Intratype Diversity Reflect Coevolution with Human Ethnic Groups. *Journal of Virology* 67(11):6424–6431.

Orchiston DW. 1971. Maori Mummification in Protohistoric New Zealand. *Anthropos* 66:753–766.

Ortner DJ. 1991. Theoretical and Missues in Paleopathology. In: Ortner DJ and Aufderheide AC, editors. *Human Paleopathology: Current Syntheses and Future Options*. Washington, DC: Smithsonian Institution Press. pp. 5–11.

Ortner DJ, and Aufderheide AC. 1991. Introduction. In: Ortner DJ and Aufderheide A, editors. *Human Paleopathology: Current Syntheses and Future Options*. Washington, DC: Smithsonian Institution Press. pp. 1–2.

Ortner DJ, Butler W, Cafarella J, and Milligan L. 2001. Evidence of Probable Scurvy in Subadults from Archeological Sites in North America. *American Journal of Physical Anthropology* 114(4):343–351.

Otten CM, and Flory LL. 1963. Blood Typing of Chilean Mummy Tissue: A New Approach. *American Journal of Physical Anthropology* 21(3):283–285.

Ottini L, Falchetti M, Marinozzi S, Angeletti LR, and Fornaciari G. 2011. Gene-Environment Interactions in the Pre—Industrial Era: The Cancer of King Ferrante I of Aragon (1431–1494). *Human Pathology* 42(3):332–339.

Ovalle IM, Torres BA, and Aufderheide AC, editors. 1993. *Acha—2 y los Orígenes del Poblamiento Humano en Arica*. Arica, Chile: University of Tarapaca.

Pääbo S. 1985a. Molecular Cloning of ancient Egyptian Mummy DNA. *Nature* 314(18):644–645.

Pääbo S. 1985b. Preservation of DNA in Ancient Egyptian Mummies. *Journal of Archaeological Science* 12(6):411–417.

Pabst MA, Letofsky-Papst I, Bock E, Moser M, Dorfer L, Egarter-Vigl E, and Hofer F. 2009. The Tattoos of the Tyrolean Iceman: A Light Microscopical, Ultrastructural and Element Analytical Study. *Journal of Archaeological Science* 36(10):2335–2341.

Pabst MA, Letofsky-Papst I, Moser M, Spindler K, Bock E, Wilhelm P, Leopold Dorfer MD, Geigl JB, Auer M, Speicher MR, and Hofer F. 2010. Different Staining Substances Were Used in Decorative and Therapeutic Tattoos in a 1000-Year-Old Peruvian Mummy. *Journal of Archaeological Science* 37(12):3256–3262.

Paddock FK, Loomis CC, and Perkons AK. 1970. An Inquest on the Death of Charles Francis Hall. *New England Journal of Medicine* 282:784–786.

Pakendorf B, Novgorodov IN, Osakovskij VL, Al'bina PD, Protod'jakonov AP, and Stoneking M. 2006. Investigating the Effects of Prehistoric Migrations in Siberia: Genetic Variation and the Origins of Yakuts. *Human Genetics* 120(3):334–353.

Panda SK, Thakral D, and Rehman S. 2007. Hepatitis E Virus. *Reviews in Medical Virology* 17(3):151–180.

Pankova SV. 2013. One More Culture with Ancient Tatoo Tradition in Southern Siberia: Tattoos on a Mummy from the Oglakhty Burial Ground, 3rd–4th Century AD. In: Della Casa P and Witt C, editors. *Tattoos and Body Modification in Antiquity Proceedings of the Sessions at the Annual Meetings of the European Association of Archaeologists in the Hague and Oslo, 2010/11*. Zurich Studies in Archaeology 9. Chronos-Verlag, Zurich. pp. 75–86.

Panzer S, Borumandi F, Wanek J, Papageorgopoulou C, Shved N, Colacicco G, and Rühli FJ. 2013a. "Modeling Ancient Egyptian Embalming": Radiological Assessment of Experimentally Mummified Human Tissue by CT and MRI. *Skeletal Radiology* 42(11):1527–1535.

Panzer S, Gill-Frerking H, Rosendahl W, Zink AR, and Piombino-Mascali D. 2013b. Multi-detector CT Investigation of the Mummy of Rosalia Lombardo (1918–1920). *Annals of Anatomy* 195:401–408.

Panzer S, Mc Coy MR, Hitzl W, Piombino-Mascali D, Jankauskas R, Zink AR, and Augat P. 2015. Checklist and Scoring System for the Assessment of Soft Tissue Preservation in CT Examinations of Human Mummies. *PLoS One* 10(8):e0133364.

Panzer S, Peschel O, Hass-Gebhard B, Bachmeier BE, Pusch CM, and Nerlich AG. 2014. Reconstructing the Life of an Unknown (ca. 500 Years Old South American Inca) Mummy—Multidisciplinary Study of a Peruvian Inca Mummy Suggests Severe Chagas Disease and Ritual Homicide. *PLoS One* 9(2):e89528.

Panzer S, Piombino-Mascali D, and Zink AR. 2012. Herniation Pits in Human Mummies: A CT Investigation in the Capuchin Catacombs of Palermo, Sicily. *PLoS One* 7(5):e36537.

Panzer S, Tamošiūnas A, Valančius R, Jankauskas R, and Piombino-Mascali D. 2013c. Radio-logical Evidence of Rickets in a Lithuanian Child Mummy. *RoFo* 185(7):670–672.

Panzer S, Zink AR, and Piombino-Mascali D. 2010. Radiologic Evidence of Anthropo-genic Mummification in the Capuchin Catacombs of Palermo, Sicily. *Radiographics* 30(4):1123–1132.

Paoli G, Tarli SMB, Klír P, Strouhal E, Tofanelli S, Del Santo Valli MT, and Pavelcová B. 1993. Paleoserology of the Christian Population at Sayala (Lower Nubia): An Evaluation of the Reliability of the Results. *American Journal of Physical Anthropology* 92(3):263–272.

Papageorgopoulou C, Rentsch K, Raghavan M, Hofmann MI, Colacicco G, Gallien V, Bia-nucci R, and Rühli F. 2010. Preservation of Cell Structures in a Medieval Infant Brain: A Paleohistological, Paleogenetic, Radiological and Physico-Chemical Study. *NeuroImage* 50:893–901.

Papageorgopoulou C, Shved N, Wanek J, and Rühli FJ. 2015. Modeling Ancient Egyptian Mummification on Fresh Human Tissue: Macroscopic and Histological Aspects. *The Ana-tomical Record* 298(6):974–987.

Papageorgopoulou C, Xirotiris NI, Iten PX, Baumgartner MR, Schmid M, and Rühli F. 2009. Indications of Embalming in Roman Greece by Physical, Chemical and Histologi-cal Analysis. *Journal of Archaeological Science* 36(1):35–42.

Paradise J, and Andrews L. 2007. Tales from the Crypt: Scientific, Ethical, and Legal Consid-erations for Biohistorical Analysis of Deceased Historical Figures. *Temple Journal of Science, Technology, and Environmental Law* 26:223–299.

Paredes UM, Prys-Jones R, Adams M, Groombridge J, Kundu S, Agapow PM, and Abel RL. 2012. Micro-CT X-rays Do Not Fragment DNA in Preserved Bird Skins. *Journal of Zoological Systematics and Evolutionary Research* 50(3):247–250.

Parker Pearson M. 1982. Mortuary Practices, Society, and Ideology. In: Hodder I, editor. *Symbolic and Structural Archaeology.* Cambridge: Cambridge University Press. pp. 99–113.

Parker Pearson M, Chamberlain A, Collins M, Cox C, Craig G, Craig O, Hiller J, Marshall P, Mulville J, and Smith H. 2007. Further Evidence for Mummification in Bronze Age Britain. *Antiquity* 81. www.antiquity.ac.uk/projgall/parker312/.

Parker Pearson M, Chamberlain A, Craig O, Marshall P, Mulville J, Smith H, Chenery C, Collins M, Cook G, Craig G et al. 2005. Evidence for Mummification in Bronze Age Britain. *Antiquity* 79:529–546.

Parsche F, Balabanova S, and Pirsig W. 1993. Drugs in Ancient Populations. *The Lancet* 341(8843):503.

Parsche F, and Nerlich A. 1995. Presence of Drugs in Different Tissues of an Egyptian Mummy. *Fresenius' Journal of Analytical Chemistry* 352(3–4):380–384.

Peintner U, Pöder R, and Pümpel T. 1998. The Iceman's Fungi. *Mycological Research* 102(10):1153–1162.

Pelo S, Correra P, Danza FM, Amenta A, Gasparini G, Marianetti TM, and Moro A. 2012. Evaluation of the Dentoskeletal Characteristics of an Egyptian Mummy with Three-Dimensional Computer Analysis. *The Journal of Craniofacial Surgery* 23(4):1159–1162.

Pernter P, Gostner P, Vigl EE, and Rühli FJ. 2007. Radiologic Proof for the Iceman's Cause of Death (ca. 5'300 BP). *Journal of Archaeological Science* 34(11):1784–1786.

Pickering RB, Conces DJ, Braunstein EM, and Yurco F. 1990. Three-Dimesional Computed Tomography of the Mummy Wenohotep. *American Journal of Physical Anthropology* 83(1):49–55.

Piepenbrink H, Frahm J, and Haase A. 1986. Nuclear Magnetic Resonance Imaging of Mummified Corpses. *American Journal of Physical Anthropology* 70(1):27–28.

Piñar G, Kraková L, Pangallo D, Piombino-Mascali D, Maixner F, Zink A, and Sterflinger K. 2014. Halophilic Bacteria Are Colonizing the Exhibition Areas of the Capuchin Catacombs in Palermo, Italy. *Extremophiles* 18:677–691.

Piombino-Mascali D, Abinion OV, Salvador-Amores A, and Beckett RG. 2013a. Human Mummification Practices Among the Igorot of North Luzon. *Bulletin der Schwiezerischen Gesellschaft fur Anthropologie* 19(2):45.

Piombino-Mascali D, Aufderheide AC, Johnson-Williams M, and Zink AR. 2009. The Salafia Method Rediscovered. *Virchows Archiv* 454:355–357.

Piombino-Mascali D, Aufderheide AC, Panzer S, and Zink AR. 2010. Mummies from Palermo. In: Wieczorek A and Rosendahl W, editors. *Mummies of the World*. New York: Prestel. pp. 357–361.

Piombino-Mascali D, Kozakaitė J, Tamošiūnas A, Ramūnas V, Panzer S, and Jankauskas R. 2014. Skeletal Pathological Conditions of Lithuanian Mummies. *Papers on Anthropology* 23:118–126.

Piombino-Mascali D, Maixner F, Zink AR, Marvelli S, Panzer S, and Aufderheide AC. 2012. The Catacomb Mummies of Sicily: A State-of-the-Art Report (2007–2011). *Antrocom Online Journal of Anthropology* 8:341–352.

Piombino-Mascali D, McKnight L, Snitkuvienė A, Jankauskas R, Tamošiūnas A, Valančius R, Rosendahl W, and Panzer S. 2015. From Egypt to Lithuania: Marija Rudzinskaitė-Arcimavičienė's Mummy and its Radiological Investigation. In: Ikram S, Kaiser J, and Walker R, editors. *Egyptian Bioarchaeology: Humans, Animals, and the Environment*. Leiden: Sidestone Press. pp. 95–104.

Piombino-Mascali D, Panzer S, Marvelli S, Lösch S, Aufderheide AC, and Zink AR. 2011. The "Sicily Mummy Project": First Results of the Scientific Campaigns (2007–2010). *Geschichte und Tradition der Mumifizierung in Europa Kasseler Studien zur Sepulkralkultur* 25–31.

Piombino-Mascali D, Zink AR, Reinhard KJ, Lein M, Panzer S, Aufderheide AC, Rachid R, De Souza W, Araújo A, Chaves SAM et al. 2013b. Dietary Analysis of Piraino 1, Sicily, Italy: The Role of Archaeopalynology in Forensic Science. *Journal of Archaeological Science* 40(4):1935–1945.

Plowman T. 1986. Coca Chewing and the Botanical Origins of Coca (Erythroxylum spp.) in South America. *Cultural Survival Report* 23:5–34.

Pöder R. 2005. The Ice Man's Fungi: Facts and Mysteries. *International Journal of Medicinal Mushrooms* 7(3).

Pöder R, and Peintner U. 1999. Laxatives and the Ice Man. *The Lancet* 353(9156):926.

Polosmak NV. 2000. Tattoos in the Pazyryk World. *Archaeology, Ethnology and Anthropology of Eurasia* 4:95–102.

Posh JC. 2015. Technical Limitations on the Use of Traditional Magnetic Resonance Imaging in the Evaluation of Mummified Remains: A View from a Hands-On Radiologic Technologist's Perspective. *The Anatomical Record* 298(6):1116–1124.

Post PW, and Donner DD. 1972. Frostbite in a Pre-Columbian Mummy. *American Journal of Physical Anthropology* 37(2):187–191.

Powell ML. 2012. The History of the Paleopathology Association. In: Buikstra JE and Roberts CA, editors. *The Global History of Paleopathology: Pioneers and Prospects*. Oxford: Oxford University Press. pp. 667–677.

Powell ML, Cook DC, Bogdan G, Buikstra JE, Castro MM, Horne PD, Hunt DR, Koritzer RT, de Souza SFM, Sandford MK, Saunders L, Sene GAM, Sullivan L, and Swetnam JJ. 2006. Invisible Hands: Women in Bioarchaeology. In: Buikstra JE and Beck LA, editors. *Bioarchaeology: The Contextual Analysis of Human Remains*. Amsterdam: Academic Press. pp. 131–194.

Prats-Muñoz G, Galtés I, Armentano N, Cases S, Fernández PL, and Malgosa A. 2013. Human Soft Tissue Preservation in Cova des Pas site (Minorca Bronze Age). *Journal of Archaeological Science* 40:4701–4710.

Prats-Muñoz G, Malgosa A, Armentano N, Galtés I, Esteban J, Bombi JA, Tortosa M, Fernández E, Jordana X, Isidro A et al. 2012. A Paleoneurohistological Study of 3,000-Year-Old Mummified Brain Tissue from the Mediterranean Bronze Age. *Pathobiology* 79:239–246.

Previgliano CH, Ceruti C, Reinhard J, Araoz FA, and Diez JG. 2003. Radiologic Evaluation of the Llullaillaco Mummies. *American Journal of Roentgenology* 181:1473–1479.

Price DT, Tiesler V, and Burton JH. 2006. Early African Diaspora in Colonial Campeche, Mexico: Strontium Isotopic Evidence. *American Journal of Physical Anthropology* 130(4):485–490.

Pullman D, and Nicholas GP. 2011. Intellectual Property and the Ethical/Legal Status of Human DNA: The (ir) Relevance of Context. *Études/Inuit/Studies* 35(1–2):143–164.

Quigley C. 1998. *Modern Mummies: The Preservation of the Human Body in the Twentieth Century*. Jefferson, NC: McFarland & Company, Inc.

Rakita GFM. 2006. Hemenway, Hrdlička, and Hawikku: A Historical Perspective on Bioarchaeological Research in the American Southwest. In: Buikstra JE and Beck LA, editors. *Bioarchaeology: The Contextual Analysis of Human Remains*. Burlington, MA: Elsevier. pp. 95–111.

Rakita GFM. 2014. Bioarchaeology as a Process: An Examination of Bioarchaeological Tribes in the USA. *Archaeological Human Remains*: Springer 213–234.

Rakita GFM, and Buikstra JE. 2005a. Introduction. In: Rakita GFM, Buikstra JE, Beck LA, and Williams SR, editors. *Interacting with the Dead: Perspectives on Mortuary Archaeology for the New Millennium*. Gainsville: University Press of Florida. pp. 1–11.

Rakita GFM, and Buikstra JE. 2005b. Corrupting Flesh: Reexamining Hertz's Perspective on Mummification and Cremation. In: Rakita GFM, Buikstra JE, Beck LA, and Williams SR, editors. *Interacting with the Dead: Perspectives on Mortuary Archaeology for the New Millennium*. Gainsville: University Press of Florida. pp. 97–106.

Rakita GFM, Buikstra JE, Beck LA, and Williams SR, editors. 2005. *Interacting with the Dead: Perspectives on Mortuary Archaeology for the New Millennium*. Gainsville: University Press of Florida.

Ramaroli V, Hamilton J, Ditchfield P, Fazeli H, Aali A, Coningham RAE, and Pollard AM. 2010. The Chehr Abad "Salt Men" and the Isotopic Ecology of Humans in Ancient Iran. *American Journal of Physical Anthropology* 143(3):343–354.

Razmilic B, Allison M, and Gonzalez M. 1987. Determinación de la edad del destete utilizando las relaciones Sr/Ca y Zn/Ca en hueso trabecular en momias de niños precolombinos. *Chungara* 18:189–194.

Reinhard KJ. 1990. Archaeoparasitology in North America. *American Journal of Physical Anthropology* 82(2):145–163.

Reinhard KJ, and Buikstra J. 2003. Louse Infestation of the Chiribaya Culture, Southern Peru: Variation in Prevalence by Age and Sex. *Memórias do Instituto Oswaldo Cruz* 98:173–179.

Reinhard KJ, Fink TM, and Skiles J. 2003. A Case of Megacolon in Rio Grande Valley as a Possible Case of Chagas Disease. *Memórias do Instituto Oswaldo Cruz* 98:165–172.

Reinhard KJ, LeRoy-Toren S, and Arriaza BT. 2011. Where Have All the Plant Foods Gone? The Search for Refined Dietary Reconstruction from Chinchorro Mummies. *Yearbook of Mummy Studies* 1:139–151.

Reinhard KJ, and Urban O. 2003. Diagnosing Ancient Diphyllobothriasis from Chinchorro Mummies. *Memórias do Instituto Oswaldo Cruz* 98:191–199.

Renaut L. 2004. Les tatouages d'Ötzi et la petite chirurgie traditionnelle. *L'anthropologie* 108(1):69–105.

Reycraft RM. 2005. Style Change and Ethnogenesis Among the Chiribaya of far South Coastal Peru. In: Reycraft RM, editor. *Us and Them: Archaeology and Ethnicity in the Andes.* Los Angeles: Cotsen Institute of Archaeology, University of California. pp. 54–72.

Reynard LM, Henderson GM, and Hedges REM. 2011. Calcium Isotopes in Archaeological Bones and Their Relationship to Diary Consumption. *Journal of Archaeological Science* 38(3):657–664.

Rick FM, Rocha GC, Dittmar K, Coimbra CEA, Jr, Reinhard K, Bouchet F, Ferreira LF, and Araújo A. 2002. Crab Louse Infestation in Pre-Columbian America. *Journal of Parasitology* 88(6):1266–1267.

Ritzinger J, and Bingenheimer M. 2006. Whole-Body Relics in Chinese Buddhism—Previous Research and Historical Overview. *The Indian International Journal of Buddhist Studies* 7:37–94.

Rivera MA, Aufderheide AC, Cartmell LW, Torres CM, and Langsjoen O. 2005. Antiquity of Coca-Leaf Chewing in the South Central Andes: A 3,000 Year Archaeological Record of Coca-Leaf Chewing from Northern Chile. *Journal of Psychoactive Drugs* 37(4):455–458.

Rivera MA, Mumcuoglu KY, Matheny RT, and Matheny DG. 2008. Huevecillos de Anthropophthirus Capitus en Momias de la Tradicion Chinchorro, Camarones 15-D, Norte de Chile. *Chungara* 40(1):31–39.

Robb J. 2002. Time and Biography: Osteobiography of the Italian Neolithic Lifespan. In: Hamilakis Y, Pluciennik M, and Tarlow S, editors. *Thinking Through the Body: Archaeologies of Corporeality.* New York: Kluwer Academic, Plenum Publishers. pp. 153–172.

Robb J. 2009. Towards a Critical Ötziography: Inventing Prehistoric Bodies. In: Lambert H and McDonald M, editors. *Social Bodies.* New York: Berghahn Books. pp. 100–128.

Robbins Schug G. 2011. *Bioarchaeology and Climate Change: A View from South Asian Prehistory.* Gainesville: University Press of Florida.

Roberts CA. 1999. Disability in the Skeletal Record: Assumptions, Problems and Some Examples. *Archaeological Review from Cambridge* 15(2):79–97.

Roberts CA. 2011. The Bioarchaeology of Leprosy and Tuberculosis: A Comparative Study of Perceptions, Stigma, Diagnosis, and Treatment. In: Argarwal SC and Glencross BA, editors. *Social Bioarchaeology.* West Sussex: Wiley-Blackwell. pp. 252–281.

Roberts CA, and Buikstra JE. 2003. *The Bioarchaeology of Tuberculosis: A Global View on a Reemerging Disease.* Gainsville: University Press of Florida.

Roberts CA, and Buikstra JE. 2014. The History of Tuberculosis from Earliest Times to the Development of Drugs. In: Davies PDO, Barnes PF, and Gordon SB, editors. *Clinical Tuberculosis.* Boca Raton: CRC Press. pp. 3–19.

Roberts CA, Powell ML, and Buikstra JE. 2012. T. Aidan Cockburn (1912–1981) and Eve Cockburn (1924–2003). In: Buikstra JE, and Roberts CA, editors. *The Global History of Paleopathology: Pioneers and Prospects.* Oxford: Oxford Oxford University Press. pp. 32–39.

Rodríguez H, Noemí I, Cerva JL, Espinoza-Navarro O, Castro ME, and Castro M. 2011. Análisis paleoparasitológico de la musculatura esquelética de la momia del cerro El Plomo, Chile: Trichinella sp. *Chungara* 43:581–588.

Rodríguez-Martin C. 1996. Guanche Mummies of Tenerife (Canary Islands): Conservation and Scientific Studies in the CRONOS Project. In: Spindler K, Wilfing H, Ratbichler-Zissernig E, zur Nedden D, and Nothdurfter H, editors. *Human Mummies: A Global Survey of Their Status and the Techniques of Conservation.* New York: Springer-Wien. pp. 183–193.

Rogan PK, and Salvo JJ. 1990. Study of Nucleic Acids Isolated from Ancient Remains. *Yearbook of Physical Anthropology* 33(S11):195–214.

Rollo F, Ermini L, Luciani S, Marota I, and Olivieri C. 2005. Studies on the Preservation of the Intestinal Microbiota's DNA in Human Mummies from Cold Environments. *Medicina nei Secoli* 18(3):725–740.

Rollo F, Ermini L, Luciani S, Marota I, Olivieri C, and Luiselli D. 2006. Fine Characterization of the Iceman's mtDNA Haplogroup. *American Journal of Physical Anthropology* 130(4):557–564.

Rollo F, Luciani S, Canapa A, and Marota I. 2000. Analysis of Bacterial DNA in Skin and Muscle of the Tyrolean Iceman Offers New Insight into the Mummification Process. *American Journal of Physical Anthropology* 111(2):211–219.

Rollo F, Luciani S, Marota I, Olivieri C, and Ermini L. 2007. Persistence and Decay of the Intestinal Microbiota's DNA in Glacier Mummies from the Alps. *Journal of Archaeological Science* 34(8):1294–1305.

Rollo F, and Marota I. 1999. How Microbial Ancient DNA, Found in Association with Human Remains, Can Be Interpreted. *Philosophical Transactions of the Royal Society of London* 354:111–119.

Rollo F, Ubaldi M, Ermini L, and Marota I. 2002. Ötzi's last meals: DNA Analysis of the Intestinal Content of the Neolithic Glacier Mummy from the Alps. *Proceedings of the National Academy of Sciences of the United States of America* 99:12594–12599.

Rosendahl W, Alt KW, Meier S, and Rühli F. 2010. Egyptian Mummies—The Reiss-Engelhorn-Museen Collection. In: Wieczorek A, and Rosendahl W, editors. *Mummies of the World.* New York: Prestel. pp. 316–318.

Rothhammer F, Allison MJ, Núñez L, Standen V, and Arriaza B. 1985. Chagas' Disease in Pre-Columbian South America. *American Journal of Physical Anthropology* 68(4):495–498.

Rubin A. 1988. *Marks of Civilization: Artistic Transformations of the Human Body.* Los Angeles: University of California.

Rudenko SI. 1970. *Frozen Tombs of Siberia: The Pazyryk Burials of Iron Age Horsemen. Tr. M. W. Thompson.* Berkeley, Los Angeles: University of California Press.

Ruff CB, Holt BM, Sladek V, Berner M, Murphy WA, zur Nedden D, Seidler H, and Recheis W. 2006. Body Size, Body Proportions, and Mobility in the Tyrolean "Iceman." *Journal of Human Evolution* 51:91–101.

Ruffer MA. 1911. On Arterial Lesions Found in Egyptian Mummies (1580 B.C–525 A.D.). *The Journal of Pathology and Bacteriology* 15(4):453–462.

Ruffer MA, and Ferguson A. 1911. Note on an Eruption Resembling That of Variola in the Skin of a Mummy of the Twentieth Dynasty (1200–1100 BC). *The Journal of Pathology and Bacteriology* 15(1):1–3.

Rühli FJ. 2015. Short Review: Magnetic Resonance Imaging of Ancient Mummies. *The Anatomical Record* 298(6):1111–1115.

Rühli FJ, and Böni T. 2000a. Radiological and Physio-Chemical Analyses of an Unusual Post Mortem Artefact in an Egyptian Mummy. *Journal of Paleopathology* 12(3):63–70.

Rühli FJ, and Böni T. 2000b. Radiological Aspects and Interpretation of Post-Mortem Artefacts in Ancient Egyptian Mummies from Swiss Collections. *International Journal of Osteoarchaeology* 10:153–157.

Rühli FJ, Böni T, Perlo J, Casanova F, Baias M, Egarter E, and Blumich B. 2007a. Non-Invasive Spatial Tissue Discrimination in Ancient Mummies and Bones in situ by Portable Nuclear Resonance. *Journal of Cultural Heritage* 8:257–263.

Rühli FJ, Chhem RK, and Böni T. 2004. Diagnostic Paleoradiology of Mummified Tissue: Interpretation and Pitfalls. *Canadian Association of Radiologists Journal* 55(4):218–227.

Rühli FJ, Hodler J, and Böni T. 2002. CT-Guided Biopsy—A New Diagnostic Method for Paleopathological Research. *American Journal of Physical Anthropology* 117(3):272–275.

Rühli FJ, and Ikram S. 2014. Purported medical diagnosis of Pharoah Tutankhamun, c. 1325 BC-. *Homo—Journal of Comparative Human Biology* 65:51–63.

Rühli FJ, von Waldburg H, Nielles-Vallespin S, Böni T, and Speier P. 2007b. Clinical Magnetic Resonance Imaging of Ancient Dry Human Mummies Without Rehydration. *Journal of the American Medical Association* 298(22):2617–2620.

Rylander CG, Stumpp OF, Milner TE, Kemp NJ, Mendenhall JM, Diller KR, and Welch AJ. 2006. Dehydration Mechanism of Optical Clearing in Tissue. *Journal of Biomedical Optics* 11(4):041117.

[SAA]. 1996. *Principles of Archaeological Ethics*. http://saa.org/AbouttheSociety/PrinciplesofArchaeologicalEthics/tabid/203/Default.aspx; Accessed January 23, 2015.

Sakurai K, Ogata T, Morimoto I, Long-Xiang P, and Zhong-Bi W. 1998. Mummies from Japan and China. In: Cockburn A, Cockburn E, and Reyman TA, editors. *Mummies, Disease & Ancient Cultures*. Cambridge: Cambridge University Press. pp. 308–335.

Saleem SN, and Hawass Z. 2013. Variability in Brain Treatment During Mummification of Royal Egyptians Dated to the 18th-20th Dynasties: MDCT Findings Correlated with the Archaeologic Literature. *American Journal of Roentgenology* 200:w336–w344.

Saleem SN, and Hawass Z. 2014. Brief Report: Ankylosing Spondylitis or Diffuse Idiopathic Skeletal Hyperostosis in Royal Egyptian Mummies of the 18th–20th Dynasties? Computed Tomography and Archaeology Studies. *Arthritis & Rheumatology* 66(12):3311–3316.

Salo WL, Aufderheide AC, Buikstra JE, and Holcomb TA. 1994. Identification of Mycobacterium Tuberculosis DNA in a Pre-Columbian Peruvian Mummy. *Proceedings of the National Academy of Sciences of the United States of America* 91(6):2091–2094.

Salomon F. 1995. "The Beautiful Grandparents": Andean Ancestor Shrines and Mortuary Ritual as Seen Through Colonial Records. In: Dillehay TD, editor. *Tombs for the Living: Andean Mortuary Practices*. Washington, DC: Dumbarton Oaks Research Library and Collection. pp. 315–353.

Salvador-Amores A. 2012. The Reconceptualization of Burik (Traditional Tattoos) of Kabayan Mummies in Benguet to Contemporary Practices. *Humanities Diliman* 9(1).

Samadelli M, Melis M, Miccoli M, Vigl EE, and Zink AR. 2015. Complete Mapping of the Tattoos of the 5300-Year-Old Tyrolean Iceman. *Journal of Cultural Heritage* 16(5):753–758.

Sampsell BM. 2015. Resolving a Mummy Mismatch. In: Ikram S, Kaiser J, and Walker R, editors. *Egyptian Bioarchaeology: Humans, Animals, and the Environment*. Leiden: Sidestone Press. pp. 119–130.

Sanders C. 1989. *Customizing the Body: The Art and Culture of Tattooing*. Philadelphia: Temple University Press.

Sandison AT. 1955. The Histological Examination of Mummified Material. *Stain Technology* 29/30:277–283.

Sandison AT. 1962. Degenerative Vascular Disease in the Egyptian Mummy. *Medical History* 6(1):77.

Santoro CM, Arriaza BT, Standen VG, and Marquet PA. 2005. People of the Coastal Atacama Desert Living Between Sand Dunes and Waves of the Pacific Ocean. *Desert Peoples* 243–260.

Santoro CM, Rivadeneira MM, Latorre C, Rothhammer F, and Standen VG. 2012. Rise and Decline of Chinchorro Sacred Landscapes Along the Hyperarid Coast of the Atacama Desert. *Chungara* 44(4):637–653.

Saul FP. 1972. *The Human Skeletal Remains of the Altar de Sacrificios:An Osteobiographic Analysis.* Cambridge, MA: Peabody Museum of Archaeology and Ethnology, Harvard University Press.

Sawicki VA, Allison MJ, Dalton HP, and Pezzia A. 1976. Presence of *Salmonella* Antigens in Feces from a Peruvian Mummy. *Bulletin of the New York Academy of Medicine* 52(7):805–813.

Sawyer DR, Allison MJ, Elzay RP, and Pezzia A. 1978. The Mylohyoid Bridge of Pre-Columbian Peruvians. *American Journal of Physical Anthropology* 48(1):9–15.

Sawyer DR, Allison MJ, Elzay RP, and Pezzia A. 1979. A Study of Torus Palatinus and Torus Mandibularis in Pre-Columbian Peruvians. *American Journal of Physical Anthropology* 50(4):525–526.

Sawyer DR, Gianfortune V, Kiely ML, and Allison MJ. 1990. Mylohyoid and Jugular Foramen Bridging in Pre-Columbian Chileans. *American Journal of Physical Anthropology* 82(2):179–181.

Sawyer DR, Mosadomi A, Allison MJ, and Pezzia A. 1982. Crown Dimensions of Deciduous Teeth from Pre-Columbian Peru. *American Journal of Physical Anthropology* 59(4):373–376.

Saxe AA. 1970. *Social Dimensions of Mortuary Practices.* PhD thesis, University of Michigan.

Scarre G. 2003. Archaeology and Respect for the Dead. *Journal of Applied Philosophy* 20(3):237–249.

Scarre G. 2006. Can Archaeology Harm the Dead? In: Scarre C and Scarre G, editors. *The Ethics of Archeology: Philosophical Perspectives on Archaeological Practice.* Cambridge: Cambridge University Press. pp. 181–198.

Scheper-Hughes N, and Lock MM. 1987. The Mindful Body: A Prolegomenon to Future Work in Medical Anthropology. *Medical Anthropology Quarterly* 1:6–41.

Schiffer MB. 2000. Social Theory in Archaeology: Building Bridges. In: Schiffer MB, editor. *Social Theory in Archaeology.* Salt Lake City: The University of Utah Press. pp. 1–13.

Schjellerup I. 1997. *Incas and Spaniards in the Conquest of the Chachapoya, Archaeological and Ethnohistorical Research in the North-eastern Andes of Peru.* GOTARC, series B, Gothenburg Archaeological Theses, 7. Götebotg: Götebotg University.

Schmidt C, Harbort J, Knecht R, Grzyska U, Muenscher A, and Dalchow CV. 2013. Measurement and Comparison of Labyrinthine Structures with the Digital Volume Tomography: Ancient Egyptian Mummies' Versus Today's Temporal Bones. *European Archives of Oto-Rhino-Laryngology* 270(3):831–840.

Schmidt RA. 2002. The Iceman Cometh: Queering the Archaeological Past. In: Lewin E and Leap WL, editors. *Out in Theory: The Emergence of Lesbian and Gay Anthropology.* Chicago: University of Illinois Press. pp. 155–184.

Schmidt WA. 1908. Chemical and Biochemical Examination of Egyptian Mummies, Including Some Observations on the Chemistry of the Embalming Process of the Ancient Egyptians. *Cairo Scientific Journal* 2:147.

Schobinger MJ. 2012. La momia inca del nevado de Chuscha (noroeste argentino): resultado preliminar de su estudio. *Boletín de Arqueología PUCP* (7):277–285.

Schoeninger MJ, and DeNiro MJ. 1984. Nitrogen and Carbon Isotopic Composition of Bone Collagen from Marine and Terrestrial Animals. *Geochimica et Cosmochimica Acta* 48:625–639.

Schroeder H, Shuler KA, and Chenery SR. 2013. Childhood Lead Exposure in an Enslaved African Community in Barbados: Implications for Birthplace and Health Status. *American Journal of Physical Anthropology* 150(2):203–209.

Schulting RJ. 1995. Preservation of Soft Tissues by Copper in the Interior Plateau of British Columbia. *Proceedings of the First World Congress on Mummy Studies* 2:771–780.

Schwarcz HP, and White CD. 2004. The Grasshopper or the Ant? Cultigen-Use Strategies in Ancient Nubia from C-13 Analyses of Human Hair. *Journal of Archaeological Science* 31(6):753–762.

Scott DL, Wolfe F, and Huizinga TWJ. 2010. Rheumatoid Arthritis. *The Lancet* 376(9746):1094–1108.

Scott JW, Horne PD, Hart GD, and Savage H. 1977. Autopsy of an Egyptian Mummy. 3. Gross Anatomic and Miscellaneous Studies. *Canadian Medical Association Journal* 117(464–469).

Searcey N, Reinhard KJ, Egarter-Vigl E, Maixner F, Piombino-Mascali D, Zink AR, van der Sanden W, Gardner SL, and Bianucci R. 2013. Parasitism of the Zweeloo Woman: Dicrocoeliasis Evidenced in a Roman Period Bog Body. *International Journal of Paleopathology* 3:224–228.

Séguéla P-E, Pierrat-Bonnefois G, and Paul J-F. 2013. A Dextrocardia in a Foetal Egyptian Mummy? *Cardiology in the Young* 23(02):287–290.

Seiler R, and Rühli F. 2015. "The Opening of the Mouth"—A New Perspective for an Ancient Egyptian Mummification Procedure. *The Anatomical Record* 298(6):1208–1216.

Seiler R, Spielman AI, Zink A, and Rühli F. 2013. Oral Pathologies of the Neolithic Iceman, c.3,300 bc. *European Journal of Oral Sciences* 121:137–141.

Selma Uysal R, Gokharman D, Kacar M, Tuncbilek I, and Kosar U. 2005. Estimation of Sex by 3D CT Measurements of the Foramen Magnum. *Journal of Forensic Sciences* 50(6):1310–1314.

Seo M, Oh CS, Chai JY, Lee SJ, Park JB, Lee BH, Park J-H, Cho GH, Hong D-W, Park HU, and Shin DH. 2010. The Influence of Differential Burial Preservation on the Recovery of Parasite Eggs in Soil Samples from Korean Medieval Tombs. *Journal of Parasitology* 96(2):366–370.

Sepúlveda M, Arriaza B, Standen VG, Rousseliére H, Van Elslande E, Santoro CM, and Walter P. 2015. Análisis Microestratigráficos de Recubriemientos Corporales de una Momia Chinchorro, Extremo Norte de Chile. *Chungará (Arica)* 47:239–247.

Shanks M, and Tilley C. 1982. Ideology, Symbolic Power and Ritual Communication: A Reinterpretation of Neolithic Mortuary Practices. In: Hodder I, editor. *Symbolic and Structural Archaeology*. Cambridge: Cambridge University Press. pp. 129–154.

Sharf RH. 1992. The Idolization of Enlightenment: On the Mummification of Ch'an Masters in Medieval China. *History of Religions* 32(1):1–31.

Sharp ZD, Atudorei V, Panarello HO, Fernández J, and Douthitt C. 2003. Hydrogen Isotope Systematics of Hair: Archeological and Forensic Applications. *Journal of Archaeological Science* 30(12):1709–1716.

Shin DH, Choi YH, Shin KJ, Han GR, Youn M, Kim C, Han SH, Seo JC, Park SS, Cho Y-J, and Change BS. 2003a. Radiological Analysis on a Mummy from a Medieval Tomb in Korea. *Annals of Anatomy* 185:377–382.

Shin DH, Lee IS, Kim MJ, Oh CS, Park JB, Bok GD, and Yoo DS. 2010. Magnetic Resonance Imaging Performed on a Hydrated Mummy of Medieval Korea. *Journal of Anatomy* 216:329–334.

Shin DH, Lim D-S, Choi K-J, Oh CS, Kim MJ, Lee IS, Kim SB, Shin JE, Bok GD, Chai JY, Seo M. 2009. Scanning Electron Microscope Study of Ancient Parasite Eggs Recovered From Korean Mummies of the Joseon Dynasty. *Journal of Parasitology* 95(1):137–145.

Shin DH, Oh CS, Chai J-Y, Lee H-J, and Seo M. 2011. Enterobius Vermicularis Eggs Discovered in Coprolites from a Medieval Korean Mummy. *Korean Journal of Parasitology* 49(3):323–326.

Shin DH, Oh CS, Lee HJ, Chai JY, Lee SJ, Hong D-W, Lee SD, and Seo M. 2013. Ancient DNA Analysis on Clonorchis Sinensis Eggs Remained in Samples from Medieval Korean Mummy. *Journal of Archaeological Science* 40(1):211–216.

Shin DH, Oh CS, Lee SJ, Lee E-J, Yim SG, Kim MJ, Kim Y-S, Lee SD, Lee YS, Lee HJ et al. 2012. Ectopic Paragonimiasis from 400-Year-Old Female Mummy of Korea. *Journal of Archaeological Science* 39(4):1103–1110.

Shin DH, Youn M, and Chang BS. 2003b. Histological Analysis on the Medieval Mummy in Korea. *Forensic Science International* 137:172–182.

Shin MH, Yi YS, Bok GD, Lee E-J, Spigelman M, Park JB, Min S-R, and Shin DH. 2008. How Did Mummification Occur in Bodies Buried in Tombs with a Lime Soil Mixture Barrier During the Joseon Dynasty in Korea. In: Peña PA, Rodriguez Martin C, and Ramírez Rodríguez Á, editors. *Mummies and Science: World Mummies Research Proceedings of the VI World Congress on Mummy Studies*. Santa Cruz de Tenerife: Academia Canaria de la Historia. pp. 105–113.

Shuler KA. 2011. Life and Death on a Barbadian Sugar Plantation: Historic and Bioarchaeological Views of Infection and Mortality at Newton Plantation. *International Journal of Osteoarchaeology* 21(1):66–81.

Silva-Pinto V, Arriaza B, and Standen V. 2010. Evaluación de la frecuencia de espina bífida oculta y su posible relación con el arsénico ambiental en una muestra prehispánica de la Quebrada de Camarones, norte de Chile. *Revista Médica de Chile* 138(4):461–469.

Smith GE. 1908. Anatomical Report. *Bulletin of the Archaeological Survey of Nubia* 1:25–35.

Smith GE. 1912. *The Royal Mummies: Cairo: Catalogue Général des Antiquitees Égyptiennes du Musée du Caire*. Nos. 61051–61100, The Royal Mummies. Cairo: L'Institut Français d'Archéologie Orientale.

Smith GS, and Zimmerman MR. 1975. Tattooing Found on a 1600 Year Old Frozen, Mummified Body from St. Lawrence Island, Alaska. *American Antiquity* 40(4):433–437.

Sofaer JR. 2006. *The Body as Material Culture: A Theoretical Osteoarchaeology*. Cambridge: Cambridge University Press.

Sofaer JR. 2011. Towards a Social Bioarchaeology of Age. In: Argarwal SC and Glencross BA, editors. *Social Bioarchaeology*. West Sussex: Wiley-Blackwell. pp. 285–311.

Song MK, and Shin DH. 2014. Joseon Mummies Before Mummy Studies Began in Korea. *Papers on Anthropology* 23:135–151.

Sonoda S, Li H-C, Cartier L, Nunez L, and Tajima K. 2000. Ancient HTLV Type 1 Provirus DNA of Andean Mummy. *AIDS Research and Human Retroviruses* 16(16):1753–1756.

Sotomayor H, Burgos J, and Arango M. 2004. [Demonstration of Tuberculosis by DNA Ribotyping of Mycobacterium Tuberculosis in a Colombian Prehispanic Mummy]. *Biomedica: Revista del Instituto Nacional de Salud* 24:18–26.

Spindler K. 1994. *The Man in the Ice: The Discovery of a 5,000-Year-Old Body Reveals the Secrets of the Stone Age*. New York: Harmony Books.

Spindler K, Wilfing H, Ratbichler-Zissernig E, zur Nedden D, and Nothdurfter H, editors. 1996. *Human Mummies: A Global Survey of Their Status and the Techniques of Conservation*. New York: Springer Wien.

Standen VG. 1997. Temprana complejidad funeraria de la cultura Chinchorro (norte de Chile). *Latin American Antiquity* 8:134–156.

Standen VG. 2003. Bienes funerarios del cementerio Chinchorro Morro 1: Descripción, análisis e interpretación. *Chungara* 35(2):175–207.

Standen VG, Allison M, and Arriaza B. 1984. Patologías óseas de la población Morro-1, asociada al complejo Chinchorro: Norte de Chile. *Chungara* 13:175–185.

Standen VG, and Arriaza BT. 2000. Trauma in the Preceramic Coastal Populations of Northern Chile: Violence or Occupational Hazards? *American Journal of Physical Anthropology* 112(2):239–249.

Standen VG, Arriaza BT, and Santoro CM. 1997. External Auditory Exostosis in Prehistoric Chilean Populations: A Test of the Cold Water Hypothesis. *American Journal of Physical Anthropology* 103(1):119–129.

Standen VG, Arriaza BT, Santoro CM, Romero Á, and Rothhammer F. 2010. Perimortem trauma in the Atacama Desert and Social Violence During the Late Formative Period (2500–1700 years BP). *International Journal of Osteoarchaeology* 20(6):693–707.

Standen VG, Arriaza BT, Santoro CM, and Santos M. 2014. La Práctica Funeraria en el Sitio Maestranza Chinchorro y el Poblamiento Costero Durante el Arcaico Medio en el Extremo Norte de Chile. *Latin American Antiquity* 25(3):300–321.

Stead M, Bourke JB, and Brothwell D, editors. 1986. *Lindow Man: The Body in the Bog*. London: British Museum.

Stodder AL, and Palkovich AM, editors. 2012. *The Bioarchaeology of Individuals*. Gainesville: University Press of Florida.

Stødkilde-Jørgensen H, Jacobsen NO, Warncke E, and Heinemeier J. 2008. The Intestines of a More Than 2000 Years Old Peat-Bog Man: Microscopy, Magnetic Resonance Imaging and 14C-Dating. *Journal of Archaeological Science* 35(3):530–534.

Stojanowski CM. 2013. *Mission Cemeteries, Mission Peoples: Historical and Evolutionary Dimensions of Intracemetery Bioarchaeology in Spanish Florida*. Gainesville: University Press of Florida.

Stojanowski CM, and Duncan WN. 2014. Engaging Bodies in the Public Imagination: Bioarchaeology as Social Science, Science, and Humanities. *American Journal of Human Biology* 27(1):51–60.

Stojanowski CM, and Knudson KJ. 2014. Changing Patterns of Mobility as a Response to Climatic Deterioration and Aridification in the Middle Holocene Southern Sahara. *American Journal of Physical Anthropology* 154(1):79–93.

Stone PK. 2012. Binding Women: Ethnology, Skeletal Deformations, and Violence Against Women. *International Journal of Paleopathology* 2:53–60.

Sutherland ML, Cox SL, Lombardi GP, Watson L, Valladolid CM, Finch CE, Zink A, Frohlich B, Kaplan HS, Michalik DE, Miyamoto MI, Allam AH, Thompson RC, Wann LS, Narula J, Thomas GS, and Sutherland JD. 2014. Funerary Artifacts, Social Status, and Atherosclerosis in Ancient Peruvian Mummy Bundles. *Global Heart* 9(2):219–228.

Sutter RC. 2005. A Bioarchaeological Assessment of Prehistoric Ethnicity Among Early Late Intermediate Period Populations of the Azapa Valley, Chile. In: Reycraft RM, editor. *Us and Them: Archaeology and Ethnicity in the Andes*. Los Angeles: Cotsen Institute of Archaeology, University of California. pp. 183–205.

Swanston T, Haakensen M, Deneer H, and Walker EG. 2011. The Characterization of *Helicobacter pylori* DNA Associated with Ancient Human Remains Recovered from a Canadian Glacier. *PLoS One* 6(2):e16864.

Sydler C, Öhrström L, Rosendahl W, Woitek U, and Rühli F. 2015. CT-Based Assessment of Relative Soft-Tissue Alteration in Different Types of Ancient Mummies. *The Anatomical Record* 298(6):1162–1174.

Tainter J. 1978. Mortuary Practices and the Study of Prehistoric Social Systems. In: Schiffer MB, editor. *Advances in Archaeological Method and Theory*. New York: Academic Press. pp. 105–141.

Tapp E, Curry A, and Anfield C. 1975. Sand Pneumoconiosis in an Egyptian Mummy. *British Medical Journal* 2(5965):276.

Tarlow S. 2006. Archaeological Ethics and the People of the Past. In: Scarre C and Scarre G, editors. *The Ethics of Archaeology: Philosophical Perspectives on Archaeological Practice*. Cambridge: Cambridge University Press. pp. 199–216.

Tarlow S. 2008. The Extraordinary History of Oliver Cromwell's Head. In: Borić D and Robb J, editors. *Past Bodies: Body-Centered Research in Archaeology*. Oxford: Oxbow Books. pp. 69–78.

Tassie GJ. 2003. Identifying the Practice of Tattooing in Ancient Egypt and Nubia. *Papers from the Institute of Archaeology* 14:85–101.

ten Berge RL, vandeGoot FR. 2002. Seqenenre Taa II, the Violent Death of a Pharaoh. *Journal of Clinical Pathology* 55:232.

Thèves C, Senescau A, Vanin S, Keyser C, Ricaut FX, Alekseev AN, Dabernat H, Ludes B, Fabre R, and Crubézy E. 2011. Molecular Identification of Bacteria by Total Sequence Screening: Determining the Cause of Death in Ancient Human Subjects. *PLoS One* 6(7):e21733.

Thompson AH, Chaix L, and Richards MP. 2008. Stable Isotopes and Diet at Ancient Kerma, Upper Nubia (Sudan). *Journal of Archaeological Science* 35:376–387.

Thompson AH, Richards MP, Shortland A, and Zakrzewski SR. 2005. Isotopic Palaeodiet Studies of Ancient Egyptian Fauna and Humans. *Journal of Archaeological Science* 32(3):451–463.

Thompson JL, Alfonso-Durruty MP, and Crandall JJ, editors. 2014. *Tracing Childhood: Bioarchaeological Investigations of Early Lives in Antiquity*. Gainesville: University Press of Florida.

Thompson RC, Allam AH, Lombardi GP, Sutherland ML, Sutherland JD, Soliman MA-T, Frohlich B, Mininberg DT, Monge JM, Vallodolid CM, Cox SL, el-Maksoud GA, Badr I, Miyamoto MI, Nur el-din AH, Narula J, Finch CE, and Thomas GS. 2013. Atherosclerosis Across 4000 Years of Human History: The Horus Study of Four Ancient Populations. *The Lancet* 381:1211–1222.

Tibbett M, and Carter DO. 2008. Cadaver Decompositon and Soil: Processes. In: Tibbett M and Carter DO, editors. *Soil Analysis in Forensic Taphonomy*. Boca Raton: CRC Press. pp. 29–50.

Tiesler V. 2012. Studying Cranial Vault Modification in Ancient Mesoamerica. *Journal of Anthropological Sciences* 90:1–26.

Tilley L. 2015. Accommodating Difference in the Prehistoric Past: Revisiting the Case of Romito 2 from a Bioarchaeology of Care Perspective. *International Journal of Paleopathology* 8:64–74.

Tilley L, and Cameron T. 2014. Introducing the Index of Care: A Web-Based Application Supporting Archaeological Research into Health-Related Care. *International Journal of Paleopathology* 6:5–9.

Tilley L, and Oxenham MF. 2011. Survival Against the Odds: Modeling the Social Implications of Care Provision to Seriously Disabled Individuals. *International Journal of Paleopathology* 1:35–42.

Tito RY, Knights D, Metcalf J, Obregon-Tito AJ, Cleeland L, Najar F, Roe B, Reinhard K, Sobolik K, Belknap S et al. 2012. Inisghts from Characterizing Extinct Human Gut Microbiomes. *PLoS One* 7(12):e51146.

Tkocz I, Bytzer P, and Bierring F. 1979. Preserved Brains in Medieval Skulls. *American Journal of Physical Anthropology* 51(2):197–202.

Torres CM. 1995. Archaeological Evidence for the Antiquity of Psychoactive Plant Use in the Central Andes. *Annals Museo Civico di Rovereto* 11:291–326.

Torres CM, Repke DB, Chan K, McKenna D, Llagostera A, and Schultes RE. 1991. Snuff Powders from Pre-Hispanic San Pedro de Atacama: Chemical and Contextual Analysis. *Current Anthropology* 32(5):640–649.

Torres-Rouff C. 2003. Oral Implications of Labret Use: A Case from Pre-Columbian Chile. *International Journal of Osteoarchaeology* 13(4):247–251.

Torres-Rouff C. 2008. The Influence of Tiwanaku on Life in the Chilean Atacama: Mortuary and Bodily Perspectives. *American Anthropologist* 110:325–337.

Torres-Rouff C. 2011. Piercing the Body: Labret Use, Identity, and Masculinity in Prehistoric Chile. In: Baadsgaard A, Boutin AT, and Buikstra JE, editors. *Breathing New Life into the Evidence of Death.* Santa Fe: School for Advanced Research. pp. 153–178.

Torres-Rouff C, Pestle WJ, and Gallardo F. 2012. Eating Fish in the Driest Desert in the World: Osteological and Biogeochemical Analyses of Human Skeletal Remains from the San Salvador Cemetery, North Chile. *Latin American Antiquity* 23(1):51–69.

Touzeau A, Blichert-Toft J, Amiot R, Fourel F, Martineau F, Cockitt J, Hall K, Flandrois J-P, and Lecuyer C. 2013. Egyptian Mummies Record Increasing Aridity in the Nile Valley from 5500 to 1500 yr Before Present. *Earth and Planetary Science Letters* 375:92–100.

Toyne JM. 2015. Tibial Surgery in Ancient Peru. *International Journal of Paleopathology* 8:29–35.

Trotter M. 1943. Hair from Paracas Indian Mummies. *American Journal of Physical Anthropology* 1(1):69–75.

Tung TA. 2014. Agency, 'Til Death Do Us Part? Inquiring About the Agency of Dead Bodies from the Ancient Andes. *Cambridge Archaeological Journal* 24(3):437–452.

Tung TA, and Knudson KJ. 2011. Identifying Locals, Migrants, and Captives in the Wari Heartland: A Bioarchaeological and Biogeochemical Study of Human Remains from Conchopata, Peru. *Journal of Anthropological Archaeology* 30:247–261.

Tunón H, and Svanberg I. 1999. Laxatives and the Ice Man. *The Lancet* 353(9156):925–926.

Turner BL, and Andrushko VA. 2011. Partnerships, Pitfalls, and Ethical Concerns in International Bioarchaeology. In: Argarwal SC and Glencross BA, editors. *Social Bioarchaeology.* West Sussex: Wiley-Blackwell. pp. 44–67.

Turner BL, Klaus HD, Livengood SV, Brown LE, Saldaña F, and Wester C. 2013. The Variable Roads to Sacrifice: Isotopic Investigations of Human Remains from Chotuna-Huaca de los Sacrificios, Lambayeque, Peru. *American Journal of Physical Anthropology* 151(1):22–37.

Turner BL, Zuckerman MK, Garofalo EM, Wilson AS, Kamenov GD, Hunt DR, Amgalantugs T, and Frohlich B. 2012. Diet and Death in Times of War: Isotopic and Osteological Analysis of Mummified Human Remains from Southern Mongolia. *Journal of Archaeological Science* 39(10):3125–3140.

Turner RC, and Scaife RG, editors. 1995. *Bog Bodies: New Discoveries and New Perspectives.* London: British Museum Press.

Ubaldi M, Luciani S, Marota I, Fornaciari G, Cano RJ, and Rollo F. 1998. Sequence Analysis of Bacterial DNA in the Colon of an Andean Mummy. *American Journal of Physical Anthropology* 107(3):285–295.

Ubelaker DH, and Zarenko KM. 2011. Adipocere: What Is Known After Over Two Centuries of Research. *Forensic Science International* 208:167–172.

Ueki Y, Tiziani V, Santanna C, Fukai N, Maulik C, Garfinkle J, Ninomiya C, do Amaral C, Peters H, Habal M, Rhee-Morris L, Doss JB, Kreiborg S, Olsen BR, and Reichenberger E. 2001. Mutations in the Gene Encoding c-Abl-Binding Protein SH3BP2 Cause Cherubism. *Nat Genet* 28:125–126.

Vahey T, and Brown D. 1984. Comely Wenuhotep: Computed Tomography of an Egyptian Mummy. *Journal of Computer Assisted Tomography* 8(5):992–997.

Vandamme A-M, Hall WW, Lewis MJ, Goubau P, and Salemi M. 2000. Origins of HTLV-1 in South America (Letter 2). *Nature Medicine* 6(3):232–233.

Vanzetti A, Vidale M, Gallinaro M, Frayer DW, and Bondioli L. 2010. The Iceman as a Burial. *Antiquity* 84:681–692.

Vargiolu R, Pailler-Mattei C, Coudert M, Lintz Y, and Zahouani H. 2013. Hair Surface and Mechanical Properties of Copt Mummies from Antinopolis. *Journal of Archaeological Science* 40(10):3686–3692.

Vásquez Sánchez VF, Jordán RF, Tham TR, Fraile IR, Cifuentes LT, and Dorda BÁ. 2013. Estudio Microquímico Mediante Med-ebs (análisis de energía dispersiva por rayos x) del pigmento utilizado en el tatuaje de la señora de cao. *Archaeobios* 1(7).

Vass AA, Bass WM, Wolt JD, Foss JF, and Ammons JT. 1992. Time Since Death Determination of Human Cadavers Using Soil Solution. *Journal of Forensic Science* 37:126–1253.

Verdery K. 1999. *The Political Lives of Dead Bodies: Reburial and Postsocialist Change*. New York: Columbia University Press.

Villa C, Buckberry J, Cattaneo C, and Lynnerup N. 2013. Technical Note: Reliability of Suchey-Brooks and Buckberry-Chamberlain Methods on 3D Visualizations from CT and Laser Scans. *American Journal of Physical Anthropology* 151(1):158–163.

Villa C, and Lynnerup N. 2012. Hounsfield Units Ranges in CT-Scans of Bog Bodies and Mummies. *Anthropologischer Anzeiger* 69(2):127–145.

Villa C, Rasmussen MM, and Lynnerup N. 2011. Age Estimation by 3D CT Scans of the Borremose Woman, a Danish Bog Body. *Yearbook of Mummy Studies* 1:165–170.

von Hagen A. 2002. Chachapoya Iconography and Society at Laguna de los Cóndores, Peru. In: Silverman H and Isbell WH, editors. *Andean Archaeology Volume II: Art, Landscape, and Society*. New York: Kluwer Academic, Plenum Publishers. pp. 137–155.

Vos RL. 1993. *The Apis Embalming Ritual. P. Vindob. 3873*. Leuven: Peeters Press.

Wade AD, Beckett RG, Conlogue GJ, Gonzalez R, Wade R, and Brier B. 2015. MUMAB: A Conversation with the Past. *The Anatomical Record* 298(6):954–973.

Wade AD, Lawson B, Nelson AJ, and Tampieri D. 2014. Hybrid Ritual: Abdominal Incision Plate Use in a Case of Transperineal Evisceration. *Yearbook of Mummy Studies* 2:103–108.

Wade AD, and Nelson AJ. 2013a. Radiological Evaluation of the Evisceration Tradition in Ancient Egyptian Mummies. *HOMO—Journal of Comparative Human Biology* 64:1–28.

Wade AD, and Nelson AJ. 2013b. Evisceration and Excerebration in the Egyptian Mummification Tradition. *Journal of Archaeological Science* 40(12):4198–4206.

Wade AD, Nelson AJ, and Garvin GJ. 2011. A Synthetic Radiological Study of Brain Treatment in Ancient Egyptian Mummies. *HOMO—Journal of Comparative Human Biology* 62:248–269.

Walker PL. 2000. Bioarchaeological Ethics: A Historical Perspective on the Value of Human Remains. In: Katzenberg MA and Saunders SR, editors. *Biological Anthropology of the Human Skeleton*. New York: Wiley-Liss.

Wallgren JE, Caple R, and Aufderheide AC. 1986. Contributions of Nuclear Magnetic Resonance Spectroscopy to the Question of Alkaptonuria (Ochronosis) in an Egyptian Mummy. In: David RA, editor. *Science in Egyptology*. Manchester: University of Manchester Press. pp. 321–327.

Wanek J, Speller R, and Rühli FJ. 2012. Direct Action of Radiation on Mummified Cells: Modeling of Computed Tomography by Monte Carlo Algorithms. *Radiation and Environmental Biophysics* 52:397–410.

Wanek J, Székely G, and Rühli F. 2011. X-ray Absorption-Based Imaging and Its Limitation in Differentiation of Ancient Mummified Tissue. *Skeletal Radiology* 40(5):595–601.

Wann LS, Lombardi G, Ojeda B, Benfer RA, Rivera R, Finch CE, Thomas GS, and Thompson RC. 2015. The Tres Ventanas Mummies of Peru. *The Anatomical Record* 298(6):1026–1035.

Washburn SL. 1951. The New Physical Anthropology. *Transactions of the New York Academy of Sciences*, Series II 13(7):298–304.

Webb E, Thomson S, Nelson A, White CD, Koren G, Rieder M, and Van Uum S. 2010. Assessing Individual Systemic Stress Through Cortisol Analysis of Archaeological Hair. *Journal of Archaeological Science* 37(4):807–812.

Webb E, White C, and Longstaffe F. 2013. Dietary Shifting in the Nasca Region as Inferred from the Carbon- and Nitrogen-Isotope Compositions of Archaeological Hair and Bone. *Journal of Archaeological Science* 40(1):129–139.

Weinstein RS, Simmons DJ, and Lovejoy CO. 1981. Ancient Bone Disease in a Peruvian Mummy Revealed by Quantitative Skeletal Histomorphometry. *American Journal of Physical Anthropology* 54(3):321–326.

Wells C, and Maxwell BM. 1962. Alkaptonuria in an Egyptian Mummy. *The British Journal of Radiology* 35(418):679–682.

Werning J. 2010. Mummies in China. In: Wieczorek A and Rosendahl W, editors. *Mummies of the World*. New York: Prestel. pp. 127–137.

White CD. 1993. Isotopic Determination of Seasonality in Diet and Death from Nubian Mummy Hair. *Journal of Archaeological Science* 20(6):657–666.

White CD, Longstaffe FJ, and Law KR. 1999. Seasonal Stability and Variation in Diet as Reflected in Human Mummy Tissue from the Kharga Oasis and the Nile Valley. *Palaeogeography, Palaeoclimatology, Palaeoecology* 147:209–222.

White CD, Longstaffe FJ, and Law KR. 2004. Exploring the Effects of Environment, Physiology and Diet on Oxygen Isotope Ratios in Ancient Nubian Bones and Teeth. *Journal of Archaeological Science* 31(2):233–250.

White CD, Nelson AJ, Longstaffe FJ, and Jung A. 2009. Landscape Bioarchaeology at Pacatnamu, Peru: Inferring Mobility from $\delta13C$ and $\delta15N$ Values from Hair. *Journal of Archaeological Science* 36(7):1527–1537.

White CD, and Schwarcz HP. 1994. Temporal Trends in Stable Isotopes for Nubian Mummy Tissues. *American Journal of Physical Anthropology* 93(2):165–187.

White CD, Spence MW, Longstaffe FJ, and Law KR. 2004b. Demography and Ethnic Continuity in the Tlailotlacan Enclave of Teotihuacan: The Evidence from Stable Oxygen Isotopes. *Journal of Anthropological Archaeology* 23:385–403.

Wieczorek A, and Rosenthal W, editors. 2010. *Mummies of the World*. Munich: Prestel.

Wild EM, Guillén S, Kutschera W, Seidler H, and Steier P. 2007. Radiocarbon Dating of the Peruvian Chachapoya/Inca Site at the Laguna de los Condores. *Nuclear Instruments and Methods in Physics Research B* 259:378–383.

Wilkinson TM. 2002. Last Rights: The Ethics of Research on the Dead. *Journal of Applied Philosophy* 19:31–41.

Willerson JT, and Teaff R. 1996. Egyptian Contributions to Cardiovascular Medicine. *Texas Heart Institute Journal* 23(3):191.

Williams AC, Edwards HGM, and Barry BW. 1995. The 'Iceman': Molecular Structure of 5200-Year-Old Skin Characterised by Raman Spectroscopy and Electron Microscopy. *Biochimica et Biophysica Acta (BBA)—Protein Structure and Molecular Enzymology* 1246(1):98–105.

Williams JS, and Katzenberg MA. 2012. Seasonal Fluctuations in Diet and Death During the Late Horizon: A Stable Isotopic Analysis of Hair and Mail from the Central Coast of Peru. *Journal of Archaeological Science* 39(1):41–57.

Williams JS, and Murphy MS. 2013. Living and Dying as Subjects of the Inca Empire: Adult Diet and Health at Puruchuco-Huaquerones, Peru. *Journal of Anthropological Archaeology* 32:165–179.

Williams JS, and White CD. 2006. Dental Modification in the Postclassic Population from Lamanai, Belize. *Ancient Mesoamerica* 17:139–151.

Williams LJ, White CD, and Longstaffe FJ. 2011. Improving Stable Isotopic Interpretations Made from Human Hair Through Reduction of Growth Cycle Error. *American Journal of Physical Anthropology* 145(1):125–136.

Wilson AS, Brown EL, Villa C, Lynnerup N, Healey A, Ceruti MC, Reinhard J, Previgliano CH, Araoz FA, Diez JG, and Taylor J. 2013. Archaeological, Radiological, and Biological Evidence Offer Insight into Inca Child Sacrifice. *Proceedings of the National Academy of Sciences of the United States of America* 110(33):13322–13327.

Wilson AS, Taylor T, Ceruti MC, Chavez JA, Reinhard J, Grimes V, Meier-Augenstein W, Cartmell L, Stern B, Richards MP, Worobey M, Barnes I, and Gilbert MTP. 2007. Stable

Isotope and DNA Evidence for Ritual Sequences in Inca Child Sacrifice. *Proceedings of the National Academy of Sciences of the United States of America* 104:16456–16461.

Wink AE. 2014. Pubic Symphyseal Age Estimation from Three-Dimensional Reconstructions of Pelvic CT Scans of Live Individuals. *Journal of Forensic Sciences* 59(3):696–702.

Winston CE, and Kittles RA. 2005. Psychological and Ethical Issues Related to Identity and Inferring Ancestry of African Americans. In: Turner TR, editor. *Biological Anthropology and Ethics: From Repatriation to Genetic Identity.* Albany: State University of New York Press. pp. 209–230.

Wisseman SU, and Hunt DR. 2014. Rescanned: New Results from a Child Mummy at the University of Illinois. *Yearbook of Mummy Studies* 2:87–94.

Wittmers LE, Aufderheide AC, and Buikstra J. 2011. Soft Tissue Preservation System: Applications. *International Journal of Paleopathology* 1:150–154.

Woide D, Zink A, and Thalhammer S. 2010. Technical Note: PCR Analysis of Minimum Target Amount of Ancient DNA. *American Journal of Physical Anthropology* 142(2):321–327.

Wood J, Milner G, Harpending HC, and Weiss K. 1992. The Osteological Paradox. *Current Anthropology* 33:343–370.

Yamada TK, Kudou T, and Takahashi-Iwanaga H. 1990. Some 320-Year-Old Soft Tissue Preserved by the Presence of Mercury. *Journal of Archaeological Science* 17(4):383–392.

Yamada TK, Kudou T, Takahasi-Iwanaga H, Ozawa T, Uchihi R, and Kasumata Y. 1996. Collagen in 300 Year-Old Tissue and a Short Introduction to the Mummies in Japan. In: Spindler K, Wilfing H, Rastbichler-Zissernig E, zur Nedden D, and Nothdurfter H, editors. *Human Mummies: A Global Survey of Their Status and the Techniques of Conservation.* New York: Springer. pp. 71–79.

Yatsenko SA. 2013. The Tattoo System in the Ancient Iranian World. In: Della Casa P and Witt C, editors. *Tattoos and Body Modification in Antiquity Proceedings of the Sessions at the Annual Meetings of the European Association of Archaeologists in the Hague and Oslo, 2010/11.* Zurich Studies in Archaeology 9. Chronos-Verlag, Zurich. pp. 97–101.

Yu C, Fan S, Sun Y, and Pickwell-MacPherson E. 2012. The Potential of Terahertz Imaging for Cancer Diagnosis: A Review of Investigations to Date. *Quantitative Imaging in Medicine and Surgery* 2(1):33–45.

Zanatta A, Zampieri F, Bonati MR, Frescura C, Scattolin G, Stramare R, and Thiene G. 2014. Situs Inversus with Dextrocardia in a Mummy Case. *Cardiovascular Pathology* 23:61–64.

Zaro G. 2007. Diversity Specialists: Coastal Resource Management and Historical Contingency in the Osmore Desert of Southern Peru. *Latin American Antiquity* 18(2):161–180.

Zaro G, and Alvarez AU. 2005. Late Chiribaya Agriculture and Risk Management Along the Arid Andean Coast of Southern Perú, A.D. 1200–1400. *Geoarchaeology: An International Journal* 20(7):717–737.

Zaro G, Nystrom KC, Umire Alvaraez A, Bar Esquivel A, and Miranda A. 2010. Tierras Olvidadas: Chiribaya Landscape Engineering and Marginality in Southern Peru. *Latin American Antiquity* 21(4):355–374.

Zimmerman MR. 1972. Histological Examination of Experimentally Mummified Tissues. *American Journal of Physical Anthropology* 37(2):271–280.

Zimmerman MR. 1977. The Mummies of the Tomb of Nebwenenef: Paleopathology and Archeology. *Journal of the American Research Center in Egypt* 14:33–36.

Zimmerman MR. 2011. The Analysis and Interpretation of Mummified Remains. In: Grauer AL, editor. *A Companion to Paleopathology.* West Sussex: John Wiley & Sons. pp. 152–169.

Zimmerman MR. 2014. Studying Mummmies: Giving Life to a Dry Subject. In: Metcalfe R, Cockitt J, and David R, editors. *Palaeopathology in Egypt and Nubia.* Oxford: Archaeopress Egyptology. pp. 119–127.

Zimmerman MR, and Aufderheide AC. 1984. The Frozen Family of Utqiagvik: The Autopsy Findings. *Arctic Anthropology* 21(1):53–64.

Zimmerman MR, Brier B, and Wade RS. 1998. Brief Communication: Twentieth Century Replication of an Egyptian Mummy: Implications for Paleopathology. *American Journal of Physical Anthropology* 107:417–420.

Zimmerman MR, and Gleeson M. 2015. PUM I Revisited: Tradeoffs in Preservation and Discovery. *The Anatomical Record* 298(6):949–953.

Zimmerman MR, Trinkaus E, LeMay M, Aufderheide AC, Reyman TA, Marrocco GR, Shultes RE, and Coughlin EA. 1981. Trauma and Trephination in a Peruvian Mummy. *American Journal of Physical Anthropology* 55(4):497–501.

Zimmerman MR, Yeatman GW, and Sprinz H. 1971. Examination of an Aleutian Mummy. *Bulletin of the New York Academy of Medicine* 47:80–103.

Zink A. 2014. *The World of Mummies: From Ötzi to Lenin*. South Yorkshire: Pen and Sword Books.

Zink AR, Graefen A, Oeggl K, Dickson JH, Leitner W, Kaufmann G, Fleckinger A, Gostner P, and Egarter-Vigl E. 2011. The Iceman is not a burial: Reply to Vanzetti et al. (2010). *Antiquity* 85.

Zink AR, Molnár E, Motamedi N, Pálfy G, Marcsik A, and Nerlich AG. 2007. Molecular History of Tuberculosis from Ancient Mummies and keletons. *International Journal of Osteoarchaeology* 17(4):380–391.

Zink AR, and Nerlich AG. 2003. Molecular Analyses of the "Pharaos": Feasibility of Molecular Studies in Ancient Egyptian Material. *American Journal of Physical Anthropology* 121(2):109–111.

Zink AR, and Nerlich AG. 2005. Long-Term Survival of Ancient DNA in Egypt: Reply to Gilbert et al. *American Journal of Physical Anthropology* 128(1):115–118.

Zink AR, Reischl U, Wolf H, Nerlich AG, Miller R. 2001. Corynebacterium in Ancient Egypt. *Medical History* 45:267–272.

Zink AR, Reischl U, Wolf H, Nerlich AG. 2000. Molecular Evidence of Bacteremia by Gastrointestinal Pathogenic Bacteria in an Infant Mummy from Ancient Egypt. *Archives of Pathology and Laboratory Medicine* 124:1614–1618.

Zink AR, Sola C, Reischl U, Grabner W, Rastogi N, Wolf H, and Nerlich AG. 2004. Molecular Identification and Characterization of Mycobacterium Tuberculosis Complex in Ancient Egyptian Mummies. *International Journal of Osteoarchaeology* 14(5):404–413.

Zink AR, Spigelman M, Schraut B, Greenblatt CL, Nerlich AG, and Donoghue HD. 2006. Leishmaniasis in Ancient Egypt and Upper Nubia. *Emerging Infectious Diseases* 12(10):1616–1617.

Zink A, Wann LS, Thompson RC, Keller A, Maixner F, Allam AH, Finch CE, Frohlich B, Kaplan H, Lombardi GP, et al. 2014. Genomic Correlates of Atherosclerosis in Ancient Humans. *Global Heart* 9(2):203–209.

Zuckerman MK, and Armelagos GJ. 2011. The Origins of Biocultural Dimensions in Bioarchaeology. In: Argarwal SC and Glencross BA, editors. *Social Bioarchaeology*. West Sussex: Wiley-Blackwell. pp. 15–43.

Zuckerman MK, Kamnikar KR, and Mathena SA. 2014. Recovering the 'Body Politic': A Relational Ethics of Meaning for Bioarchaeology. *Cambridge Archaeological Journal* 24:513–522.

Zuckerman MK, Turner BL, and Armelagos GJ. 2012. Evolutionary Thought in Paleopathology and the Rise of the Biocultural Approach. In: Grauer AL, editor. *A Companion to Paleopathology*. West Sussex: Wiley-Blackwell. pp. 34–57.

Zweifel L, Böni T, and Rühli FJ. 2009. Evidence-Based Palaeopathology: Meta-Analysis of PebMed-Listed Scientific Studies on Ancient Egyptian Mummies. *HOMO—Journal of Comparative Human Biology* 60:405–427.

INDEX

Page numbers in *italic* indicate a figure on the corresponding page